# OPTION FOR THE POOR

# OPTION FOR THE POOR

## A HUNDRED YEARS
## OF VATICAN SOCIAL TEACHING

# DONAL DORR

GILL AND MACMILLAN
Dublin

ORBIS BOOKS
Maryknoll, New York

First published 1983 by
Gill and Macmillan Ltd
Goldenbridge,
Dublin 8
with associated companies in Auckland, Dallas, Delhi,
Hong Kong, Johannesburg, Lagos, London, Manzini,
Melbourne, Nairobi, New York, Singapore, Tokyo, Washington

Published in the USA and Canada by
Orbis Books, Maryknoll
Maryknoll, New York 10545

0  7171  1298  5 (Gill and Macmillan)
0  88344  365  1 (Orbis Books)

Second Printing, March 1985

# Table of Contents

# Preface

I would like to express my gratitude to a number of people and institutions that helped me during the period I was writing this book. First of all I must acknowledge the contribution of *Trocaire*, the Irish Catholic Agency for World Development, which, in conjunction with the theology faculty of Maynooth College, established the Cardinal Conway Research Fellowship in the Theology of Development; the book was written during the time I was the holder of this fellowship. I am especially grateful to Bishop Casey, the chairman of *Trocaire*, and to Brian McKeown, its director, for their vision and commitment, which they shared with me. I was also greatly encouraged and helped by other members of the staff and committees of *Trocaire*. I wish also to thank the president and staff of Maynooth College, who welcomed me and provided an ambiance which encouraged me to study.

A number of good friends read the manuscript and helped me with their advice. I particularly want to mention Padraig Ó Máille, now in Malawi, and my brother Noel, for helping me to clarify what I wanted to say. I would like also to thank Michael Gill and John Eagleson for their encouragement and advice, and to express my appreciation and gratitude to Bridget Lunn, of Gill and Macmillan, fo her kindness and very professional help in preparing the book for publication and for her invaluable work on the index.

During the three and a half years in which I held the fellowship I did not spend all my time studying and writing. At irregular intervals I spent a good deal of time trying to experience at first hand what it might mean for a Church to make an 'option for the poor'. I am deeply grateful to many friends and fellow-workers — in East, West, Central, and

Southern Africa, as well as in Brazil and Ireland — who took part with me in workshops about justice, development, and human liberation; they kept me sane and helped me to grow in understanding and commitment during these years. I did not experience these interludes as an escape from doing theology; but they were a welcome change from looking up Church documents and trying to understand the nuances of their meaning. In writing this book I was writing for those fellow-workers and for people like them in many parts of the world — Christians who feel called to work for justice and who turn to Church social teaching for inspiration and for guidance about how to answer the call.

Earlier drafts of Chapters Three and Five were published in *Doctrine and Life* and *The Irish Theological Quarterly*, and some paragraphs of Chapter Eleven have appeared in *The Furrow*.

Donal Dorr
Easter 1983

# Introduction

This book is about the social teaching of the Catholic Church over the past hundred years. It sets out to look at this teaching from a particular point of view — the extent to which the Church has committed itself to being on the side of those who are poor or oppressed. That is why I chose the title 'Option for the Poor'. This phrase burst on to the ecclesiastical scene only a few years ago. Since then it has become the most controversial religious term since the Reformers' cry, 'Salvation through faith alone'. Hostile critics dismiss the term and all that it has come to represent as an unlikely cross between Marxism and Latin American Catholicism. On the other hand, there are some enthusiasts who welcome it precisely because of its Marxist and Latin American associations. More commonly, those who invoke the idea of such an option maintain that its origin lies in the Bible rather than in Marx; and they believe that the Church needs to make an 'option for the poor' not merely in Latin America but everywhere else as well.

In recent years many earnest Christians who have been trying to discern 'the signs of the times' in renewal courses and assemblies have come to believe that they are called to make this 'option for the poor'. Yet, having worked with many groups of this kind, I am keenly aware that some people who feel called to make such a commitment do not really know what it involves. A lot of people in the Western world — and also in many parts of the Third World — find the term 'option for the poor' both confusing and threatening. I suspect that the confusion arises from the sense of threat; for the most obvious thing about the whole idea is that it puts a question mark over people's present way of life and

1

previous commitments. Fears and guilt create an aura of ambiguity around the term, as well as some selective blindness. People demand 'a simple explanation' of the term. When that is given they often respond with questions that begin: 'But surely . . . ?' These 'but surely' questions are an indication that the questioner has reached the point of resistance. Too direct a response to such questions may arouse defensiveness. Frequently it is more useful to provide some kind of biblical background and to trace the recent development in Church action, reflection, and teaching. This allows people space to answer the questions for themselves.

Though this book is about 'option for the poor' it does not set out to give a comprehensive treatment of the whole topic. For − as I have said already and as the subtitle indicates − my concern has been with the social teaching of the Church over the past hundred years. Indeed I have limited myself to the official teaching of just one Church, namely, the Roman Catholic Church. Furthermore, I have confined my attention mainly to Vatican teaching. In general I did not set out to deal with official documents of regional groups of bishops, except in the cases of the documents of Medellín and Puebla. To attempt to examine the teaching of other Christian Churches, or of all the regional meetings of bishops in the Catholic Church, would have made the book too long and unwieldy; so I reluctantly decided to confine my attention to Vatican teaching. The subtitle of the book is intended to limit and qualify the main title, by indicating that I am dealing here only with one aspect of the topic 'option for the poor'.

Since it is only recently that the term 'option for the poor' has come into common usage, it would have been pointless to expect to find in Vatican documents of even twenty years ago any formal or explicit treatment of the topic. What I have had to do, especially in the earlier parts of the book, is to get behind the *term* 'option for the poor', so as to look at the *reality* that is designated by the term. I have tried to see what kind of stances were taken by the highest authorities in the Catholic Church in relation to the issue of poverty and oppression in society.

This means that I have not attempted to cover all aspects of Catholic social teaching. The documents and statements that I have used in this book would have provided the raw

2

materials for a more comprehensive study of what might be called 'the social justice agenda' — including such topics as civil rights, ownership and use of goods, participation in decision-making, and ecological questions. But my present concern is not this wider agenda; it is rather the less differentiated question that must be the first item on the social justice agenda and at the same time underpins all the rest: what does the Church have to say to, or about, those who are the victims of a society that is structurally unjust?

*A Response to Structural Injustice*

It seems appropriate to indicate briefly at this point what I understand by an 'option for the poor'. What it involves is a response to the structural injustice that characterises our world. The word 'option' suggests a personal choice. While continuing to put emphasis on this personal aspect, I would want to insist that the choice in question is not essentially an act of private asceticism or even of face-to-face compassion for a poor person. It is specifically a response at the level of the wider society as a whole, a response to the unjust ordering of society. Therefore it makes sense only in the context of an awareness of how society is in fact structured.

We live in a stratified society where certain economic, political, cultural, and religious structures maintain and promote the dominance of the rich and powerful over the mass of ordinary people and peoples. These structures operate through agencies and institutions that are staffed mainly by middle-class people — those who provide the professional and commercial services of society. Whatever their private loyalties and values, these service people contribute to structural injustice through the kind of work they are doing. The possibility of making an 'option for the poor' arises for such people and it is mainly to them that the challenge is issued. Some of the services provided by the Churches are an integral part of the institutions of society — for instance of the educational or medical system of the country. Those who are working in, or responsible for, Church services of this kind are asking themselves whether their work, however good it may be in itself, is an adequate embodiment of the Church's commitment to justice in society.

An 'option for the poor', in the sense in which it is intended

3

here, means a series of choices, personal or communal, made by individuals, by communities, or even by corporate entities such as a religious congregation, a diocese, or a Church (as represented by its central administration, and, in varying degrees, by its ordinary members). It is the choice to disentangle themselves from serving the interests of those at the 'top' of society and to begin instead to come into solidarity with those at or near the bottom. Such solidarity means commitment to working and living within structures and agencies that promote the interests of the less favoured sectors of society. These would include those who are economically poor, the groups that are politically marginalised or oppressed, people discriminated against on sexual grounds, peoples that have been culturally silenced or oppressed, and those who have been religiously disinherited or deprived.

However, the above description focuses attention on what has to be *done*. But what needs to be done cannot in fact be done successfully unless there is a prior, and continuing, attempt to find solidarity with 'the poor' in a more experiential way — by sharing their lives, sorrows, joys, hopes, and fears. Without this, the attempt to serve the interests of these people will be patronising — and it will make them feel more powerless and dependent than ever.

It should be noted that in the remainder of this book I have not set out to give a more detailed and systematic explanation of what an 'option for the poor' means. Certain aspects of the question have, however, been examined in an incidental way, in the course of my study of Vatican teaching. Furthermore, I have not tried to suggest how the more experiential aspect of such an option (sharing the life of 'the poor') might be fitted together with the more organisational aspects (building alternative structures); this topic is, however, referred to briefly in Chapter Eight where the Medellín documents are examined. The outline I have just given of the meaning of an 'option for the poor' is intended merely to help the reader of the book to understand why I have chosen certain material as significant, out of a very large body of documents and addresses which I have been studying.

*The Biblical Concept of Poverty*
As I have noted already, this book does not set out to give

a full treatment of the topic 'option for the poor'; it is limited to an examination of the Vatican teaching relevant to the issue. However, in view of the particular importance of the biblical basis for making such an option it seems appropriate to offer, in this introduction, some general ideas about what the Bible has to say on the subject of poverty and oppression.

In the Old Testament the term 'the poor' refers especially to those groups of people who are economically deprived, who have no social status, who are treated unjustly by foreign rulers or by the authorities in their own land. These people are oppressed because they are poor, and are therefore at the mercy of the unscrupulous. Furthermore, they are poor because they are oppressed: they have been further impoverished by being cheated and deprived of their rights. Some groups of 'the poor' are doubly oppressed. They are the people who are at risk not only because they are economically poor but also because they happen to be widows, orphans, or resident aliens — categories of people who have nobody to defend them against exploitation. The Old Testament leaves us in no doubt that God has a special care for the poor. The oppression of his people in Egypt moved him to save them, as the Book of Exodus recounts. After the Israelites had settled in 'the Promised Land' the poor among them found themselves oppressed by the wealthy and powerful of their own people. Time after time God sent the prophets to protest against this injustice and to proclaim his care for the poor.

The New Testament deepens our understanding of what it means to be poor. In some important respects, Jesus himself should be seen as one of 'the poor'. Having 'emptied himself' to share our humanity (*Phil.* 2:7), he became a native of a despised village (*Jn.* 1:46) and was known as a carpenter's son (*Mt.* 13:55). He resisted the temptation to carry out his mission through the use of glory and power (*Mt.* 4:5-10). He was the innocent victim of persecution and was executed as a criminal after an unjust trial.

The Bible makes it clear that there can be an unjust use of power by religious leaders as well as by civil authorities. The reaction of Christ to the scribes and pharisees, as portrayed in the New Testament, suggests that he sees them as oppressors, imposing their will on the mass of ordinary believers (e.g.

5

*Mt.* 15:3-20; 23:4-38). In challenging this abuse of power, Christ was standing in the tradition of Moses and the prophets who cried out against economic injustice and political oppression. Defence of the poor includes standing up for those who are powerless before religious authorities that abuse their power.

Some religious people today hold that the Bible — especially the New Testament — is more concerned about 'poverty of spirit' than about material poverty. However, a study of the theme of poverty in the Bible suggests that it is not helpful to make too sharp a distinction between 'the poor' and those who are 'poor in spirit'. The Scriptures indicate that those who are poor and defenceless have nobody to turn to but God. He has a special care for the victims of injustice and those who are poor; and they in turn can more easily accept his care and protection. Of course, poor people can also turn away from God — through bitterness and lack of hope. But in general it is more likely that those who are economically and politically poor will also be 'poor in spirit', dependent on and open to God. On the other hand the rich and powerful tend to rely on themselves and therefore to close themselves off from God. Their reliance on wealth and power makes it difficult for them to be 'poor in spirit' and to enter God's kingdom (cf. *Mt.* 19:24).

These brief points from Scripture go some way towards clarifying what an 'option for the poor' means — and what it does not mean. Such an option, seen in a biblical perspective, would mean some special care or preference for people or groups who are marginalised in human society. It is quite true that there is a sense in which *everybody* is 'poor before God'. But this idea can be invoked as a way of evading the central thrust of the biblical teaching about poverty. The meaning of the word 'poor' can be extended and redefined to a point where the challenge of the scriptural position gets lost. In Chapter Eleven of the book the question of the meaning of the word 'poor' is treated in a little more detail; and there I have examined the different senses in which one might speak of the 'poverty' of rich people.

*Content and Interpretation*

Before finishing this introduction I want to say a little

6

more about the material I set out to cover and to add a few remarks about the way in which I have interpreted the material. The book begins with an examination of the first of the great social encyclicals — *Rerum Novarum*, issued by Leo XIII in 1891. But in order to throw light on the background to this document, several other encyclicals of Leo XIII are dealt with in Chapter Two. Some of these were issued a number of years before *Rerum Novarum* in 1891; so in fact the subtitle of the book is accurate when it refers to 'a hundred years of Vatican social teaching'.

In the subtitle I refer to 'Vatican' social teaching rather than just to 'papal' social teaching. This is because the materials I have dealt with include not merely the major social encyclicals but also the documents issued by the Second Vatican Council and the Synod of Bishops in Rome. I have also treated (fairly briefly) the documents issued by the Conferences of Latin American Bishops at Medellín in 1968 and at Puebla in 1979. Although these are not Vatican documents, they merit attention in this study because of the impact they had on the wider Church and on the Vatican.

This study is not confined to the most formal documents such as papal encyclicals. In order to present the teaching of some popes — especially Pius XII and John Paul II — I found it necessary to take account of some of the more important addresses which these popes saw as being in some sense authoritative.

Apart from some special cases I have not gone into the question of who drafted the various documents. Information on this point is not readily available in regard to recent Vatican documents. The attempt to discover such information leads one into the realm of investigative journalism rather than historical research. I have decided to adopt the position that the various documents and statements represent the considered views of their official authors, no matter who may have prepared the drafts.

The issue of the criteria of evaluation is of central importance in a study of this kind. Until twenty years ago most Catholic commentaries on the social encyclicals treated them as quite beyond any overt criticism. In practice, of course, the commentators gave an emphasis and interpretation that favoured their own views. It would have been less confusing

7

if they had made explicit the basis for their varying interpretations. But that could hardly have been expected in the climate of the time. Nowadays this kind of approach is less excusable — though it is perhaps understandable that a certain sycophantic fundamentalism should arise as a reaction against biased criticism of Vatican statements.

At the other extreme one finds a corrosively critical type of evaluation that can be quite perceptive but is lacking in any sympathetic feeling for what the Vatican teaching is trying to achieve. For instance, some critics suggest that Pope John Paul's encyclical on human work was worse than useless; they saw it as an attempt to impose an outdated Catholic blueprint on the world. Vatican documents are often criticised as being 'unrealistic' or as not being sufficiently 'radical'. Realism and radicality are both useful criteria for evaluation. But by implicitly invoking these two different criteria at different times a hostile critic can dismiss a Vatican statement as both unrealistic and lacking in radicality. This seems rather unfair, since a 'radical' critique of society inevitably espouses views that are 'unrealistic' in terms of the accepted patterns of society.

In this book the evaluation of social teaching from the time of Leo XIII up to fairly recent times has been based on 'hindsight'. In other words, I have used the present understanding of the Church as a basis for evaluating what was said in the past. For instance, I believe that John XXIII and the Vatican Council were unduly optimistic about the effects of modern economic development. This view is supported by the critical remarks made by John Paul II about the kind of development that has taken place in recent times. An evaluation of the past based on 'hindsight' must not, of course, judge the views and actions of people without taking account of their historical situation. On the contrary, the aim is to understand why people thought and acted the way they did. A more ultimate aim is to discern an overall pattern, and in this way to come to a better understanding of the background to our present positions.

It is not so easy to specify precisely the criteria I have used in evaluating more recent documents and statements. I have looked especially for consistency; social teaching has to be internally coherent if it is to be credible. I have also evaluated what is being said in the light of the understanding of poverty and of 'option for the poor' as outlined briefly earlier in this introduction, and as examined further towards the end of the book. A person's commitments affect his or her choice of materials and the evaluation of the material. Objectivity is not attained by abandoning all commitment; and commitment to social justice is part of the Christian faith in the light of which I have done this theological study. That commitment to social justice calls for some kind of 'option for the poor' is one of the main points that has emerged in Catholic social teaching in recent years.

In my subtitle I have used the phrase 'social teaching'. This calls for a brief comment. A generation ago the term 'Catholic social doctrine' was used very frequently. More recently, however, this term fell into theological disrepute. Some theologians felt it smacked of a timeless dogmatism; and that would be particularly inappropriate in matters of social morality where in fact Church authorities have changed at least the emphasis, if not the substance, of their teaching over the years. Others objected to the notion of a 'Catholic social doctrine' or even a 'Catholic social teaching' on the grounds that this phrase suggests that the Church has a body of principles and a model of society that amount to a 'third way', that is, an alternative to the capitalist and socialist models; this they considered unacceptable.

In the course of Chapters Ten and Eleven of the book I have discussed these issues. Here in the introduction it suffices to say that Pope John Paul II has succeeded to some extent in reinstating the term 'social doctrine', using it alongside 'social teaching' and similar terms. But this does not mean a return to the situation of the 1930s when many Catholics thought the Church had a blueprint for society. It is clear that, for John Paul, social 'doctrine' or teaching does not mean a readymade pattern or an immutable set of truths. He sees it as an organic tradition of teaching by the Church on social issues. This tradition is open to development; and the pope believes that he himself has a contribution to make to it. It is not primarily a question of laying down rules for how society must be organised; but he believes that the Church has a duty to teach and witness to certain basic truths about the human person and certain fundamental human values that ought to be respected in society. It is within the context of such an organic tradition of social teaching that the notion of an 'option for the poor' can best be understood.

# 1

# *Rerum Novarum:* A Call for Justice

The first of the great social encyclicals, *Rerum Novarum*, was issued by Leo XIII in 1891.[1] In it the pope protested strongly against the harsh conditions which industrial workers had to endure. It is sometimes said that Leo was inspired to write his encyclical more by the loss of the working classes to the Church than by their plight. No doubt he was anxious to ensure that the Church should not be rejected by the mass of the new urban poor. But that is no reason to cast doubt on the genuineness of his protest about their treatment. In any case I am concerned here mainly with the content and impact of the encyclical rather than with speculations about why it was written.

Somebody who reads *Rerum Novarum* today, more than ninety years after it was written, may feel that the changes it calls for are not very radical, and that it is rather vague in regard to how they should be brought about. Clearly, it does not go nearly so far as the encyclicals of more recent popes in articulating the requirements of social justice, and in offering specific criticisms of the structures and practices which lead to poverty and oppression. Nevertheless, it lays a solid foundation on which the later social encyclicals and other Church documents could build.

Though the content of Leo's encyclical was important and remains important, what was perhaps even more important was the character of the document as a cry of protest against the exploitation of poor workers. It is not so much the detail of what Leo had to say that was significant but the fact that he chose to speak out at that time, intervening in a most solemn way in a burning issue of the day. His intervention meant that the Church could not be taken to be indifferent

11

to the injustices of the time. Rather, the Church was seen to be taking a stand on behalf of the poor.

The fact that Catholic Church leaders since that time have frequently spoken out strongly on issues of social injustice makes it difficult to appreciate just how significant it was that Pope Leo should issue his encyclical at that time. An analogy may help. Suppose the present pope were to issue an encyclical maintaining that it is quite immoral for any nation or individual to make or handle nuclear weapons. Commentators might say that this was simply an application of known principles of morality. But the document would have enormous significance as an intervention which committed the Vatican firmly to a specific practical application of general moral principles. It would put the pope firmly on the side of the nuclear disarmers, and against those who hold that nuclear weapons are necessary. In a somewhat similar way, *Rerum Novarum* represents a definite moral stance by the pope. It committed the Catholic Church officially to a rejection of a central thesis of the prevailing capitalist 'realism' of the Western world, namely, that labour is a commodity to be bought at market prices determined by the law of supply and demand rather than by the human needs of the worker.[2] So already in this first of the social encyclicals there was a strong protest against the prevailing order.

It is clear that Leo XIII *intended* his encyclical to be a major intervention in defence of the poor. He solemnly and firmly proposed his teaching as a remedy for the social problems of the time,[3] the core of which was 'the misery and wretchedness pressing so unjustly on the majority of the working class';[4] and he saw such an intervention as necessary in view of the fact that 'a small number of very rich men have been able to lay upon the teeming masses of the labouring poor a yoke little better than that of slavery itself.'[5]

Looked at from the point of view of its *effect*, this first of the social encyclicals must be seen as a very significant move of the Church towards the side of the poor. It ensured that social issues could no longer be treated as marginal or secondary to the mission of the Church, or as an 'optional extra'. This applied not merely in the sphere of official teaching but also in practical commitment. *Rerum Novarum* gave great encouragement to those of the clergy and laity who had been

12

working for years to get the Catholic Church more involved in social issues; and it had the long-term effect of greatly increasing the numbers of such committed activists. So, if one judges in terms of the effects over a considerable period of years, it is correct to say with Vidler that the encyclical 'had a truly epoch-making effect in driving home the idea that Catholics must have a social conscience'.[6] But this did not happen overnight. There were practical and theological obstacles which made for a progress that was uneven and very slow in some sectors. In fact the encyclical was at first largely ignored by many of the people with whom it was most directly concerned — employers, industrial workers, and even some Churchmen. In some places, such as Latin America, it was scarcely read at all. Where it was read it was not always accepted. It gave rise to some scandal, not only in society but even within the Church itself.[7]

The reason for this shocked reaction and the resistance that accompanied it was not so much any specific course of action proposed by the pope. It was rather the much more fundamental point that he challenged the current assumption that the 'laws' of economics should be treated as though they were laws of nature, and therefore the basis for morality. Pope Leo issued this challenge at the most obvious point of all, which is also the most sensitive point: he questioned the sacrosanctness of the wage contract. He rejected the assumption that the employer's obligations in justice can be taken to have been fulfilled once the agreed wage has been paid. Leo insisted that 'there underlies a dictate of natural justice more imperious and ancient than any bargain between man and man, namely that wages ought not to be insufficient to support a frugal and well-behaved wage-earner.'[8] He drew the conclusion that if, 'through necessity or fear of a worse evil' the worker accepts a wage less than that required for frugal living then 'he is made the victim of force and injustice.'[9] None of this involved any radical new departure in Catholic moral theology; and the same general principles were applied in the theology of 'secret compensation', which allowed workers to supplement an unjust wage by petty pilfering. But that Leo should apply the general principle so bluntly to a situation that was so widespread was really quite shocking in the atmosphere of the time. For it was a clear and

13

outspoken contradiction of the taken-for-granted views of those who held power in the Western world.

The basic principle behind Leo's stance is that human labour cannot be treated simply as a commodity because to do so is a denial of human dignity and a reduction of the worker to the status of a thing. Needless to say, there is nothing startling in Leo's assertion that it is shameful and inhuman to treat people as though they were things. But for a pope to invoke this principle in defence of underpaid workers was quite startling — shocking for some and inspiring for others. That is why it can be claimed that the importance of *Rerum Novarum* is to be measured not merely in terms of its contribution to the body of teaching (or 'doctrine') of the Catholic Church but also in terms of its impact as an intervention on the side of the poor: that is what we may call the *'effective'* meaning of the document in contrast to its 'doctrinal' meaning.

Various aspects of the teaching contained in the encyclical can be seen in a new light when account is taken of this overriding purpose and effective meaning of *Rerum Novarum*. For instance, a fairly lengthy section is devoted to a treatment of socialism.[10] Leo had already spoken out against socialism on a number of occasions. In *Rerum Novarum*, however, he set out not merely to reject it but also to refute it.[11] Undoubtedly Leo considered this part of the encyclical to have an importance in its own right: it warned off the small but significant number of radical Catholics who were flirting with social ideas. However, his formal rejection of socialism also served a different and wider purpose. It gave Leo the freedom to condemn the abuses within the existing capitalist system without leaving himself open to the accusation that he was encouraging those who advocated a socialist alternative.

In spite of its strong rejection of socialism the encyclical must have appeared to many to be tainted with socialist principles on one vital issue — the question of intervention by the State. It is true that in the early part of the document the pope lays down very strict limits to the right of the State to intervene in the affairs of the individual and the family.[12] But on the other hand he makes particular mention later on of the duty of the State to be concerned for the interests of the working classes.[13] He then goes on even to give the working class a certain privileged place in this regard:

... when there is question of defending the rights of individuals, the poor and badly-off have a claim to especial consideration. The richer class have many ways of shielding themselves ... whereas the mass of the poor ... must chiefly depend upon the assistance of the State.[14]

In later paragraphs the pope specifies various ways in which the State should protect workers from abuse and exploitation.[15] This whole approach involved a rejection of the principles of *laissez faire* capitalism, especially as expounded by the Manchester school.

From the point of view of its 'doctrine', *Rerum Novarum* can be seen as a balanced statement of general principles which rejects the two extremes – socialism on the one hand and uncontrolled capitalism on the other. But when one considers its effective meaning as an intervention by the pope in the social issues of the time it is clear that it is an attempt to place the Catholic Church on the side of the poor – or of the working class, which at that time was more or less the same thing.[16] It succeeded in doing so to a considerable extent – at least in so far as it was the first major official step in a long process which has been continuing, with some 'ups and downs', up to the present. However, a clarification is called for at once: the encyclical did not attempt to put the Church on the side of the working class *against* another class. What it was against was not a group or class but simply the fact of exploitation. So it did not represent a 'class option' in the usual sense of the term. In fact its whole thrust was to lessen the barriers between the classes of society.[17] Nevertheless, this in no way detracts from the fact that in this encyclical Leo XIII took a firm stand on the side of the mass of exploited workers in the society of the time. It would be overstating the case to claim that *Rerum Novarum* represents or calls for 'an option for the poor' in the sense in which that term is generally understood today; but it indicates a particular concern for the poor and it can now be seen as a major step on the road which eventually led to such an option.

*The Proposed Remedy*

In *Rerum Novarum* Leo XIII was proposing his 'remedy'[18] for the social problem, a remedy which he believed could, if applied, eliminate the grave injustices of the existing system and bring harmony to the social and economic order. But how realistic was this solution? Granted that the pope was seeking to defend the poor against exploitation, was he also proposing a coherent programme which could bring this about in practice? Or was there a gap between the aim he wished to attain and the means he proposed?

What kind of changes does Leo XIII have in mind? As already noted, *Rerum Novarum* insists on the duty of the State to protect the poor.[19] This amounts to a call for a major change in the role which the State had been playing in society in Leo's time. In order to understand and assess the pope's call, it is helpful to consider an issue frequently overlooked by moralists — the relation between economic power and political power.

We can look briefly at two contrasting views of the role of the State in society. (By 'the State' I understand here the apparatus of government that has power to control the way people act in society.) First, there is the classical theory of liberal capitalism. It held that the State should mainly confine itself to 'political' matters such as defending society from external aggression and ensuring internal order and stability; normally the government should not 'interfere' in the economic sphere, but should rather allow private enterprise, open competition, and the forces of the market to operate freely. The assumption here is that the State and its agencies (the judiciary, the security forces, the civil service, etc.) are 'neutral' and independent in relation to any economic rivalries or conflicts that take place in society; their task is to provide the framework within which economic activity can take place peacefully and effectively.

In sharp contrast to this is the Marxist theory. It holds that in fact the State is not neutral; political power is normally held by those with economic power — and, as one might expect, they use the apparatus of the State to further their own interests; the lower classes find that the laws and the security forces are being used to oppress them and to ensure that they cannot escape from the economic exploitation practised by those who control the wealth.

What was the view of Leo XIII? He disagreed with both of the above views. But in speaking about the role of the State in *Rerum Novarum* he comes fairly close to each of the two views at different times. His *ideal* of what the State ought to be, though it differs significantly from that of the liberal capitalist, nevertheless shares with the latter the assumption that the State is neutral and 'above' economics. But, on the other hand, Leo's account of what happens *in practice* is closer to the Marxist view.

According to the principles laid down by Leo, economic power ought not to overlap with political power. In society as it ought to be, the wealthy would not control the apparatus of the State. Instead, the State would be above the interests of all classes and would keep a balance between them.[20] Leo maintains that cooperation rather than conflict is to be the basis of the social order: 'The great mistake . . . is to take up the notion that class is naturally hostile to class, and that the wealthy and the working-men are intended by nature to live in mutual conflict.'[21] The reason this mistaken view was held, the pope believed, lay in the failure to appreciate the design of nature for the body politic:

> Just as the symmetry of the human frame is the result of the suitable arrangement of the different parts of the body, so in a State is it ordained by nature that these two classes should dwell in harmony and agreement, so as to maintain the balance of the body politic. Each needs the other: Capital cannot do without Labour, nor Labour without Capital.[22]

The institutions of the State have the task of preserving and fostering the cooperation of the different classes. So the State is neutral, not the instrument of the richer class.

However, a quite different account of the State is suggested by the actual situation as it had evolved up to the time at which the encyclical was written. Looking at what had taken place all around him, Pope Leo did not gloss over the obvious fact that in practice the rich were the ones who held the effective power, a power that extended into the apparatus of the State:

> On the one side there is the party which holds power because it holds wealth; . . . which manipulates for its own benefit . . . all the sources of supply, and which is even

represented in the councils of the State itself. On the other side there is the needy and powerless multitude . . .[23]

Faced with this reality, Leo proposed his long-term solution: the gulf between the classes should be narrowed by enabling as many workers as possible to become owners of property.[24] This indicates that he recognised that, in practice, so long as wealth is concentrated in the hands of the few, these few are likely to have undue political power; they will be able to use this power for their own benefit. In practice this means not allowing the State to play its role effectively in protecting the rights of the poor. Leo was well aware that this was actually happening; that is why he insisted so strongly on the need for the State to protect the rights of workers, and why he went on to list several of these rights.[25]

We have now noted two of the key changes which Leo proposed as a remedy for the social problem: immediate action by the State to protect the interests of the working classes and a more long-term effort to distribute ownership of property much more widely. The next question is, who or what are to be the *agents* of change that can ensure that the remedy is really applied and the changes take place? How can one make sure that those who have the power to make the changes have the will to do so — and that those who want to do it are able to get it done?

Leo XIII gives a double answer to this question. First, he puts forward religion as the most powerful intermediary of all in drawing the rich and the working class together; and he presents the Church as the interpreter of religion in reminding each class of its duties to the other and especially of the obligations of justice.[26] Secondly, he vindicates the right of workers to band together in trade unions or other associations for their own protection.[27] Unfortunately, however, each of these two sources or agents of change is open to serious challenge in the form in which it is presented in *Rerum Novarum*. In the following two sections of this chapter, I shall consider each of these points in turn.


*How Prophetic can the Church dare to be?*
In Leo's view the Church has a task which would nowadays be called 'prophetic' — that of challenging each of the classes

18

of society to meet its obligations in justice to the others. But how can the Church best promote cooperation and respect, combined with justice, in the relations between the classes? Leo's view — and his difficulties — can best be understood by looking at two contrasting strategies. One possible approach is to call the rich and powerful to conversion, while exhorting the poor and powerless to be patient — and especially to respect public order in the way they seek their rights. In this approach those who hold power would be encouraged not merely to change their hearts but also to change the structures of society so that injustice would be eliminated.

A very different strategy would be to animate the poor to demand their rights. They would be encouraged not simply to wait patiently for justice but rather to confront the rich and powerful when this proves necessary. The Church could assure them that God is the God of the poor, who supports those who feel called to act like Moses in challenging the injustice of the powerful.

Are the two policies mutually exclusive? Partly, but not entirely. It is possible for Church leaders to appeal to the rich while animating the poor. But the two strategies differ fundamentally on one major point — whether the poor ought to be encouraged to wait patiently or to engage in active confrontation. The difference between the two approaches is based above all on the different degree of importance each gives to the value of stability in society. In the first approach it is seen as a very high value, so indispensable that one dare not put it at risk. In the second approach, stability is seen as an important value but one that must at times be risked in order to ensure justice in society; furthermore, it is considered that the best guarantee of long-term stability is to ensure that society is just.

How does Leo's approach relate to these two possible strategies? It must be said that his conviction about the importance of stability in society led him to adopt a position much nearer to the first approach than to the second. There is no doubt that he wanted changes to take place in society. But what he had in mind was change 'from the top down' rather than 'from the bottom up'. He issued a ringing call to conversion to the people who held economic power. But what if this call goes largely unheeded? Then it appears that the poor working class have little option but to put up with their sad situation.

Various encyclicals issued by Leo XIII give indications that for him the changes in society that would make for social justice depended to a very considerable degree on a change of heart by those who held economic and political power. In the next chapter I shall make a detailed study of various writings of Leo in order to provide a background against which his approach in *Rerum Novarum* can be understood more clearly. But *Rerum Novarum* itself throws quite a lot of light on the pope's attitude, both in what it says and in what it fails to say.

A central paragraph in the encyclical lists the reciprocal duties of employers and workers, duties of which the Church reminds them in order to promote harmony and justice. First, those of the employers:

> The following duties bind the wealthy owner and the employer: not to look upon their work-people as their bondsmen but to respect in every man his dignity and worth. . . . They are reminded that . . . to misuse men as though they were things in the pursuit of gain . . . is truly shameful and inhuman. . . . Furthermore, the employer must never tax his work-people beyond their strength, or employ them in work unsuited to their sex and age. His great and principal duty is to give every one what is just. . . . to gather one's profit out of the need of another, is condemned by all laws human and divine. . . . Lastly, the rich must religiously refrain from cutting down the workmen's earnings, whether by force, by fraud, or by usurious dealing . . .[28]

The whole passage constitutes a very moving call for conversion — and not just a change of heart but significant changes in business practice and standards of behaviour in the economic world. But there is an element of unrealism in it. For, unfortunately, Leo is making a rhetorical statement rather than one that is literally true when he says that, 'all laws human and divine' condemn those who gather their profit out of the need of another. There are some human laws which allow such exploitation. It is precisely at this point that a wide gap exists between the laws of a capitalist society and what the Church sees as the divine law.

What if this gap still remains, in spite of Pope Leo's eloquent appeal? What is the pope's response if employers continue to neglect the duties he has listed, if they fail to respect their workers, if they still fail to pay a just wage and if they tax them beyond their strength? What if the wealthy continue to make a profit out of the need of the poor? Above all, what if the laws of the State continue to allow this exploitation to take place and if the law-courts and security forces fail to offer the poor adequate protection against these injustices? These are not hypothetical questions. The pope was well aware that injustices of this kind were a permanent feature of the social situation of his time. One is entitled, therefore, to ask what action he recommends to workers in the face of such abuses.

The following is a list of some of the duties which *Rerum Novarum* lays down for workers:

> ... fully and faithfully to perform the work which has been freely and equitably agreed upon; never to injure the property, nor outrage the person, of an employer; never to resort to violence in defending their own cause, nor to engage in riot or disorder; and to have nothing to do with men of evil principles, who ... excite foolish hopes ...[29]

This catalogue gives very little encouragement to activism on the part of workers in the struggle for rights. Not merely does it not give any guidelines by which workers might determine how far they could go in a situation of confrontation, but it does not appear to envisage that they might be entitled to engage in serious confrontation. For instance, workers are told that they must not injure the property of an employer. But it is not clear whether Leo adverted to the implications of this teaching. If taken strictly it would seem to imply that a strike is wrong whenever it causes damage to the property of an employer; but the pope may not have wanted to go as far as that. In a later paragraph of the encyclical he acknowledges that strikes occur, points out their causes and consequences, but does not make an explicit judgment about their morality. [30] Elsewhere he says that when a strike poses an imminent threat of public disturbance the law may be invoked to protect the peace;[31] this implies, of course, that a strike may be lawful where it does not pose such a threat. But it is significant that

Leo's main emphasis is on circumstances which would make a strike wrong rather than on those which would justify it.

Leo XIII was well aware that insistence by workers on their rights in the economic sphere could quickly spill over into the political area and give rise to a threat to public order. His reluctance to encourage the working class to press militantly for their rights stems from his belief that nothing should be done that might cause such a 'disturbance'. The pope wanted to preserve a clear line of distinction between the socio-economic sphere and the political sphere,[32] so that his challenge to the *status quo* in the economic order would not be taken as sanction for challenge in the political field.

Was Leo entitled to rely on this distinction? Perhaps the best answer is to say that the distinction is very useful in principle but that in the late nineteenth century it could be used to evade the more difficult social issues. It is certainly very useful to carve out a clearly defined area called 'the economic' as distinct from the area called 'the political'. Within this economic area a certain clash of interest and a struggle between competing groups is accepted and 'contained'. But this presupposes that the richer classes are not allowed to use their economic power to exert political pressure on others. A limited degree of struggle in the economic area is tolerable if the State can ensure that its laws and institutions remain neutral, so as to serve all classes with impartial justice. In the time of Leo XIII this political impartiality was not maintained. As he himself pointed out, the wealthy exercised undue political power.[33] In practice this meant that the institutions of the State – laws, courts, police – showed a greater or lesser degree of bias against the poor. Such a bias is not merely something personal but a structural imbalance. In this situation only *political* changes could ensure that the *economic* rights of the poor were protected. To confine the struggle of workers to the purely economic order would very frequently mean condemning them to futility. For as soon as a really effective economic weapon was developed – for instance a general strike – it could at once be countered by political means, for instance by making its use illegal or subject to crippling restrictions.

In these circumstances it would amount to an option against the poor if Church authorities were to say that the

22

poor were not entitled to work for major political changes, structural changes. It would be giving ideological support to those who were oppressing the poor. Leo XIII did not make such an option. But he failed to give clear guidelines for political and quasi-political action by the working class — the only kind of action which was likely to bring about the changes that would make society just. He allowed such words and phrases as 'disorder'[34] and 'danger of disturbance to the public peace'[35] to remain vague in meaning and therefore capable of being invoked to cover almost any situation which threatened the interests of the rich and powerful. He did not distinguish clearly between, on the one hand, an altogether unacceptable level of violent or disruptive action and, on the other hand, a certain level of disturbance and instability which may be necessary if structural injustices are to be overcome despite the resistance of powerful groups. In other words, he failed to develop guidelines for confrontation.

Pope Leo set up an ideal of harmony in society that was so exalted and perfect that it remained abstract and unreal. Instead of envisaging a whole series of possible situations, approximating to a greater or lesser degree to the ideal, he seemed to consider only two alternatives to his ideal. The first of these was 'disorder' or 'disturbance'; and this was something he felt he had to condemn. The second alternative was the existing state of what would now be called 'structural injustice'. This was the situation where the institutions of the State supported and reinforced the gap between rich and poor. This too was something that he had to condemn. But if the condemnation had little or no practical effect then it seemed as though the Church would have to acquiesce reluctantly in the existing unjust situation rather than opt for 'disorder'. This acquiescence, reluctant though it was, gave a considerable degree of religious support to a society that was structurally unjust. It undoubtedly diminished the effectiveness of *Rerum Novarum* as a cry of protest and a call for justice on behalf of the poor.

To understand why Leo XIII found himself in this awkward position one must look beyond *Rerum Novarum* to the writings in which he presented his teaching on political questions. This will be the subject of the next chapter. But before moving on to that study it is well to look more closely at what *Rerum Novarum* has to say on the question of workers' associations.

## Workers' Organisations

In the previous section we have been considering religion and the Church as a possible agent of change in society, a force that might be able to bring about the transformation required to make it a structurally just society. We have seen that the pope felt reluctant to encourage workers to take organised militant action to secure their rights. What then was the teaching of the pope in regard to trade unions or other associations which could give some power to the workers? This is an important question because, apart from the Church and religion, the other possible agent of social change which has to be considered in the context of Leo's encyclical is the trade union movement. (For the pope entirely ruled out revolutionary movements as acceptable agents of change; and in *Rerum Novarum* he did not consider the question of political change brought about by democratic action — that did not enter into the socio-economic question with which he was concerned in this encyclical.)[36]

At the beginning of *Rerum Novarum* there is a perceptive passage in which the pope points to one of the basic reasons why workers at that time could be so exploited. He says: '. . . the ancient working-men's guilds were abolished in the last century, and no other protective organisation took their place.'[37] This statement has sometimes been dismissed as a pointless pining for an out-dated social order. No doubt there is a certain nostalgia there. But the following lines show that this passage contains one of the most important insights in the whole encyclical.[38] The pope adverts to the fact that, partly as a result of the abolition of the guilds, 'working-men have been surrendered, isolated and helpless, to the hard-heartedness of employers and the greed of unchecked competition.'[39] The point to note here is that the plight of the workers is not attributed simply to the hard-heartedness of employers or to greed and competition. Rather the problem arises because the workers no longer have protective organisations or other defences. It is this that has now left them 'isolated and helpless' at the mercy of employers. It is for this reason that greed and competition remain 'unchecked'. At

24

this point the pope is not saying whether he considers that employers are now more hard-hearted and greedy than in the past. Instead, he is focusing attention on the safeguards which society offers, or fails to offer, to workers; and this is a question of the *structures* of society, rather than a purely *moral* matter, such as how virtuous the employers are.

This passage indicates that Leo XIII had gone some way towards analysing the structures of the society of his time and pinpointing the relationship between poverty and the powerlessness of workers. So it would not be quite fair to suggest that *Rerum Novarum* fails entirely to offer a 'structural analysis' of the causes of poverty.[40] What is true, however, is that there is little coherent development of the basic insight about the importance of protective organisations for workers. Perhaps even more important is the fact that Leo's prophetic voice seemed to falter when it came to drawing practical conclusions from the insight.

Since Leo had noted the disastrous effect of the loss of the workers' guilds, one might have expected that he would go on to point out the need for strong and united movements of workers, to ensure adequate protection from the hard-heartedness and greed of employers. The existence of such movements would constitute a significant change in the structures of society. The development of the trade union movement in Western countries in this century indicates how effectively society can be changed by their action. Through them the workers can bargain with employers from a position of some strength. They can generally ensure that the solidarity of workers is not weakened by the use of non-union labour to break strikes. They can also have some involvement in the formulation of government policy. This quasi-political role is a necessary check on the political influence which can be exerted on government by the employers. This means there is a somewhat better chance that the State will protect the interests of workers, as Pope Leo wished.[41] The result so far of all this leaves much to be desired, both with regard to the internal organisation of Western countries and in their relationship with the poor countries of the Third World. But it represents a considerable advance on the society of Leo's time in so far as the internal structures of these countries are concerned; it goes some way towards having that balance in the body politic which Leo considered to be essential.[42]

The central point that emerges from this brief look at the role of trade unions is that major social injustices can be overcome even if the rich and powerful are not 'converted'. The greed and hard-heartedness of employers may still be present. But now they are no longer 'unchecked', to use Leo's word.[43] Workers are no longer 'isolated and helpless'. They have a structure that protects them. It is a good example of what is meant when people say that social injustice must be dealt with at the *structural* level, not merely by working for the moral conversion of the oppressors.

Despite its obvious advantages, *Rerum Novarum* does not come out clearly in favour of such an approach. This may have been partly due to an inability of the pope and his advisors to anticipate the kind of developments that might come about as a result of a strong and united trade union movement. But it would appear that it was at least partly due to hesitation about giving encouragement to the kind of movement that could bring about significant structural change. Such changes could come as a result of pressure from a workers' movement whose strength lay in its unity and whose activity would at times seem quite militant. But the practical proposals put forward by the pope fall quite short of this.

The pope defends the basic right of workers to form associations. The most important of these, he says are 'Workingmen's Unions'.[44] But the encyclical goes on to speak in general terms of associations in a way that could scarcely be applied to trade unions in the modern sense. The paragraphs that deal with associations[45] are quite vague. They refer to a wide variety of associations ranging from sodalities to trade unions; and it is difficult if not impossible to know which of Leo's remarks are intended to refer to which type of organisation. [46] Having said that working-men's unions are the most important form of association the pope immediately goes on to speak in very general terms about unions or associations some of which are open in their membership to employers as well as workers.[47] When he goes on to speak of organisations which aim to promote the cause of workers, he carefully avoids the use of such militant phrases as 'struggling for rights'; his main emphasis is on self-restraint and harmony. Working-men's associations, he says, must give their 'chief attention to the duties of religion and morality' and their concept of

26

social betterment should have this chiefly in view.[48] Indeed there is no clear evidence that the pope approved of the idea of a trade union as presently understood, namely, an organisation which has limited goals of a secular nature.

The reluctance of the pope to dissociate spiritual from temporal welfare is very important. He wanted to ensure that Catholic workers would not be 'led astray' by associations that were not explicitly Catholic. So he encouraged Catholic workers to form their own associations as an alternative to those which might expose their religion to peril.[49] There were two unfortunate results of this policy. In the first place it minimised the influence that Catholic social activists could have on those of other Churches, or of no Church, and *vice versa*; so the Catholic social movement remained rather cut off from similar movements outside the Church, while the emerging 'secular' trade unions tended to become secularist and even anti-Catholic at times. The second result was even more significant: Leo's policy contributed notably to a fragmentation of the trade union movement. Instead of uniting with other activists in a strong united workers' movement, very many socially-oriented Catholics formed Catholic trade unions in several European countries. This had the effect of greatly weakening the whole trade union movement, especially in view of the fact that the different unions competed with each other and adopted different policies and strategies on particular issues.

There was, then, a clear disparity between the kind of working-men's associations that Leo XIII actually wanted to have and the kind of workers' movement that would have a real chance of bringing about the major structural changes required if society were to become just. The main reason for this seems to be that Leo XIII was not prepared to take the risks involved in calling for, and actively supporting, a united militant workers' movement. The encyclical itself indicates some of the pope's reservations. He believed that many of the existing unions were 'in the hands of secret leaders and . . . managed on principles ill-according with Christianity and the public well-being'.[50] Furthermore, he was convinced that these unions and their leaders were trying to bring about what would now be called a 'closed shop' — a situation where only those who joined that union would be able to get a job.

27

The combination of these two features was seen by the pope as posing a very grave danger for Catholic workers; for he felt that for them to be forced to join such unions would put their faith, and therefore their salvation, at risk.[51] There can be little doubt that the principles which he saw as incompatible with Christianity were socialist and revolutionary ones — the two being, for Leo, more or less inseparable.

The attitude of Leo XIII to trade unions was largely determined by two major concerns of his. On the one hand he wanted to vindicate the right of the individual to free association in the protection of personal interests; so he affirmed the basic right of the worker to join a union or form a new one. But on the other hand the pope had an overriding concern for public order. It was this that made him oppose any movement that sought to change the social structures of society by vigorous action 'from below'. If an assessment of *Rerum Novarum* is to be fair it must take account of both of these points. It must not play down the importance of the pope's vindication of the right to form trade unions. But it must also acknowledge that Leo was a very long way from encouraging militant action by workers to reconstruct society. The reason for this should emerge more clearly in the next chapter which sets out to examine his socio-political teaching as enunciated in a wide variety of documents issued prior to, and subsequent to, *Rerum Novarum*.

# 2

# Leo XIII and Allegiance to the State

A nineteenth-century industrialist is reported to have said that the best way to prevent strikes would be to establish an association of St Francis Xavier.[1] The implication is that the Catholic Church and its associations served the function, whether deliberately or not, of making workers less likely to take militant action in pursuit of better pay and conditions. To what extent was this true? No simple answer can be given to the question, since, as we saw in the last chapter, even the pope felt himself pulled in two directions. He certainly wanted to defend the rights of exploited workers. But he was also reluctant to sanction any activity that could disturb public order. In this chapter I shall look more closely at Leo XIII's teaching on allegiance to the civil authorities, in order to understand why he laid so much stress on public order. The pope's teaching on these matters is to be found only peripherally in *Rerum Novarum*; the main sources are a series of other encyclicals and documents issued by the pope at various times during his long pontificate. A study of the teaching in these sources will help one to see *Rerum Novarum* in context.

## *Authority is from God*

There are good reasons for saying that in the mind of Leo XIII one of the purposes of Catholic associations was to discourage militancy on the part of workers. The following passage provides evidence for this:

> ... it seems expedient to encourage associations for handicraftsmen and labouring men, which, placed under the sheltering care of religion, may render the members content with their lot and resigned to toil, inducing them to lead a peaceful and tranquil life.[2]

One can distinguish three very different kinds of reason why the pope laid so much emphasis on workers being content with their lot:

— At the practical level he was anxious to have close co-operation between Church and State, so he offered the support of the Church to governments so far as possible.
— At the more philosophical-theological level he had a conception of civil authority which required that he stress the duty of obedience and submission.
— At the psychological level, he was personally very perturbed about the danger of revolution.

In Leo XIII these three levels of motivation interlock and support each other; so it would be pointless to focus exclusively on one or other as the primary reason for a particular statement or action. Nevertheless, it is useful to make the distinction because the earnestness with which the pope pursued his policy of practical cooperation with governments, and the tirelessness with which he propounded his philosophy on the nature of authority, can be understood more clearly and sympathetically in the light of his real anxiety about the danger of anarchy and the disintegration of society.

In the encyclical *Inscrutabili*, issued just two months after he became pope, Leo XIII made a strong appeal to civil authorities that they should cooperate with the Church and accept the support the Church offered them:

> We address ourselves to princes and chief rulers of the nations and earnestly beseech them . . . not to refuse the Church's aid . . . but with united and friendly aims to join themselves to her as the source of authority and salvation . . . considering that their own peace and safety, as well as that of their people, is bound up with the safety of the Church and the reverence due to her . . .[3]

Some months later, in the encyclical *Quod Apostolici Muneris*, he indicated the kind of support the Church can give to rulers of the State: the Church teaches that the authority of civil rulers must be accepted because it comes from God himself: 'From the heads of States, to whom as the Apostle admonishes, all owe submission, and on whom the rights of authority are bestowed by God Himself, these sectaries withhold obedience . . .'[4] He maintains that it is 'impious' to rise

30

up against one's rulers.[5] Later in the same encyclical he says that the Church constantly urges on everybody the apostolic precept that one should obey rulers as a matter of conscience.[6]

Two and a half years later, in 1881, Leo issued an encyclical, *Diuturnum*, devoted to the specific question of the origin of civil power. Rejecting the 'modern' view that it comes from a mandate of the people, he insisted that civil power has its source in God. In support of this position he invokes the Old Testament, the New Testament, the Fathers of the Church,[7] and arguments from reason.[8] Central to his case is his claim that a purely human origin for civil authority is too weak and fragile a basis for it.[9] The authority of rulers requires a religious foundation. Leo points out that the Church had recognised this, even in early Christian times when believers were being persecuted; even then they saw the power of the rulers as coming from God.[10] The pope goes on to note that once states came to have Christian rulers the Church redoubled its efforts to promote the awareness of the sacredness of authority; in this way people were drawn to reverence and love their rulers by the aura of religious majesty that surrounded them.[11] Leo maintains that reliance on force provided rulers with an insecure basis for obedience; what is required is something loftier — and more effective. Strict laws will not have the desired effect unless people are motivated by a sense of obligation and a salutary fear of God.[12] It is not surprising, then, to find Leo saying, later in the encyclical, that the Church strengthens the authority of rulers and helps it in many ways.[13] As he pointed out in the following year, 'those who are imbued with the Christian religion know with certainty that they are bound in conscience to submit to those who lawfully rule them'; and he concluded that religion is the most effective way to root out violence, envy between different classes, and the desire for a new order in society.[14]

In 1885, in his classical encyclical *Immortale Dei*, on the Christian constitution of states, Pope Leo covered much the same ground, with some additional nuances:

> ... every civilised community must have a ruling authority and this authority, no less than society itself, has its source in nature, and has, consequently, God for its author. Hence it follows that all public power must proceed from God ...[15]

He goes on to draw the conclusions. It is a matter of justice and duty to obey rulers. To despise legitimate authority, in whomsoever invested, is a rebellion against the divine will. To cast aside obedience, and by popular violence to incite revolt, is treason not merely against man but against God.[16] Later in the same encyclical he remarks that the order of the commonwealth should be maintained as sacred; obedience to rulers is submission to God, because God is exercising his sovereignty through the medium of humans.[17]

Four years later Leo remarked that while it is true that the poor and manual workers have the right to escape from their poverty to a better condition by lawful means, nevertheless reason and justice require that they should not overturn the order established by God's providence.[18] This is an important statement. It suggests that not only is God the source of political power in a general way but also that God gives his support to whatever particular form of government has emerged in a given country — for this is attributed to God's providence.

In the encyclical *Quod Multum*, which Leo XIII wrote in 1886 to the bishops of Hungary, there is a passage which not only sums up several of the points already noted but also conveys a sense of the *spirituality* which the pope was promoting:

> The best and most effective way of avoiding the horrors of socialism . . . is for the citizens to be completely imbued with religion. . . . For just as religion requires the worship and fear of God so also it demands submission and obedience to lawful authority; it forbids any kind of seditious activity and wills that the property and the rights of everybody be safeguarded; and those who are more wealthy should magnanimously help the poor masses. Religion cares for the poor with every form of charity; it fills the stricken with the sweetest comfort by offering them the hope of very great and immortal good things which are all the more plentiful in the future in proportion to the extent to which one has been weighed down more heavily or for a longer time.[19]

Perhaps the most significant feature of Leo's approach here is the way in which he quite consciously links economics and politics with life after death. He recognises that it is those who are economically deprived who pose a threat to political stability. And he spells out the role of religion in helping to meet and overcome that threat by placating the poor. This is done most effectively by promising them rewards in heaven proportionate to the miseries they have endured patiently on earth.

This spirituality was applied by Pope Leo even in situations where rulers abuse their God-given authority. In his early encyclical *Quod Apostolici Muneris*, directed against socialism, communism, and nihilism, the pope makes it clear that abuses by rulers give subjects no right to rebel:

> Should it, however, happen at any time, that in the public exercise of authority rulers act rashly and arbitrarily, the teaching of the Catholic Church does not allow subjects to rise against them without further warrantry, lest peace and order become more and more disturbed, and society run the risk of greater detriment. And when things have come to such a pass as to hold out no further hope, she teaches that a remedy is to be sought in the virtue of Christian patience and in urgent prayer to God.[20]

This passage not merely forbids rebellion but reinforces the prohibition by offering what would now be called an 'escapist' answer to problems of injustice: prayer is presented as an alternative to the kind of action that might change the unjust situation. Further on, Pope Leo unashamedly speaks of how the Church cheers and comforts the hearts of the poor by setting before them the example of Christ, or by reminding them that Jesus called them 'blessed' and told them to hope for the reward of eternal happiness. The pope adds that this is obviously the best way to appease the undying struggle between rich and poor.[21]

All this adds up to a comprehensive spirituality which damps down any inclination the poor might have to put up active resistance to situations of injustice. Three forms of religious argument or persuasion are involved:

— First, they are told that resistance is sinful because the authority exercised by the government comes from God, and to resist is to disobey God.

— Secondly, the promise of reward in the next life is offered

to those who suffer patiently under unjust rulers in this life.
— Thirdly, the example of the patient suffering Christ is held up as a model to the poor.
To reinforce these arguments the Christian religion contributes to the lessening of tension between rich and poor in two other ways — by urging the rich to be generous in helping the poor, and by itself engaging in charitable activity to ease the misery of the poor. In view of the teaching of Pope Leo on the nature of civil authority and the submission it calls for, and in view of the spirituality which is built on this basis and which the pope so earnestly promoted, one can certainly understand his claim that the Church offers invaluable support to State governments.

*Some Qualifications*

Does all this mean that according to Leo's teaching the Church gives unqualified support to all governments, and condemns every instance of disobedience and every attempt to bring about change? By no means. There are certain qualifications to be made. These constitute a quite significant feature of the theoretical synthesis presented by the pope. In the practical sphere they also have a certain importance, though they are rather severely limited in the area to which they apply.

The first qualification concerns a situation where a ruler commands something that is evidently wrong, opposed to the law or will of God. One is then entitled — and indeed obliged — not to obey the command.[22] This apparent exception fits into the overall pattern of Leo's teaching because, 'the right to command and to require obedience exists only so far as it is in accordance with the authority of God, and is within the measure that He has laid down'; and in the situation now envisaged 'there is a wide departure from this divinely constituted order and at the same time a direct conflict with the divine authority'.[23] Strictly speaking this is not an exception at all, not really a case of disobedience in the proper sense. For those rulers whose will is in opposition to the will and law of God have gone beyond the limits of their authority. Leo adds an interesting remark which brings out the relationship which he sees between authority and justice. Such rulers, he says, have contravened justice and therefore their authority can no longer have validity, since there is no authority where there is no justice.[24]

It may be noted in passing that this 'exception' has a some-what different connotation from that of the modern under-standing of conscientious objection — although the two obviously have a common basis and overlap to some extent. The pope's presentation, which is the traditional Catholic one, puts less emphasis on the rights of the individual (subjective) conscience and more on the objective will and law of God. It would appear that Leo was not thinking primarily of the isolated individual. The kind of situation he would have had mostly in mind was that of Christians assured by Church authorities that certain kinds of action are contrary to the objective law of God.

The case just described seems to envisage a certain passive resistance on a specific issue; it is simply a refusal to obey a particular command or law. But is there room for any more active form of resistance, for some positive line of action which could bring about a change in the situation? Leo's answer is 'yes'. He gives it quite strongly. But he gives it with a significant lack of concrete indications about how such active resistance can take place. The pope's teaching on this matter came in a very delicate political situation where he had to be quite circumspect in what he said. In 1892 some royalists in France were suggesting that the French Republic of the time was 'animated by such anti-Christian sentiments that honest men, Catholics particularly, could not conscien-tiously accept it'.[25] The pope did not accept this argument. He drew a careful distinction between the 'constituted powers' of the State on the one hand, and 'legislation' on the other. The fact that odious legislation is passed by a regime does not prove that it is not a duly constituted political authority. One owes respect to such authorities. But this does not mean that one is bound to give unlimited respect — and still less unlimited obedience — to all legislative measures, of whatever kind, enacted by those who hold lawful political authority. The pope concludes that one should never approve of those points of legislation which are hostile to religion and to God; in fact one's duty is to condemn them.[26]

So far Pope Leo was simply giving a somewhat more elaborated version of the general principle that one must obey God above all. But he also says to the French of the time that, 'good people should put aside all political dissensions and unite as one to combat, by all legal and upright means, progressive abuses of legislation'.[27] This is an exhortation to something much more than mere passive refusal to obey evil laws. It recommends active resistance. But the significant point is that this resistance is to employ only 'legal and upright means'. It is clear that what the pope had in mind is the use of those forms of political representation or activity that do not undermine the security of the State nor challenge the legitimacy of the authority of those in power.

The next question is whether there are any circumstances in which one would be entitled to go even further: to engage in a kind of political planning and action that would aim at replacing the existing rulers by new rulers or by a different structure of government. Clearly there is no difficulty about seeking to replace one government by another through the process of a free election in a state which is constituted in such a way as to require such elections; for in that situation there is an agreed and orderly transfer of authority from one group of office-holders to another. But is this the only kind of situation in which it is legitimate to seek to oust one's rulers? To answer this question it is necessary to sift very carefully through the teaching of the pope in regard to the relationship between authority and 'social need', as well as the relation between the moral right to exercise political authority and the actual possession of political power.

In 1881 Pope Leo taught that people are not forbidden to choose for themselves the type of government that is appropriate to their nature and traditions — provided justice is preserved.[28] At that time, and again in *Immortale Dei* (1885), he held that the right to rule is not tied to any particular form of government.[29] But when and how are people entitled to choose for themselves a particular form of government? This question has to be made more specific in order to apply it to the real world where people normally live under some existing form of government. The question becomes: when and how — if at all — are people entitled to *change* their existing form of government? In 1888 Leo XIII said that it is lawful to seek a different constitution or structure of government 'where there exists, or there is reason to fear, an unjust

36

oppression of the people . . . or a deprivation of the liberty of the Church'; and a few lines further on he added that 'it is not of itself wrong to prefer a democratic form of government'.[30] The vague Latin phrase translated here as 'a different constitution or structure of government' seems to mean more than the normal replacement through elections of one democratic government by another.[31] This teaching raises considerable difficulties in regard to the coherence of Leo's teaching. For if the situation is one of 'unjust oppression of the people' it must be presumed that those who hold the political power and are guilty of this oppression will be most unwilling to relinquish their power. How then is the person who seeks a different structure of government to avoid being guilty of subversion? To answer this one must find out what is the precise nature of subversion and, in particular, whether there is any way in which a new form of government can replace an old one without the intervention of any subversive activity.

## Social Need in a Revolutionary Situation

The French political situation of 1892 pushed Pope Leo to a very deep analysis of the issues of legitimacy and allegiance. In an encyclical of that year to the Church in France,[32] he offered a very carefully nuanced political philosophy. It included the general principles which he had already laid down in earlier encyclicals. But it set them within a wider theoretical framework and it also applied his overall vision to the specific situation in France.

First of all the pope recalls that over the preceding century a variety of different political systems have existed in France. He maintains that in 'the sphere of speculative ideas' a person is free to prefer one political form or structure to another. But as a matter of contingent historical fact each nation has a particular form of government. Then the pope says: 'It is hardly necessary to repeat that all individuals are bound to accept these governments and not to attempt to overthrow them or change their form.'[33] He goes on to recall that the Church has always condemned those who rebelled against legimimate authority. Next he points out that 'whatever be the form of civil power in a nation it cannot be considered so definitive as to have the right to remain immutable'.[34] Time, he says, brings fundamental changes in the political institutions of human societies.[35] Then he comes to the crucial question: 'How do these political changes come about?' His answer deserves to be quoted at some length:

> They sometimes follow in the wake of violent crises, too often of a bloody character, in the midst of which pre-existing governments totally disappear; then anarchy holds sway, and soon public order is shaken to its foundations and finally overthrown. From that time onward a *social need* obtrudes itself upon the nation; it must provide for itself without delay. . . . Now this social need justifies the creation and the existence of new governments, whatever form they take; since, in the hypothesis wherein we reason, these new governments are a requisite to public order, all public order being impossible without a government.[36]

This is a very significant passage, in both what it says and what it omits. The pope does not claim to be speaking of all situations where the structures of government have undergone major change. He concentrates on one particular 'scenario' which, he says, *sometimes* happens. It is the situation in which a regime dissolves into anarchy and out of this anarchy a new regime emerges; the pope sets out to show how such a regime can have legitimacy. The crucial point is this: *the legitimacy of the new government does not depend on the legitimacy of the rebellion against the previous regime*. The new rulers are now entitled to demand obedience from the people; but that does not imply that the previous rulers had already lost this right prior to their downfall. Quite the contrary. They never lost the *right* to rule until they lost the *power* to rule, that is, until their government collapsed. So long as the previous government remained in power all attempts to overthrow it were unlawful and sinful. The neatness of Leo's teaching is that it succeeds in explaining how there can be a transition of lawful authority from the old regime to the new one — but it does so without offering any moral justification or support to attempts to bring about such a transition! It explains the legitimacy of post-revolutionary governments without conceding anything to those who seek to bring about a revolution.

Presumably Leo XIII felt entitled to limit himself to the

kind of situation he outlined because he considered that it was exemplified in France at least in the case of the original French Revolution. (Its application to changes of regime in France during the nineteenth century may be more doubtful.) The pope did not consider other kinds of situation — ones where existing governments were forced out of power and were replaced by fundamentally different regimes without any intervening period of anarchy. Nevertheless, it appears that one could extend the application of Leo's principles to cover such situations as well. Suppose a particular government is losing its power to rule, either gradually or quite suddenly. Suppose this loss of ability to govern is, practically speaking, irreversible. There comes a point in the process where anarchy, though not yet a reality, has become an imminent likelihood. Presumably the 'social need' of the people (of which the pope speaks) would at that point require the emergence of an alternative ruling power. The acceptance of this new form of government would then be 'not only permissible but even obligatory', to use Leo's own phrase.[37]

*Pragmatism or Principle?*

The key to the whole argument presented by Leo XIII on this issue lies in his conception of the source of political authority. He insists always that authority comes from God. 'Social need' merely determines who is to exercise this authority and the form the government is to take.[38] What gives the new regime the moral right to exact obedience from the citizens is the fact that God is supporting it, exercising his sovereignty through it. But why has God now given this moral authority to the new regime? Not because its structures are better, or its office-holders more just, than those of the previous regime, but simply because it now holds effective power. To put it very crudely one might say: 'God backs only the winners.' He gives the right to demand allegiance and obedience only to those who successfully retain or gain actual control. The determining factor is not justice but power.

Now at last we are in a position to answer the question posed a few pages back, namely, when and how — if at all — are people entitled to change their existing form of government. Putting together the various elements in Pope Leo's teaching (and its implications) the answer comes out as follows:

1. *When* is a change justified? When there is abuse of power by the rulers over some time, to a point where unjust oppression exists or can reasonably be feared.

2. *How* may such a change be sought? By 'legal and upright means'. And who decides whether a given means is legal? Apparently it is the existing regime. At this point one must envisage two possible situations. The first case is one where people, using whatever means the regime permits, succeed in compelling the rulers either to abandon their injustice or to yield power in an orderly way to a different government. The second case is where the regime resists all such pressures; when those who hold power find the pressure becoming intolerable they simply pass a law banning the use of whatever effective means is being used against them. If the regime is a really unjust and corrupt one it is most likely that it will refuse to bow to purely moral pressures and that it will declare illegal any activity that threatens its existence. In this extreme case the answer to the question, 'How can people work for change?' amounts to, 'Only by ineffective means'! That is precisely why the pope had to include as part of his teaching the point that in the last resort one has to endure evil and turn to prayer, rather than seek to oust the regime.

Does this mean that concern for justice can never entitle one to seek political change? No, because, as noted earlier, Leo teaches that citizens may and must exert pressure to get evil legislation changed.[39] But the presupposition here is that they are working within the existing system, continuing to give it their allegiance. If citizens cannot obtain justice within the existing system they may not take the further step of trying to topple it by means declared illegal by the regime itself. At that point the limit has been reached; injustice must then be endured. For to challenge the system, even in defence of justice, is to challenge the authority of God himself. Questions about the injustice of the regime are not relevant at this point, for injustices do not entitle one to rebel. It would appear that according to the teaching of Leo XIII there can be no such thing as a justified revolution.[40]

It is interesting to note that one of Pope Leo's own advisers, the noted philosopher and theologian Cardinal Zigliara, followed the scholastic tradition in accepting that active resistance to tyrannical abuse of power could sometimes be justified. He argued that this was resistance not to authority but to violence, not to the ruler but to an unjust aggressor who was in the very act of violating a genuine right.[41] Leo XIII, in his carefully constructed teaching on political authority, does not invoke these nice distinctions; it seems that he decided not to follow Zigliara's view. It is possible, of course, that he accepted it at the level of abstract theory; but, if so, he must have decided that the argument was not applicable to the kind of situations he faced. The traditional theory itself included the notion that there should be a proportion between the evil to be corrected and the means used to correct it. It seems that Leo held that a revolution would cause so much damage to society that it would certainly be a greater evil than the injustices that provoked it. Holding such a view, Leo did not need to reject formally the traditional teaching about justified rebellion; he could simply maintain that in the world of his time no revolution could be justified.

One important implication of Leo's position needs to be noted. According to the pope's argument the wrongness of subversion is not due solely to the violence which those involved in it may practice. Its evil is more basic. It is the fact that the order of society is being overturned and its stability disrupted; and this damage inflicted on the common good is at the same time a flouting of God's authority, since the existing authorities are his agents. It follows that to seek to overthrow a regime *even by non-violent means* would also be fundamentally wrong. Questions about just means do not arise, since there can be no just means by which one could reject God's authority as embodied in the regime. This is the logic of Leo's position. It is true that he speaks of citizens uniting to combat abuses and of the lawfulness of seeking a different form of government.[42] But this allows only such questioning of the system as the system itself tolerates. It appears then that those who accept Pope Leo's teaching on political authority are morally obliged to avoid planning or organising any serious attempt to replace the regime under which they live, or at least any attempt which is forbidden by that regime. They cannot give support to revolutionaries, however non-violent, until these have actually succeeded in undermining the regime; and at that point they must suddenly transfer their allegiance since they are then bound to support the new regime!

41

When spelled out in this blunt fashion Pope Leo's teaching on political authority may seem shockingly pragmatic. Does this mean that the pope subordinated the value of justice to the values of order and stability? To put the question in this way is hardly fair to the pattern of his thinking. As he would see it, public order is not an alternative to justice in society. Rather, stability and order are a fundamental precondition for justice and might even be called an integral part of the just society. This explains why they have an overriding importance in his teaching, so much so that other instances of injustice have to be tolerated rather than have the order of society disturbed.

Leo XIII's desire to promote stability in society fitted well with his commitment to presenting a body of socio-political teaching which would clearly demonstrate how useful the Church could be to civil authorities and how unjustified were any accusations that the Church promoted disloyalty. His teaching served this purpose admirably:

— It showed how the Church could recognise the legitimacy of any and every regime and could negotiate with any government, even when disapproving of particular legislation which such a government might have enacted.

— It established the neutrality of the Church vis-à-vis any particular political party,[43] and even in relation to different political systems — monarchy, democracy, etc.

— It explained how individual Christians or the local Church could dissent from particular laws or edicts which they found unacceptable, and could even exert pressure on the government to have them changed — but using only the means allowed by law.

— It provided a convincing answer to those who accused the Church of undermining the loyalty of citizens; for it gave to every existing regime the highest level of legitimation and support, namely, the assurance that the rulers derived their authority from God and were to be obeyed for this reason; and it unequivocally condemned all revolutionary activity and seditious plotting.

— While giving no support to political movements for radical change, it left Leo room to express deep concern about the plight of the poor and serious misgivings about the capitalist order, which he held responsible for much of their suffering;

and it left him free to call for changes in the socio-economic order; in this way there was an opening for a bridging of the wide gap between the Church and the industrial workers.

Pope Leo's effort to establish the credibility of the Church as a force for stability was not undertaken merely to promote the Church itself but also because Leo was passionately concerned that order should be preserved or restored in society. He believed the world had been seriously damaged by anarchy, revolution, and a spirit of licence. He was convinced that there was 'grave need for society to return to the true principles of order, so imprudently abandoned and neglected'.[44] The Church, he believed, had an important role to play in restoring public order. It could teach each group in society its proper obligations.[45] It could be a mediating influence between the rulers and the people in cases of excess by either side.[46] But above all it could throw the full weight of its authority — and of God's authority — behind existing regimes and against subversion and revolution. This task was the high moral purpose which rescued Leo from any taint of mere pragmatism in his political teaching. His sincerity is shown by the fact that he insisted on the duty of allegiance even to regimes that were harassing the Church. The promotion of public order was for Leo a major service to humanity, a fundamental element in the task of the Church.

There has always been a certain pragmatic element in the teaching of the Church in political questions, particularly in regard to issues about a just war and about obedience to civil authority. At first sight it may seem that the Church adopts and inculcates an attitude of compromise — a readiness to tolerate injustice rather than challenge those who hold power. But in fact what the Church proposes is a healthy pragmatism, a rejection of the kind of romantic idealism that would want to pull down a whole society rather than endure any injustice. What the Church's traditional teaching insists on is that there should be some proportion between the evil and the proposed remedy; the harm done to society by the attempt to correct injustices must be less than that done by the original abuses. Leo XIII is therefore quite within the tradition when he gives a high priority to order and stability in society. He is not going beyond the traditional outlook in giving a certain moral weight to the fact that a particular individual or group actually holds political power; that is not pragmatism in the bad sense but realistic concern for the common good. The question that needs to be asked is not, 'Why does Leo set a high importance on stability in society and stress the value of loyalty to existing governments?'; rather the question is, 'Why does he give *overriding* importance to stability and order, so that resistance beyond the bounds of the laws of the regime can *never* be countenanced, no matter how unjust the regime may be?' For it is on this issue that Leo XIII departs from the traditional teaching worked out by the scholastics. To understand his attitude one has to look more closely at the political and social situation of Leo's time and the kind of concerns and fears the situation aroused in him — above all, his anxiety about revolution.

## Fear of Revolution

Pope Leo XIII's teaching on political issues was not worked out in an academic environment where his thinking might be protected in some degree from the pressures of practical political affairs. His teaching was immediately related to actual situations and was intended to be a major part of his pastoral ministry. So his perceptions of the political situation — and of the role of the Church in it — had a considerable influence on his political philosophy.

In this, Leo XIII was by no means unique. Many other churchmen of the late nineteenth century were genuinely shocked by the poverty and defencelessness of the working class. A considerable number of them became deeply involved in the efforts of voluntary agencies to relieve distress and give some help to the victims of social injustice. A rather smaller number were prepared, like Leo XIII, to go so far as to be quite outspoken in condemning the causes of such injustice. But very few churchmen were prepared to give support or approval to efforts to bring about radical changes in the order of society. It was widely accepted by leaders of the Christian Churches that loyalty to the existing State authorities and structures was a fundamental Christian obligation. The Churches played a conservative role in society by propounding a theology and a spirituality that discouraged any radical questioning in the political sphere.

It should, however, be noted that in the second half of the

nineteenth century significant groups of Christians in several European countries were proposing alternative models of society. Some Christians were flirting with socialist notions. But the ideal favoured most widely by socially aware groups of Christians was that of a society organised along corporatist lines.[47] Pope Leo XIII had some sympathy with certain Catholic social reformers with leanings in this direction; indeed he was influenced by them in writing *Rerum Novarum*. But it would probably be fair to say that their influence on him was more in causing him to write the encyclical than in the actual content of it. He agreed with them that the abolition of the guilds was a major cause of the social problem.[48] But he did not endorse their proposals for a corporatist state. He probably felt that these were unrealisable at that time. But he must also have felt that they were too radical: the proposals involved a major reconstruction of the social and political order. And the last thing Leo wanted was that the Catholic Church should be identified in any degree with something that might smack of revolutionary change.

So, whatever about theoretical dreams of a new kind of society, in practice the Catholic Church, led by the Vatican, was firmly against any significant attempts to bring about radical changes in the structures of society. The Protestant and Orthodox Churches were also socially conservative. Some of the factors influencing the Churches were common to all of them; others were specific to particular Churches. My intention here is to consider briefly some particular reasons why the Catholic Church (and, more specifically, the Vatican) was especially resistant at that time to radical social change. The central point to be noted is what the word 'revolution' conjured up for the pope and the Vatican. The previous hundred years had dealt the Catholic Church two wounds so serious that they called in question its self-understanding and seemed like a threat to its very existence; both of them were associated with the word 'revolution'.

The first of these happenings was the French revolution which overthrew the old order in France; it was followed by major social and political changes in other European countries, changes that were less sudden and perhaps less profound but which affected the Church in a very serious way. The second happening was the loss by the Papacy of its temporal power, a process in which a key psychological moment was the Roman Republic of 1848, the memory of which caused shudders in the Vatican.[49] The Catholic Church, and particularly the papacy, had made a remarkable come-back with the growth of what might be called a cult of the pope, and the development of Catholic institutions and new forms of spirituality. But this growth in new directions had by no means numbed the pain of the political-social wounds associated with 'revolution'. There was an almost neurotic fear of social disorder — so much so that nearly every other social value was in practice subordinated to the values of stability and harmony in society.

One effect of this conservative stance was that many of those who worked for radical change in society perceived the Church as part of the established order; so they tended to be anti-Christian, or at least anti-Church. The effect of the sharp polarisation was that each side lived up to the worst expectations of the other. The revolutionaries fulfilled the fears of Church leaders that their aims were anti-Christian. And the churchmen lived up to the Marxist accusation that they were allies of the dominant class, using religion to inhibit radical social change.

Against this background one can begin to understand Pope Leo's concern for stability and public order, leading to his support for existing regimes. The priority he gave to order in society left him in the ironic position of giving moral support and religious legitimation to regimes that were quite hostile to much of what the Church stood for. The Vatican still felt itself to be manning the defences of the old order (despite the significantly new elements in the approach of Leo XIII, as compared with that of Pius IX).[50] But in fact the old order had largely been swept away. The new regimes had taken away from the Church almost everything they could take: the position of Rome as an independent state; the Church's establishment position in some 'Catholic' states; many of the traditional institutions and rights of the Church. Furthermore, the new economic order (with its social consequences) had cost the Church the allegiance of the industrial working class. Meanwhile the new middle class were more willing to 'use' the Church than to share the pope's concern about the plight of the poor. The new elite had a 'liberal' ideology which was

46

hostile to the influence of the Church and indifferent to many traditional Christian values. Nevertheless this new elite had succeeded not merely in gaining power but in presenting themselves as the representatives of 'order', the only realistic alternative to the utter lawlessness of revolution. So the pope's concern to promote social stability and public order made it almost impossible for him to offer an effective challenge to the new order — even though he recognised and even condemned verbally the gross injustices within it.

A lot of the difficulty stemmed from a failure by the pope to make adequate distinctions between various kinds of left-wing thinking and various levels of challenge to the existing structures of society. Leo seems to have thought of socialism as the summit and source of practically every social evil one could imagine. He paints a lurid picture: '. . . the beginning and the instruments of "Socialism" are violence, violations of injustice, the craze for a new order and envy between the different classes of society.'[51] He generally linked socialism with revolution. He traced the two to a common origin in the Reformation, which, he said, led to rationalism and so to the exclusion of God from public life; the notion of reward and punishment in the future life was eliminated, so it was not surprising that the poor should become discontented and should covet the wealth of the rich.[52] From the same roots, in Leo's view, there sprang the idea that government arises only from the will of the people.[53] To him this suggested not just democracy but anarchism and nihilism — and so he bracketed these theories with socialism.[54] For good measure he added in Freemasonry, which he saw as favouring the same aim, namely, the overthrow of the order of society.[55]

It would seem, then, that 'socialism' became for Pope Leo XIII a kind of short-hand word whose meaning included all kinds of political extremism. That is why he could say in 1901 that he saw in the growing power of the socialist movement a threat of 'the most disastrous national upheavals'.[56] When he spoke of socialism he probably had in mind the Paris Commune of 1871 and the violence that attended its brief life and bloody death. He was genuinely fearful that the vast majority of humankind would fall back in a 'most abject condition of bondage', or else that human society would be 'agitated by constant outbreaks and ravaged by plunder and rapine'; that is why he wanted the Church to appease the conflict between rich and poor, by warning the rich of eternal punishment if they refuse 'to give of their superfluity to the poor', and by comforting the hearts of the poor with the hope of reward in heaven.[57]

The pope's fear of 'socialism' led him to modify an earlier draft of *Rerum Novarum* in which the right to private property had been subordinated to the wider principle that the goods of the earth are for the common good.[58] He felt, it seems, that a statement of this kind would be, or would appear to be, too close to the socialist view. So he gave a very restrictive interpretation to the traditional teaching that 'God has granted the earth to mankind in general'; this simply means, he says, 'that no part of it was assigned to anyone in particular, and that the limits of private possession have been left to be fixed by man's own industry, and by the laws of individual races.'[59] This was quite a different emphasis from that of traditional scholastic teaching. Another departure from the scholastic tradition has already been noted — the refusal to accept that rebellion could ever be justified. It too came from Leo's concern for stability and fear of revolution.

The horror evoked by 'socialism' in many Church leaders in the late nineteenth century might be compared to the almost paranoid fear of 'communism' that pervades the ruling strata of South American and South African society today. There was the same failure to make distinctions, to avoid being limited to just two alternatives — either total revolution or support for existing unjust regimes. Under Leo XIII the Catholic Church was just beginning to take the first steps towards extricating itself from this awkward dilemma. In the political sphere the Church was coming to terms with democracy. And in the economic sphere the publication of *Rerum Novarum* represented a major advance. For this encyclical was a strong challenge to the *status quo*. However, it has now become evident that Leo XIII's political philosophy, his spirituality, and his fear of revolution, all imposed severe limits to the extent to which the pope could carry through that challenge. Leo called for a change of attitude by the rich and the acceptance of practices and laws that would protect the poor. But if such changes 'from the top' were not introduced, the pope had no very effective way in which he could promote fundamental changes in society. In the last resort he felt that the Church was obliged to encourage allegiance to the liberal capitalist regimes of the time, even while speaking out against the injustices that were so evident in them.

## Inadequate Solution — but a Major Advance

Leo XIII did not experience any contradiction in his approach. For him there was a clear distinction between the existing socio-economic order, whose abuses he condemned, and the political order, which he felt obliged to support. Where he failed was in not paying sufficient attention to the crucial question of *who* was exercising effective power in society. He noted the fact that the wealthy had gained power in the State.[60] But he did not advert to the consequent inconsistency in his own position. He was defending the existing political order while condemning the existing economic order — despite his acknowledgment of the fact that the two were so closely interlinked that the rich could use the machinery of the State to promote their interests at the expense of the poor.

For the most part, Leo XIII seems to have forgotten that his ideal conception of the State was not realised in practice. Apart from the passing remark in *Rerum Novarum* which I have just referred to, he seems to assume that the government, in exercising its political function, is not biased in favour of the rich. Leo wanted governments to protect the poor in various ways which he did not specify in detail. Nevertheless, he did not want them to 'interfere' very much in economic affairs. So what he wanted was a 'middle way' between socialism and liberal capitalism. The main difficulty with this does not lie in the proposal itself but in the assumption that the governments of Leo's time could implement it in practice. For, as he himself acknowledged, the rich had gained control of the governments, and therefore of the apparatus of the State.

In the civil and criminal law enacted and enforced by most if not all of the states of the time there was a bias in favour of the people of property. This bias in favour of the rich extended also into the day-to-day administration of 'justice' by police, law-courts, and other branches of government. Like any other bias, this was of course largely imperceptible to those who benefited from it. They were convinced that the State, and especially 'the Law' were embodiments of justice and quite impartial. They did not realise what was really implied in their demand that the State should 'interfere' only minimally in economic affairs. What it really meant was a demand that their privileged position be preserved, that the structural inequality between rich and poor be maintained and supported by political means. One example of this has already been noted in the previous chapter: when poor workers found really effective means to defend their economic rights (for instance, a general strike), these could be labelled 'subversive' and declared illegal.

Pope Leo XIII seems to have presumed that socio-economic reform could come without significant political changes and even without major challenge to existing political structures. This presumption helps to explain how he could combine the real concern for the poor expressed in *Rerum Novarum* with a total rejection of anything that might be considered subversive. But it was rather unrealistic to expect that the rich and powerful could be persuaded by moral exhortations to relinquish their privileged position. If they chose to be intransigent, Leo's teaching offered little by way of remedy for this. I would therefore conclude that what Leo XIII presented as the official Church teaching on socio-political questions did not measure up to the deeply Christian instinct that led him to cry out against mistreatment of the poor. I would go further and say that the attitudes and spirituality that were linked to, and reflected, his teaching contributed to the failure of the Church to gain the confidence of the mass of industrial workers.

On the other hand it must not be forgotten that *Rerum Novarum* was a major intervention by the pope in defence of the poor. As such it helped to put the Church firmly on their side. The effect was two-fold. The encyclical led Church people to make a deeper study of the causes of poverty and to seek more effective means of overcoming them. And at the same time it gave heart to those of the workers and the poor who were able and willing to hear its message; this inspirational effect was quite important, especially when over the years it became apparent that many Church leaders were taking the encyclical seriously.

A further reason for saying that *Rerum Novarum* was an important step towards putting the Church on the side of the poor has to do with its teaching, its 'doctrine'. It laid a solid basis for the emergence of the concept of 'social justice'. This term was not used regularly in papal documents until much later. But what it eventually came to mean was largely what Pope Leo wrote about in his encyclical. He specified a range of obligations quite different from those that fall under the category of commutative justice. It is true that he did not neatly specify all the different categories of obligation.[61] But what seems to emerge is that it is a matter of justice (not 'merely' of charity) to ensure that the social order is not such as to facilitate the exploitation of the poor. Such teaching had a basis in the moral teaching of the scholastics. But it was an important contribution to the Church of more recent centuries: it widened the whole concept of justice in Church thinking and teaching and helped to rescue it from a tendency to fall into narrow individualism. It also helped to lay the foundation for the eventual development of the notion of an 'option for the poor' — and of the kind of spirituality that would embody such an option.

Taken as a whole, the economic, social, and political teaching of Leo XIII represents a major achievement. Despite the weaknesses or inadequacies that have been noted, it is a powerful synthesis, comprehensive and systematic. While rooted in tradition, it offers an opening to the new situation, including the emergence of democratic governments, the reality or threat of political revolution, and the development of an industrial proletariat ground down by poverty. It is not surprising, then, that Leo's teaching has remained the basis of the official Catholic position on social issues. Later popes constantly referred back to the teachings of Leo XIII and seldom attempted to change them. Indeed for a long time *Rerum Novarum* was seen not just as the foundation for the Church's teaching on 'the social question' but as the more or less definitive statement of that teaching; and on political issues Leo's other encyclicals, notably *Immortale Dei*, were given a similar definitive position. Forty years were to pass before any pope set out even to up-date the teaching of Pope Leo XIII on social questions.

## ADDENDUM TO CHAPTER TWO:
## PIUS X AND BENEDICT XV

The social question was not very high on the agenda of Pope
Pius X. Though he did not entirely ignore, it,[62] he was more
concerned with practical religious reform[63] and with the
crisis of modernism. The British author Alec Vidler remarks
that Pius X was determined to stamp out social as well as
doctrinal modernism.[64] What this meant in practice was
mostly that he wanted to ensure hierarchical and clerical
control of all kinds of 'Catholic Action' concerned with
social reform.[65] Richard Camp claims that the call of Leo
XIII for social and economic reform was 'supported in word
but stifled in deed' by Pius X.[66] This claim may be somewhat
exaggerated but it has in it an element of truth. It is an over-
statement to the extent that Pius was not opposed to a slow
and cautious movement towards economic reform and an
overcoming of the misery of the poor; and certainly he did
not want to lend support to social injustice. But on the other
hand it is true that he was instrumental in stifling two social
reform movements, one in Italy in 1903 and one in France in
1910. His opposition was largely aroused by the relative
independence which the lay leadership had achieved in these
movements; this gave rise to practical problems about obedience to ecclesiastical authority. But there was also an issue
that had more to do with theory and official teaching: the
question of the equality of human beings. On this matter
Pius spoke out sharply:

> . . . it is in accordance with the pattern established by God
> that human society should have rulers and subjects, em-
> ployers and employees, rich and poor, wise and ignorant,
> nobles and common people . . .[67]

The French movement which Pius condemned was in favour
of a system of cooperatives which would enable every worker
to become in some sense an owner-employer. Even though
*Rerum Novarum* had explicitly called for a widening of ownership,[68] Pius X was not happy with the cooperative proposal.
He felt it was inspired by the ideal of levelling out the differences between different classes in society — and he seems
to have considered this ideal to be too utopian.[69] One can

only conclude that, for a variety of reasons, Pius was in practice opposed to a movement which might have been able to put into effect in some degree one of the most important proposals of *Rerum Novarum*.

The most notable document issued by Pius X on social questions was the *Motu Proprio* of 1903 called *Fin dalla prima*. It consists mainly of a schematic summary of major points from the teaching of Leo XIII, with references to Pope Leo's documents. The style of *Fin dalla prima*, as well as the points which Pius X chose to emphasise, give the document the character of a manual of discipline. Notably absent is any sense of Leo's passionate concern for the plight of the working classes; the concern of Pius X seemed to be to ensure unity within the Church and stability in society.

*Fin dalla prima* differs subtly but significantly from *Rerum Novarum* on one important point, which it mentions twice:

VI. To calm the strife between rich and poor, it is necessary to distinguish between justice and charity. Only when justice has been violated is there a right to make a claim, in the strict sense of the word.

XIX. Finally, let Catholic writers, while upholding the cause of the people and of the poor, beware of using language which may inspire the masses with hatred of the upper classes of society. Let them not talk of claims and of justice, when it is a question of mere charity . . .[70]

In the first of these passages a reference is given to the text of *Rerum Novarum*. But the fact is that while the latter encyclical undoubtedly speaks both of obligations of justice and of obligations of charity it does not by any means draw the same conclusions as Pope Pius X.[71]

The way in which Pius applies the distinction between justice and charity is unfortunate. He says that there is a 'claim, in the strict sense of the word' only when justice has been violated. When this is put together with the second quotation, the effect is to suggest that it is 'merely' an obligation of charity to bring about an equitable social order. This set back the emerging concept of 'social justice' to which *Rerum Novarum* had made such a notable contribution. It gave the impression that any social obligation which could not be specified in the strict interpersonal terms of commutative justice was not really a matter of justice at all and was for that reason less compelling or could be ignored with greater impunity.

*Benedict XV*

From the point of view of the general history of the Church there was a major difference between Pius X and his successor, Benedict XV. The latter was much more liberal in approach than Pius; indeed it is even said that Benedict had been suspected by his predecessor of being tainted with modernism! Certainly, when he took over as pope, Benedict curbed the excesses of anti-modernism and began to open up the Catholic Church to a cautious dialogue with the modern world. In the field of socio-political activity, Benedict was much more advanced in his approach than Pius. For instance, he allowed Catholics to play a more active role in Italian political life, thus opening the way for a *rapprochement* between Church and State. Benedict was also very concerned about the problems of war and peace. The First World War dominated his pontificate and he spent a good deal of his energy in working for peace and in trying to have the Church accepted as a mediator. His concern with national and international political matters meant that he paid less attention to the socio-economic aspects of 'the social question'.

My concern here with Benedict XV is not with his general impact on the life of the papacy and the Church but with the much more limited question of his *teaching* on social issues. In this regard the difference between himself and his predecessor is much less striking than in the area of practical action and policy. He did not speak very often about socio-economic matters; and when he did so his statements were conservative in tone and content. This may have been partly due to a lingering anti-modernism and suspicion of new thinking on social issues. Perhaps also it suited Benedict to sound rather more conservative than he was in practice.

In the encyclical *Ad Beatissimi*, issued in 1914, Benedict insists that since political power has its source in God, it is to be obeyed as a matter of conscience.[72] He adds that experience shows that when rulers despise divine authority, their people tend to despise human authority; therefore

54

governments ought not to divorce their governing of the country and the education of the young from the teaching of the Church.[73]

Pope Benedict also insisted that a diversity of classes in society was part of the natural order and was willed by God. [74] Although he encouraged Catholics to help the poor, at the same time he wanted the poor to be imbued with a spirituality that would discourage them from seeking vainly for a higher situation than they could reach and from trying to escape from evils they could not avoid; they should rather be encouraged to put up with their troubles peacefully in the hope of the good things of heaven.[75]

Benedict held that envy and hatred between the classes in society was fomented by socialist agitators whose fallacies led the proletariat to forget that though people are equal by nature this does not mean that they must all occupy an equal place in the community.[76] Having given this legitimation for the inequalities in society, Benedict went on to make the following revealing remarks:

> . . . who will ever make them see that the position of each one is that which each by use of his natural gifts — unless prevented by force of circumstances — is able to make for himself? And so the poor who strive against the rich as though they had taken part of the goods of others, not merely act contrary to justice and charity but also act irrationally, particularly as they themselves by honest industry can improve their fortunes if they choose.[77]

This passage shows the extent to which the pope had come to accept the belief that, more than anything else, gives a moral legitimation to the 'free enterprise' or capitalist system. This is the belief that under such a system everybody, or at least nearly everybody, has a reasonable chance to 'make good'; in fact there is frequently the suggestion that everybody has more or less an equal chance, at least in principle. Of course one then adds on some such qualifying phrase as that used by the pope — 'unless prevented by force of circumstances'. This makes his statement technically true; but it fails to note that the 'circumstances' which handicap poor people are so widespread and so inhibiting that in fact it is these which are the main cause of poverty, and not simply the failure to use personal talents. In other words, the system itself is biased against the poor, so that they seldom get the opportunity to develop and use their talents to the extent that would enable them to escape their poverty. It was this bias which Pope Leo XIII had seen, and which he had spoken out against in *Rerum Novarum*. So it is rather unfortunate that Benedict XV should have lent his authority as pope to what might be called 'the mythological basis of the capitalist order.' This looks like a backward step from *Rerum Novarum*.

# 3

# Pius XI and a New Social Order

The second of the great social encyclicals was issued by
Pope Pius XI in 1931. It was written to commemorate the
fortieth anniversary of Leo XIII's *Rerum Novarum* so it is
known as *Quadragesimo Anno*; and the usual English title is
'The Social Order'. . .[1] In this chapter I shall examine the contribution to Catholic social teaching made by Pius XI in
*Quadragesimo Anno* and some of his other encyclical letters.
But I shall be doing this from a particular point of view. The
main emphasis will not be on the point that is usually associated with Pius XI, namely, on his proposal for a corporative
or vocational ordering of society; though this question will
of course have to be considered. The main concern of this
study will be on a prior question: did the pope commit the
Church to supporting a radical transformation of the structures
of society, an alternative to the capitalist or free enterprise
model; and, if so, how far was he prepared to go in challenging
the existing order?

*Quadragesimo Anno* is a worthy successor to *Rerum
Novarum*. It has the same sense of moral outrage at the
suffering of the poor[2] as one finds in Leo's encyclical; and
the same kind of criticism of the economic liberalism which
had caused that suffering.[3] However, Pius's encyclical, like
that of his predecessor, also rejects communism and socialism.[4]
Pius, like Leo, sees himself as presenting a 'middle way'
between economic liberalism and socialism.

The new social encyclical sets out to vindicate and develop
the teaching of *Rerum Novarum*. But then it goes on to look
at current social issues in a radical way, with the aim of showing how they can be tackled according to Christian principles.
Pius XI was very conscious that major changes had taken

place over the previous forty years. He wanted to ensure that the Church's social teaching was fully up to date and clearly relevant to the actual situation of the time.[5] In his view there were several particularly urgent reasons why the Church should be actively involved in social issues at that time:

— Wealth had come to be concentrated in the hands of a relatively small number of people.[6]

—This concentration of wealth had led to a concentration of economic power and even of political power.[7]

— While the condition of the workers in the West had improved since the time of Leo, there was now, in the Americas and in the Far East, a vast increase in the number of very poor industrial workers 'whose groans rise from earth to heaven'; there was also 'the immense army of agricultural wage-earners whose condition is depressed in the extreme'.[8]

— There was the further problem of widespread unemployment at the time the encyclical was written.[9]

Pius XI was not content merely to repeat, develop, and apply the teaching of Leo XIII. As the French theologian Chenu rightly remarks, he was concerned not just with the condition of workers but with the whole socio-economic order of society.[10] He wanted to focus attention on the basic *causes* of injustice and poverty. He was prepared to go much further than Leo in doing what would now be called a 'structural analysis' of society, locating the inadequacies and built-in injustices in its structures. He avoided the mistake of adopting a purely 'moralising' approach, an attitude which explains social evils in terms of the sinfulness of individuals. On the other hand he also avoids the opposite mistake, namely, that of blaming the structures of society for all its ills. *Quadragesimo Anno* insists on the need for *both* 'a reform of social institutions and the improvement of conduct'.[11] The encyclical treats these two aspects of the problem separately for the most part. But at one point it comes close to expressing an important insight about the relationship between the two, namely, that evil conduct can solidify into a set of practices and traditions which are themselves real 'structures' of society, affecting the more obvious political, social and economic structures. The pope does not quite say this. But he gives an impressive account of how moral standards tend to become eroded in the existing economic order.[12]

The main concern of this study is with what Pius had to say about the *structures* of society and the need for radical change in them. But before moving on to this question it is worthwhile considering one point about the reform of *conduct*. Perhaps the most effective way in which the Church can influence human behaviour is by promoting a particular kind of spirituality. Leo XIII encouraged what might be termed 'a spirituality of stability': he laid emphasis on obedience to lawful authorities to a point where in the last analysis people were asked to endure gross injustices rather than overthrow the regimes that perpetrated them; and the promise of future reward was held out to those who were patient in this way. Pius XI seems to give less emphasis to this kind of spirituality. The author of *Quadragesimo Anno* is clearly aware of the Marxist accusation that the Church condones injustice by offering happiness in the next life as a reward for patience in the face of oppression in this life. He responds by denying that the Church in general does this, though he admits that some people in the Church do so. The pope condemns the conduct of those who 'abuse religion itself, trying to cloak their own unjust impositions under its name'.[13]

It is true that Pius XI maintains that workers should not feel 'discontent at the position assigned them by divine Providence in human society'.[14] But that comment should not be taken to indicate that he sees stability in society as something to be promoted at all costs. His remark is simply an expression of his concern that feelings of envy and hatred should be overcome through a theology and spirituality of human work.[15] In general, there is a slight but noticeable shift in emphasis from a more 'escapist' to a more 'worldly' spirituality, as one moves from *Rerum Novarum* to *Quadragesimo Anno*. This is a good example of how the 'doctrinal' continuity between Leo and Pius XI is combined with subtle but significant changes. One can sense in *Quadragesimo Anno* the emergence of a new spirituality of justice; but it has not yet succeeded fully in maintaining its autonomy. On some occasions it almost seems as though concern for justice is little more than a means to the end of bringing workers into the Church, or ensuring that they are not led astray.[16] But *Quadragesimo Anno* shows that its author does see concern

59

for justice as a fundamental value in its own right. It speaks, for instance, of choosing people who 'show themselves endowed with a keen sense of justice, ready to oppose with manly constancy unjust claims and unjust actions'.[17] The pope goes on to add that such people should show great prudence and should above all be filled with the charity of Christ.[18] Here we find linked together four major virtues — justice, courage, prudence and the love of Christ; for Pius XI these constitute the heart of a Christian spirituality of justice.

*The need for Structural Change*

However important a change of heart and conduct may be, Pius XI was well aware that it is not sufficient on its own to overcome modern social problems. He believed that well-meaning employers were often trapped by the system, by structures in society that embodied injustice and created further injustice:

> We turn again in a special way to you, Christian employers and industrialists, whose problem is often so difficult for the reason that you are saddled with the heavy heritage of an unjust economic regime whose ruinous influence has been felt through many generations.[19]

One instance of the difficulty is the fact that competition may be so keen that individual employers know that any increase in their costs would put them out of business. Consequently they find themselves unable to pay their employees a just wage. The pope insisted that in these kind of situations there is an obligation to establish structures or institutions designed to limit the competition which causes the injustice. [20]

When Pius XI turns his attention in *Quadragesimo Anno* to the question of the reform of the structures of society he points out the key factor: *wealth gives power*. He goes much further than his predecessors in recognising that in a capitalist society the State is largely controlled by a wealthy group, [21] 'so that its resources and authority may be abused in economic struggles': [22]

> The State which should be the supreme arbiter, ruling in kingly fashion far above all party contention, intent only upon justice and the common good, has become instead a slave . . .[23]

At this point Pius makes his most radical criticism of the capitalist system as it has developed since the time of Leo XIII: 'Free competition has destroyed itself; economic domination has taken the place of the open market.'[24] Here the pope has pointed to a fatal weakness in capitalism, the point where it fails to be what it essentiallly claims to be. It begins as free enterprise; and this includes free competition. But a 'natural result'[25] of the competition is that only the toughest survive. Before long the free competition is only a myth and an ideology; the reality is the elimination of competition and the securing of economic and even political domination by the most ruthless.[26] That is why Pius XI insists that 'the proper ordering of economic life cannot be left to free competition'; it must be 'subjected to and governed by a true and effective guiding principle'.[27] Public authorities must ensure that free competition is kept within just and definite limits and that economic power is kept under control.[28] This amounts to a radical change in the structures that had shaped the Western world.

In dealing with the question of the restructuring of society the pope is quite subtle. His encyclical cleverly combines the advantages of being broad and general with the advantages of being rather specific. Three paragraphs give a specific and fairly detailed account of the type of corporative State that was being introduced at that time in Italy by Mussolini.[29] But the pope does not identify this as his own position. Instead he lists some of its advantages and disadvantages. In this way he succeeds in distancing himself somewhat from the model of society adopted by the Italian fascists; while at the same time he outlines its main features with a measure of what he himself called 'attentive benevolence'.[30] On the other hand when Pius is making his own proposals he carefully avoids details and specific applications. Instead, he gives general norms such as the following:

— 'The aim of social policy must . . . be the re-establishment of vocational groups.'[31]
— Professional corporations may take a variety of different forms.[32]
— Wages should be determined not with a view to private advantage but on the basis of providing employment for as many as possible.[33]

61

— No larger or higher association should 'arrogate to itself the functions which can be performed efficiently by smaller and lower societies'.[34]

Pius XI reaffirmed the right of workers to form voluntary trade unions.[35] He even had strong words of criticism for those who were reluctant to acknowledge this right.[36] A comparison of the descriptions of the role of trade unions in *Rerum Novarum* and *Quadragesimo Anno* shows an interesting shift of emphasis. There is an almost militant ring to what Pius says about unions, a tone quite different to that of Leo. Pius XI stresses the importance of unions as a means by which workers can protect themselves against oppression.[37] He implies that the trade unions are the defenders and champions of the lowly and oppressed.[38] He even sees them as having what would now be called a conscientising role.[39] In spite of all this, Pius XI did not envisage a solution to 'the social problem' as being reached through workers' organisations. The whole bent of his thinking was in a very different direction. He envisaged the elimination or at least the minimising of the division of society into classes (upper, middle and lower). This would be brought about by ensuring that the main divisions would be on the basis of the different sectors of society (e.g. agriculture, transport, various branches of industry).[40] These 'vocational' structures would cut across class structures. Within each vocational sphere there could be opportunities for employers and employees to meet separately on occasion.[41] But the whole order of society would be designed in such a way as to ensure that there would be no opposition or confrontation between the whole class of workers and the class of employers as a whole. The division into vocational sectors would be a matter of organisational convenience; it would not be so rigid and total that it would itself give rise to the kind of destructive competition and group selfishness it was supposed to eliminate.

## A Rejection of Capitalism?

Pope Pius XI, like Leo XIII, was very concerned to lessen hostility between the classes of society.[42] His teaching, following that of Leo, proposed a conception of society as an ordered harmony, rather than a battleground where workers and employers confront each other.[43] But Pius went much further than Leo in indicating how this was to be brought about. Leo had relied mainly on a reform of conduct rather than proposing any major change in the structures of society. Pius XI wanted structural as well as moral changes. A basic feature of the restructured society he proposed was that its main components would not be classes but vocational groups.[44] Such a society would, he believed, be more natural than one stratified into different classes.[45] Harmonious relationships could be expected to develop both *within* the vocational groups and *between* them.[46]

The pope did not go into detail about how these groupings should be organised or how their internal and external relationships should be structured. In fact he specifically said that people could choose for themselves the form they wished the professional groups to take.[47] But even though he does not give a blueprint covering such details, nevertheless it is clear that the type of society he was calling for represents a major change from the typical country where capitalism is in operation. The question therefore arises whether Pius was definitely rejecting the capitalist system. This calls for a nuanced answer.

When the encyclical insists that 'the proper ordering of economic life cannot be left to free competition',[48] this is more than an objection to abuses of the system. It is a repudiation of the central principle of capitalism, its ideological foundation. At the heart of capitalist thinking is the belief that market forces should be the determining factor in the economic order, regulating prices, profits, and wages — as well as who succeeds and who fails. In rejecting this principle Pius rejects capitalism not just in its present form but in its essential nature.[49]

However, a certain qualification must be added at once. Capitalism has an attenuated meaning which might be summed up as 'a system in which ownership of land and business is mostly in private hands'. In so far as the word is understood in this sense the pope was certainly not rejecting it.[50] Indeed he explicitly states that a system where capital and labour are normally provided by different people is not in itself to be condemned and certainly is not evil of its very nature.[51] Pius also held that free competition is 'justified and certainly useful provided it is kept within certain limits'.[52] He did not favour the extreme corporatist position which, paradoxically, had certain similarities to socialism, especially in the matter of restrictions on the use of private property.[53]

Perhaps the attitude of Pius may be expressed by saying that he did not want capitalism in the strict sense, but he undoubtedly wanted a large measure of *free enterprise*. He wanted people to be free to own and use land, free to found and conduct businesses without undue interference by either public authorities or capitalistic monopolies. Furthermore, he believed that such regulation and control as was required should be carried out at a 'lower' rather than a 'higher' level; it should as far as possible be done through a vocational structure rather than by the State. All this is clear from the general principles he lays down.[54] It is supported by the tenor of the critical comments he makes about the fascist-corporative system. (In fact he does not give this criticism as his own; instead he notes that some people consider the system to be excessively bureaucratic and see it as giving to the State a role that should be left to private initiative.)[55]

## Ambivalence

It has been said with some justification that Pius XI was ambivalent in regard to the capitalist system of his time. [56] There is no doubt that some of his statements give the impression that he wanted a *reform* of the system while at other times it seems as though he wanted the system to be entirely *replaced*. A good deal of the confusion can be removed by invoking the distinction made above between 'free enterprise' and 'capitalism'; one might say that the pope wanted the former to be reformed and the latter to be replaced. But even this distinction does not clear up the sense of ambivalence entirely. Should we, however, judge such ambivalence to be a fault? It would be, if one could expect the pope to opt unambiguously in favour of one particular socio-economic order. But it is arguable that the fact that he did not do this is a good thing. In that case the element of ambivalence should be seen as a virtue rather than a fault!

In order to clarify the issue further it is helpful to distinguish clearly between two different questions which have frequently been jumbled together. The first question is the one we have been considering, namely, did Pius XI reject capitalism — or, more accurately, in what sense did he reject it? The second question is: what economic system does *Quadragesimo Anno* propose? It has sometimes been assumed that one should answer this second question first; and in this way the first question will also be answered. But in fact there is *no* answer to the second question. An economic system would include 'technical' economic details which, according to Pius XI, are outside the competence and mission of the Church.[57] The reason he gives is that 'economic science' covers a sphere distinct from that of 'moral science', even though the two are closely related to each other.[58] So the pope could not be expected to teach that a given economic system is *the* correct one. Rather he lays down general principles to which any system should conform; and he uses these principles to assess and criticise existing or proposed systems, namely, capitalism, communism, different varieties of socialism, and the fascist-corporatist system. Anybody who expects the encyclical to say definitely which is the correct system will certainly find its statements about capitalism a cause of 'bewilderment' and open to different interpretations, as Camp does.[59] But to somebody who adopts another conception of the role and competence of the teaching authority of the Church, the apparent ambivalence of the encyclical will be simply an indication that Pius XI resisted the temptation to exceed that competence by making a pronouncement on a 'technical' issue of economics; not merely that, but he refused to be dogmatic on a matter where uncertainty and openness were the appropriate response.

It would be an exaggeration, however, to claim that all this was quite clear in the encyclical or even in the mind of the pope himself. In fact the way in which he treats the relationship between economic science and moral science[60] is not entirely satisfactory. There is a suggestion of a kind of dualism and a reduction of economics to a purely instrumental role. The distinction Pius XI makes between the proper object of papal teaching and the technical aspects of economics[61] is made only in passing and is not fully developed. It is only a first step, though an important one. It is important because it entitles the pope to refrain from giving specific teaching on 'technical' matters. But it is only a first step because its frame of reference is too static. It divides the issues too neatly into those which lie within the 'technical' sphere and those in the moral sphere where the pope sees himself as having the right and the duty to make pronouncements. The real life situation is by no means so amenable to such a clear distinction. The Church (community and authorities) has to assess concrete situations in the light of Christian experience and of the principles which distil and express the wisdom of past and present. The distinction between 'technical' matters and moral issues, in so far as it exists, is itself an end-product of such assessment rather than a ready-made self-evident framework whose application is obvious and almost automatic. Furthermore, the dividing line between the two is a shifting one, since moral issues can open up in matters which had seemed to be purely 'technical'. Because of this complexity Church authorities must recognise that it may be necessary to live with a good deal of uncertainty; at times the best they can do is commit themselves to searching for the best way forward.

## Desire for Certainty

At the time of *Quadragesimo Anno*, and for thirty years afterwards, it was not easy for the Catholic community or its leaders to experience themselves as uncertain and searching on important social issues. There was considerable pressure on Church authorities to present themselves as 'having the answers'. A lot of this pressure came from the believing community who looked to the leadership for clear and authoritative teaching on all issues which had a moral dimension.[62] Such an authoritative response had a double advantage: it gave a clear sense of self-identity both to the teaching authority within the Church and to the Catholic Church as a whole vis-à-vis the non-Catholic world. It is understandable then that both the authorities and the Catholic community tended to speak about *Quadragesimo Anno* as though it provided 'the answer to the social question'.

If the encyclical is seen as 'the answer' or 'the solution' to the social problem it is a very short step to interpreting this to mean that it offers its readers 'the correct system'. The unanswered questions, the deliberate vagueness, and the slightly different emphases in different places are then no longer seen as indications of search and some uncertainty. No, the truth must be there. It has only to be brought forth by means of a careful exegesis of the text. Controversy then springs up on certain key issues — above all on the question of whether corporatism is being proposed as *the* Catholic solution.[63] The controversy tends to centre not so much on the arguments for or against corporatism as on the proper interpretation of the text of the encyclical; for the text is presumed to contain the truth. In this way the prevailing theology and spirituality of authority and of the role of the Church led to a playing down of the fact that the pope did not commit himself on some important socio-economic issues.[64] The effect is that this reserve, which is an important feature of the encyclical, is not appreciated for what it is; instead it becomes the occasion for a rather fruitless exegetical controversy.

### Why was Pius XI so Radical?

*Quadragesimo Anno* has been understood by some to be proposing an alternative socio-economic system, a replacement for the capitalist system. But in the light of what has just been said it seems more accurate to see the encyclical as laying down some fundamental principles of social morality, using these as a basis for evaluation, and concluding that they rule out the acceptance of socialism in any form, and of capitalism both in its basic ideological principle and in its actual historical development. If this account is true (and *a fortiori* if the encyclical is really proposing a specific socio-economic system as some have assumed) then Pius XI is reacting against Western capitalism in a much more radical way than his predecessor. Why was he less inhibited than Leo was forty years earlier, in calling for an abandonment of the system on which modern Europe and America had been built?

Three factors may be mentioned as likely to have encouraged Pius XI to go much further than his predecessor:

— The economic collapse and 'the Great Depression' of the time had raised questions about the viability of an economic system which, whatever its moral weaknesses, had until 1929 at least appeared to be extraordinarily successful in giving rise to 'progress' and a fair measure of stability, as well as meeting many human needs. Now the system seemed to have broken down; and unemployment was creating a great pool of disillusioned and alienated people, eagerly searching for some alternative to the system that had let them down.

— Since the time of Leo XIII the inevitable and 'natural' consequences of the system had had the opportunity to emerge and develop further. Particularly significant was the fact noted earlier that the system had to a considerable extent ceased to be what it claimed to be, one of *free* enterprise. Instead of giving most people a chance to become entrepreneurs, the system actually concentrated wealth and power in the hands of a privileged few.[65]

— The liberal capitalist system no longer seemed to be the only effective alternative to communism or socialism. Portugal and Italy were offering an approach that seemed as if it might be both more acceptable morally and also more successful. The corporatist-fascist model had one great advantage at this time: it still had the sparkle of newness. The problems intrinsic to it had not yet had time to develop fully. The difficulties the new system was encountering could plausibly be considered as 'teething troubles' which would soon be overcome.

Taken together these three factors constituted a powerful argument for envisaging radical change in the structures of society. For over a hundred years the popes had all experienced an overriding concern for political and social stability; the alternative had seemed to be some form of anarchy. But now the situation had changed in two respects. On the one hand there was no guarantee that the capitalist order as it had developed could in fact ensure social and political stability. On the other hand it seemed possible that there was an alternative socio-economic model which could ensure such stability, and at the same time be more equitable. An added bonus was that one could find at least some measure of resemblance between the corporatist model now being proposed and the ancient guild system so admired by both Leo and Pius XI.[66] And there was a much closer similarity between the new fascist-corporatist model of society and the version of corporatism that had been advocated for over fifty years by many Catholic social reformers. This lent some respectability to the new system and perhaps helped to off-set the doubts that must have arisen as a result of the political philosophy and behaviour of some of its proponents. The effect of all this was that it could no longer be presumed that the Catholic Church would, in the last analysis, provide support for the *status quo* rather than take the risk of being an agent of major socio-political change.

## Authority and Subversion

Although one can make a distinction between economics and politics, the two are closely interrelated. To seek to change the economic structures of society is itself a political action. So the question arises whether or to what extent Pius XI had thought through the political implications of his call for new socio-economic structures. How far was he prepared to go in supporting political activity designed to replace existing institutions? The question is not an abstract one, since it was during his pontificate that right-wing fascist-type movements came to power in a number of European countries and were active in many others.

In the area of political philosophy Pius XI put forward nothing at all comparable to the comprehensive socio-economic principles which he had proposed in *Quadragesimo Anno*. It must be assumed that he adhered to the general position presented by Leo XIII. There is, however, one significant difference between Leo and Pius; it has to do with the matter of obedience to civil authority. The first thing to note is that, for the reasons just outlined, the question of accepting the *status quo* presented itself in a different light to Pius XI than it had to his predecessor. Leo's attitude was that existing regimes had to be supported even when their rulers' behaviour and policies were very unsatisfactory. The reason was that opposition to them meant lending support to the forces of communism and anarchy. Pius had an equal or even greater horror of communism.[67] But in the atmosphere of his time it was clear that communism was not the only alternative — or even the most likely one — to the politico-economic structures that had developed in Western countries. This left him greater freedom in working out a theory about the boundary between subversion and legitimate opposition to injustice.

69

This issue scarcely arises in *Quadragesimo Anno*. But in three major encyclicals issued in March 1937 Pius XI confronted the question of obedience to civil authorities. In the first, *Mit brennender Sorge*, he made an outspoken attack on the Nazi regime in Germany. He repeated the traditional teaching that the moral authority of the State has to be anchored in the authority of God.[68] He protested strongly against the situation where young people and their parents were being called by the State to disobey God.[69] But the pope said nothing that could in any way be taken as an incitement to subversion. This is not too surprising, in view of the total dominance of the Nazis in Germany at that time, and the fact that the Church was already being severely harassed if not persecuted.

The second of the three encyclicals, *Divini Redemptoris*, is dated five days later than the first.[70] This time the object of condemnation is communism. Here the pope repeats the traditional Catholic teaching that the human person has 'divinely-imposed obligations towards civil society', and civil authorities have the right to impose these duties.[71] He then goes on to insist that it is an 'unjust usurpation' for communism to seek to enforce its own programme instead of the divine law.[72] But he does not really address himself to the dilemma of allegiance faced by those who have to live under a communist government; for the pope's main concern was not with such people but with the threat of communism to the Western world.

The issue of allegiance was, however, taken up by Pius XI just nine days later in the third of these encyclicals. This was entitled *Firmissimum* and it dealt with the situation of Catholics in Mexico.[73] Towards the end of it there are a few paragraphs where the pope bluntly faces the question of active resistance to the civil authorities. The central teaching runs as follows:

> ... the Church ... condemns every unjust rebellion or act of violence against the properly constituted civil power. On the other hand, ... if the case arose where the civil power should so trample on justice and truth as to destroy even the very foundations of authority, there would appear no reason to condemn citizens for uniting to defend the nation and themselves by lawful and appropriate means

against those who make use of the power of the State to drag the nation to ruin.[74]

In the following paragraph the pope adds that the means used must not be intrinsically evil and should 'not bring greater harm to the community than the harm they were intended to remedy'.

This is indeed a notable departure from what had been taught by Leo XIII, Pius X, Benedict XV and by Pius XI himself up to that time. A departure, but not necessarily a total contradiction in teaching. It can be argued with some credibility that Pius XI believed he was dealing with a situation that had special features which made it morally different from the kind of situation faced by his predecessors; consequently he invoked aspects of traditional teaching which were not mentioned by them simply because they were not relevant for their situations. This argument would safeguard 'doctrinal' consistency, which has always been a high priority in the social teaching of the popes — though the consistency is, at best, somewhat strained. But whatever about coherence in the theory, there is another sense in which the present statement represents a sharp break with the past. Its effect is to put 'on the agenda' of Catholics seeking social reform a question which Leo XIII and his successors had deliberately closed off. That question is whether a particular regime is so utterly unjust that the obligation of allegiance may be superseded by a more primordial obligation. Could it be legitimate to rebel? Could it even be a duty to do so, in order to replace an incorrigibly corrupt or unjust regime with one that would promote justice and the common good?

It could be claimed that the situation in Mexico at that time was morally unique and that therefore the pope's remarks in *Firmissimum* do not establish any precedent that might be invoked in other situations. But the way in which the pope's teaching is given rules out such an interpretation. Pius XI says, 'it is . . . Our duty to remind you of some general principles which must always be kept in mind';[75] and twice he mentions that how one is to act depends on circumstances. [76] This indicates that he was judging the Mexican situation in the light of universal norms. In one sense every situation is unique and unrepeatable. But the implication of what the

71

pope was saying is that morally similar situations could occur elsewhere; and, if so, the same judgments should be made.

It must at once be added, however, that the Mexican situation, though not in principle morally unique, had certain features that made it highly unusual. These help one to see why the question of withdrawing allegiance from the existing government was considered by the pope in the case of Mexico rather than in the case of Russia or of Germany. The first, and probably the most important, of these distinctive features was the fact that there was already a good deal of organised resistance to the government within Mexico.[77] This meant that it was relevant to take account of the traditional theology that laid down 'reasonable hope of success' as one of the criteria for a just war or rebellion. Furthermore, the resistance in Mexico was a source of instability and might even bring about the overthrow of the government. So it would make sense to suggest that there might be a proportion between the existing evil and the proposed remedy; this is another of the traditional criteria to be used in an evaluation of this kind. In other words, the rightness of resistance to the regime would be judged not merely in terms of the extent of its injustices (a purely moral criterion) but also in terms of another criterion which is pragmatic at an immediate level but turns out to be moral also, because morality has to be judged also in terms of what is likely to happen in practice. This pragmatic criterion is the extent to which resistance to the existing regime is likely to lead to a more stable and effective public order.

Another feature that was significant in the Mexican situation was the fact that its population was largely Catholic and it was seen as in some sense 'a Catholic country', which made it different from Germany and Russia. In medieval times the papacy claimed the right to declare that a people no longer owed allegiance to their ruler; and this right was widely acknowledged. Because Mexico was 'a Catholic country' a statement by the pope about allegiance ought to be taken seriously; there could be a *de facto* approximation to the *de jure* situation of medieval times. At least the regime could not afford to assume that any such statement would have no practical effect on their ability to retain power. In these circumstances the statement by Pius XI could be seen

72

as a warning to the Mexican government. The pope was not saying openly that the people no longer owed allegiance to the government; but that might be implied; and, furthermore, it might be implied that the pope was threatening to make an even more explicit statement unless the harassment of the Church was moderated. If this interpretation is taken, one can see how the pope could see his statement as being not primarily an incitement to rebellion but rather a warning issued in an effort to promote peace and stability.

In conjunction with the previous two points, one must recall the pope was dealing here with a left-wing regime — a regime which Pius XI explicitly linked to the communism of Russia.[78] The Vatican at this time was still inclined to assume that communism was inimical to all genuine civil authority.[79] This means that the pope would look at a left-wing regime such as Mexico's in quite a different light to the way he would consider a right-wing government. The latter might be seen as unsatisfactory in many respects, but the pope would see it as having a *prima facie* right to exercise legitimate authority. In the case of a regime which he considered to be 'communist' this would be more questionable, since for quite a long time there had been a tendency in Church circles to equate communism with anarchy. So it is unlikely that Pius would have made such a strong statement on the question of resistance if he had been dealing with a right-wing regime.

The unusual bluntness of this part of *Firmissimum* may be largely explained by the combination of the various factors mentioned. One might add that Pius XI was a rather forceful character at the best of times, but perhaps never more so than at this particular time. *Firmissimum* was the third of three major encyclicals all on burning political questions and all issued in the space of a fortnight; one might be forgiven for thinking that there was feeling in the Vatican (or at least in the pope) that it was 'time for a showdown'! But whatever the historical explanation, the fact remains that the pope's statement gave the tradition of papal teaching a quite distinct swing away from what it had been.[80] Since the time of Leo XIII (and before) the effect of papal teaching had been to give a notable measure of canonisation to the *status quo*, despite the protests of popes about injustices. That had now changed at least in this one instance. And what is perhaps most significant is that the change was a return to an older tradition, where the possibility of a legitimate rebellion was considered. So the statement of Pius XI cannot easily be dismissed as a temporary aberration.

Almost six years intervened between *Quadragesimo Anno* and *Firmissimum*. But there is a link between the two. The first represents a major challenge to the existing socio-economic order; but it gives little guidance on the political question of how these changes could be brought about. The later encyclical opens up the possibility of disobedience and resistance to civil authorities and even a justified rebellion in certain exceptional circumstances. It would be contrived and historically inaccurate to suggest that the pope intended *Firmissimum* to 'give teeth' to his earlier encyclical. But the radicality of his views on the political issue is of a piece with that of his position on the socio-economic question. In this sense, at least, each of the two encyclicals supports and complements the other.

## Conclusion

The experience of the years since the pontificate of Pius XI suggests that it would be unwise of Church leaders today to identify themselves very closely with his views on either socio-economic or political issues. In both of these areas he showed a sympathy for the right wing. This approach would find little echo in the present trend of Catholic social teaching. But if one goes behind these historically conditioned opinions one reaches a more fundamental level where Pope Pius XI has a lot to offer. In these two encyclicals he takes a 'prophetic' stand on political and economic questions. His stand shows that the role played by the Church in society does not always have to be a conservative one. Concern for stability is important; but stability is not the only social value, or even the highest. Justice ranks higher. There may be times when the value of justice calls the Christian community and its leaders to take risks — not merely personal risks but what might be called 'social risks'. They may feel called to challenge the basic economic and political structures which seem necessary for the survival of our society — and even for the world as we know it. In taking such a radical stance they may be encouraged

74

by the example of Pope Pius XI, who, while staying within the tradition of Catholic social teaching, nevertheless gave that tradition a distinctly 'prophetic' emphasis.

# 4

# The Contribution of Pius XII

When Pius XII became pope in 1939 he took charge of a Church that was highly centralised not merely administratively but also in the sphere of theology and spirituality. His style as pope fostered this centralisation. He produced an almost endless stream of addresses and documents in which he gave a 'teaching' on a very wide range of issues. Social, economic, and political questions were among the many topics on which he made pronouncements. But in his teaching he tended to concentrate more on political issues than on strictly economic ones. The reason for this was the situation in which he found himself — and perhaps also his own character and interests.

## The Preoccupations of Pius XII

During most of the papacy of Pius XII the world was so dominated by political issues that socio-economic questions seemed less pressing and were given less prominence. The first few years of his time as pope were overshadowed by World War II. In that war the issues of ideology and of racist nationalism were so much to the fore that underlying economic issues tended to be overlooked. The war also had the effect of overshadowing socio-economic tensions within the various countries involved. It provided governments with a justification for an exceptionally high degree of control of economic, social, cultural, and political life. Some of this governmental control had the effect of ensuring that tensions between the richer and poorer classes found little means of expression. Freedom of speech and of organisation were severely restricted; and there was harsh treatment of anybody thought to be 'subversive'. Some of the government interventions in the economic sphere were designed to lessen

76

the *causes* of social tension, by curbing exploitation — for instance by rationing the supply of scarce commodities and by controlling prices and profits. The effect of all this in the non-communist world was to bring about a notable shift from a 'free enterprise' model of society towards a bureaucratic model; and this was done in a climate that damped down social tensions. By the end of the war Western society had changed considerably. But most of the changes had happened — or appeared to have happened — as a result of extrinsic political factors rather than through a 'normal' development of the socio-economic system.

In the years following the war the dominant issue was once again political rather than overtly economic. Relations between East and West had quickly deteriorated into a 'cold war'; and in Asia there was open, but localised, war. No doubt economic and social questions were very much at stake in the East-West struggle. But, ironically, the differences about the economic structuring of society had been raised to such an ideological level and had become so politicised that the purely economic and social aspects were less obvious. The struggle between communism and capitalism was now identified with an international political conflict between East and West.[1]

This situation naturally had a considerable influence on what Pius XII felt the world needed to hear from him. Peace, and the conditions for a lasting peace, were major themes for him during the years of the war.[2] Following the tradition of Benedict XV, he adopted a neutral stance and sought to be seen as a potential mediator. But as the war developed it became increasingly clear that the sympathy of the Vatican lay with the allies. To speak more accurately, one should say that the pope's sympathy lay with the *Western* allies. For during the war years the communist threat from Russia troubled Pius XII far more than it troubled the Western leaders.

## Preference for Democracy

In his teaching, Pius XII showed a clear preference for democracy over other forms of political organisation. This is not surprising, for he could see the effects of German, Russian, and Japanese totalitarianism, as well as Italian fascism, on

77

their own people and on their neighbours. As the war drew to a close the pope took democracy as his theme in his Christmas message of 1944.[3] In order to ensure consistency in papal teaching he recalled the statement of Leo XIII that the Church does not condemn any of the various forms of government.[4] But he left little doubt that he saw democracy as the system of the future,[5] because it is more in conformity with the dignity and liberty of the citizen.[6] He even went so far as to say that 'a democratic form of government is considered by many today to be a natural postulate of reason itself', precisely because the modern State is so deeply involved in the lives of people[7] — and because people want a more effective share in shaping their lives and society.[8]

Pius XII evidently believed that one of his tasks as pope was to educate people to a deeper understanding of democracy and a greater commitment to it. It is interesting to read the series of addresses which this aristocratic pope gave over a number of years to the nobility of Rome.[9] In speaking to this 'elite' audience the pope interprets the words 'nobility' and 'elite' in a way that puts the emphasis on service,[10] high moral ideals,[11] courtesy, and the ability to cross class barriers so as to have a 'compassionate solidarity' with others.[12] He insists that the nobility should not look to their high birth to give them a privileged place, but should rather give a 'tone' to the life of the area where they live, and should educate people to genuine democracy.[13] The attitude of Pius XII towards democracy represents a significant option for the common people, a real trust in them, and a commitment to the principle of participation.

But the leaning of Pius towards democracy also had what would now be called a geo-political dimension. It identified the pope with 'the West' in the struggle against communism as a world power. In the years immediately after the war this struggle was focused on Europe. But within a few years China, Korea, and other Asian countries came to the fore as the battleground. The United States came to see itself as the policeman of what was called 'the free world'; and the Churches tended to play the role of chaplain. It is hardly surprising therefore that Pius XII was not inclined at this time to make sweeping condemnations of the capitalist order; for it was on this foundation that 'the free world' rested.

In some respects the situation facing Pius XII was more like that which faced Leo XIII than the situation at the time of *Quadragesimo Anno*. There appeared to be only one realistic alternative to capitalism. That was communism — and it was seen as the ultimate abomination in the political order. There was even doubt about whether a communist state would have the fundamental right to command the allegiance of its citiziens.[14] The 'third way', represented by fascist-inspired corporatism, had been greatly discredited by World War II.[15] It is true that Spain and Portugal still retained something of this approach. But it no longer seemed a very realistic or attractive option for 'the West' as a whole. On the other hand the capitalist system had survived the economic crisis of the 1930s — at the cost of a good deal of Keynesian-inspired tampering by the State with the market economy. In many respects the war gave an important boost to the capitalist system — and proved that the system could flourish in much closer partnership with a bureaucratic State than had been envisaged in its earlier ideology. After the war, the Marshall Plan linked to massive American investment contributed to a quick recovery of capitalism in Europe (and considerable control exerted by the U.S.); and before long Japan became the new showpiece for the great 'free enterprise' system.

So capitalism could again present itself as the system that works, that brings progress. In its new guise it could even claim to have gone most of the way towards solving the traditional 'social problem', namely, the poverty of the working class. This apparent success seemed so obvious to the people of the West that by 1952 Pius XII was inclined to accept that, essentially, the problem had been solved.[16] Equally and perhaps more important than the effects of the 'free enterprise' system in the social field was the fact that it was seen as the economic face of political democracy; that was what made it particularly difficult for the pope to challenge it in any radical way.

*From Corporatism to Capitalism?*
One scholar claims that Pius XII changed his emphasis between the mid-nineteen forties and 1950: in the earlier stage he was still issuing 'diatribes against capitalist abuses'

79

while later he came to have 'a growing appreciation of the contribution which capitalism made to general welfare'.[17] This contrast is rather over-stated. It would perhaps be more accurate to say that from the beginning of his pontificate the pope realised that the social situation had changed greatly since his predecessor wrote *Quadragesimo Anno*. During the war he saw that the future had become unpredictable.[18] After the war he felt obliged to give support to 'the West' in the struggle against communism. At no time did he condone capitalist abuses; in fact he spoke out at various times against the subordination of the common good to private greed.[19] But his tone is rather closer to that of Leo XIII than to that of Pius XI. It is significant that he refers far more frequently to *Rerum Novarum* than to *Quadragesimo Anno*. The radio message in which he commemorated the fiftieth anniversary of Leo's encyclical paid surprisingly little attention to *Quadragesimo Anno*, which of course had its tenth anniversary at the same time.[20]

Like his predecessors, Pius XII was opposed to the underlying philosophy of the capitalist system. He found it unduly individualistic. Though he favoured free enterprise, he did not want personal advancement to be the chief motive for people's actions. He envisaged an organically united society where the service of the common good would be the basic motivation of all the different groupings of which it would be composed.[21] For him, as for previous popes, the way to minimise class tensions was to promote the organic unity of society. In outlining how this unity was to be achieved, Pius XII invoked in a rather vague and general way the principles laid down in *Quadragesimo Anno*. The State, he held, requires structures of cooperation.[22] But these should not normally be structures of the State itself.[23] Rather, the State should preside over the cooperation and ensure that it takes place, while remaining aloof except where State involvement is obviously needed. It should be particularly careful not to take on a major degree of involvement in the economic sphere, since that is not its field.

When it comes to the question of how these general principles are to be put into effect in the concrete, Pius XII was notably less specific than Pius XI. He was perhaps more aware that there is no easy formula which would be *the* practical solution to the social problem. For instance, he accepts that the mere existence of intermediate organisations is not in itself a solution — for there is no guarantee that these will in fact cooperate unselfishly for the common good.[24] In one interesting and significant passage he refers explicitly to the professional organisations so favoured by Pius XI. He says they offered a 'concrete and opportune formula'. He defends this formula against the accusation that it was a surrender to fascism — and also against the suggestion that what Pius XI proposed meant a return to medievalism. But then Pius XII goes on to say that this section of *Quadragesimo Anno* must now be seen as an instance of *an opportunity missed*, because it was not seized on at the opportune time.[25] This is a good example of how Pius XII preserved a 'doctrinal' consistency with his immediate predecessor while at the same time changing the emphasis and the practical implications to a significant extent. It is clear that by 1949, when he made this statement, Pius XII felt that it would be unrealistic and perhaps even counter-productive for the Church to commit itself unreservedly to working for the acceptance of a corporative-type State in most Western countries. For the foreseeable future the most realistic approach for the Church seemed to be to rest content with a tempered version of capitalist society, while working for a further tempering of its more obnoxious features.

*Concern for Personal Freedom*

Having referred to the 'missed opportunity' to implement the kind of society Pius XI would have wished, Pius XII goes on to address himself to the possibilities and dangers of the current situation. At present, he says, there is an attempt to work towards a very different kind of society: the preference is for nationalisation. So the pope clarifies the Church's attitude to this issue of the nationalisation of the means of production. He recalls the teaching of *Quadragesimo Anno* that some degree of this may be acceptable. But he maintains that the economy is not of its nature an institution of the State; the role of the public authorities is not to replace private rights and initiative but rather to serve them.[26] It soon becomes clear that the chief concern of the pope at this stage was not so much the dangers of capitalism but rather the threat of the erosion of free enterprise through excessive nationalisation.

This resistance to nationalisation is an indication of the basic social value that Pius XII felt called to defend, especially in the post-war period. Unlike his predecessor he was not campaigning eagerly for the replacement of the capitalist order by some alternative system. For he believed that the problem was not chiefly the iniquity of one 'system' rather than another. Rather it was that all the massive systems of the modern world tend to swallow up the individual person. The pope wanted to defend individual freedom, rights, and responsibilities against any such 'system'. So he rejected the great systems of the right as well as those of the left, believing that both leave the individual at the mercy of the State.[27] This rejection of systems was not confined to communism and fascism. For he held that slavery of the person could result from the tyranny of private capital as well as from the power of the State.[28] Similarly, he was concerned that the power of trade unions would increase to a point where the freedom of the individual worker would almost be lost.[29]

It is interesting to note that Pius XII saw a particular danger arising as a result of war and 'cold war' between East and West: this kind of situation leads to restrictions of the freedom of the person 'in what is called the free world'.[30] Clearly the pope was aware of the dangers of what is now called 'the National Security State' and the ideology on which it is based. Fear of enemies abroad and of 'subversives' within the State creates an atmosphere of suspicion. This gives rise to serious intrusions into the lives of citizens and curtailment or infringement of human rights.

### Distribution of Goods

From what has been said so far it is clear that Pius XII was much more concerned about socio-political matters than about strictly economic ones. However, as one might have expected from a pope who gave addresses on such a very wide range of topics, he did have some important things to say on economic quesions as well. He did not issue any document or make any statement which as an *intervention* had the same kind of impact as the two great social encyclicals of his predecessors. But he made a most significant contribution to the body of social teaching or 'doctrine' of the Catholic Church. This contribution has to do mainly with the question of the ownership and distribution of property. It came quite early in his pontificate, in the broadcast he made to commemorate the fiftieth anniversary of Rerum Novarum.

At this point we need only to advert briefly to two important points in this address.[31] The first is that economic prosperity is not to be measured purely in material or quantitative terms. Other factors may be more important. For instance, if people are living all the time in uncertainty, the here-and-now possession of goods is not sufficient; so there is need for a certain stability in society.[32] Furthermore, and perhaps even more significantly, he insists that there must be an equitable distribution of whatever goods are available. For, no matter how much wealth there may be in a given area, the country cannot be said to be economically prosperous if its people do not have the opportunity to share equitably in its wealth. But on the other hand the economy is healthy if there is a just distribution of the available goods, even if there is less to share.[33] In defining economic prosperity in this way Pius XII was well ahead of the economists and planners of his time. Right into the 1960s it was widely held that the best way for a country to become economically prosperous and 'developed' as quickly as possible was to subordinate equitable distribution to rapid growth of the gross national product. Indeed this view still prevails among many politicians and decision-makers. The 'national cake' is to be enlarged first; later on will be the time to consider a more fair distribution. In recent years this assumption is coming to be questioned fairly widely. Certain more enlightened economists are adopting a view similar to that outlined in 1941 by Pius XII.

The second major contribution of Pius XII to the socio-economic teaching of the Church concerns private property. Like his predecessors he insisted on the right and value of private ownership. But, in contrast to Leo XIII, he did not hesitate to give the first priority to the general right of all people to the use of the goods of the earth. The right of the individual to a particular item of private property does not negate the more general and fundamental right; rather it is to be a means of actualising the right of all to the use of material goods.[34] This way of treating the question of private property represents an important development in Catholic social teaching because it is clearer and more explicit than the treatment of private property in *Rerum Novarum* and *Quadragesimo Anno*.[35]

The acceptance of the idea that the right to private ownership is subordinate to the more general right of all to the goods of the earth provides a solid base for the social teaching of subsequent popes. It was only many years later that the full importance of the statement of Pius XII could be seen. For his teaching came at the height of a world war when few had time or interest in such matters. So this contribution of Pius XII was not very important as an intervention by the pope in an immediate and pressing social problem. Rather its importance lies in the way in which it contributes to the development of the corpus of social teaching. It was left to later popes to draw out the practical implications. The way in which they applied this principle attracted the attention of the world; and their position was strengthened by the fact that they could refer back to the teaching of Pius XII. They could invoke his authority for their playing down of the sacrosanctness of the right of private property in order to put the stress on social responsibilities and rights.

## Conclusion

The most notable feature of the approach of Pius XII to socio-economic issues was his 'realism', that is, his practical acceptance, especially in the second half of his pontificate, of a capitalistic society. He did not repudiate the call of Pius XI for major restructuring of the social order along lines that would be at least vaguely corporative. But, during the years that Pius XII was pope this ideal does not seem to have ever appeared to him to be very feasible in practice. So the ideal came to have what one might call an 'eschatological' character — something that was to come about in an indefinite future.[36] Indeed Pius XII on one occasion sharply rejected the idea of implementing one of his predecessor's proposals (namely, a degree of co-management) on the grounds that this was one element in an integral scheme and was therefore not to be separated from the whole.[37] This means in effect that while giving ritual approval to the proposal for radical reform of existing structures, he was in practice resisting an important step towards a piecemeal implementation of such restructuring.

It would appear that the practical ideal of Pius XII would have been an unbureaucratic free enterprise economy, with non-centralised agencies to facilitiate cooperation between various sectors of the economy. The State would play an un-obtrusive 'watchdog' role to ensure that the common good would be served. The pope believed that this ideal was threatened in Western countries both by overgrown unbridled capitalism and by socialistic tendencies — especially national-isation of the means of production and the introduction of 'the welfare state'. He could only protest and appeal against these tendencies since he was not inclined to encourage any radical political movement which would offer an alternative to the existing capitalist society of the West.

The pope believed in the possibility of gradual and peaceful improvement of the existing system. He held that justice can be promoted not through revolution but through a harmonious evolution.[38] In fact he considered that changes of this kind had already taken place, so that capitalism had not in fact been applied in its full rigour. He believed that the Western economic system had gone a long way towards overcoming poverty. In practice, then, it offered the best hope for the future — not an ideal 'best' but the best available at the present time. Consequently, his stance represents a practical option of support for a capitalist order, with the qualifica-tion that he disapproved of certain aspects of it. In the socio-economic area, therefore, he effectively, though not 'doc-trinally', retreated from the call of Pius XI for a fundamental restructuring of society and even from Leo XIII's outraged protest against the capitalist system.

There is a danger that one might stop at this point and conclude that if 'an option for the poor' meant anything to Pius XII it was largely confined to charitable works rather than the transformation of society. But that would be to overlook the fact that 'the poor' is a term that should be applied not merely to those who have little wealth but also to those who find themselves *powerless*. In other words, there is a political as well as a socio-economic connotation to the word; and this is very relevant when one is considering the views of Pius XII. One of his greatest concerns about modern society was that more and more people were being left practically powerless in the face of massive systems of one kind or another. The kind of deep concern that was aroused in Leo XIII by the plight of the mass of the industrial workers crushed by economic poverty was awakened in Pius XII by the thought of masses of ordinary people deprived of the possibility of taking personal responsibility for many aspects of their daily lives. He spoke out strongly and repeatedly about this powerlessness, as Leo spoke out about economic poverty. In this sense he was on the side of the 'poor'. But, again like Leo, he could do little more than protest. He saw what was wrong; and he proposed an ideal in which people would have all the freedoms of a genuine democracy, unencumbered by bureaucracy. But he did not focus attention on any really practical and effective steps that could be taken towards the overcoming of powerlessness and the achievement of real participation and freedom. Had he done so his words would inevitably have been taken by many as a challenge to Western-style democracy — and possibly as an encouragement to its enemies. That was a risk that Pius XII felt he could not afford to take.

# 5

# Pope John XXIII — A New Direction?

It is generally agreed that Pope John made a major contribution to the social teaching of the Catholic Church. My purpose in this chapter is to examine the overall effect of his stance on social questions, rather than considering the details of what he had to say about such matters as private property or international aid. This should help one to see whether, or in what sense, he gave a new direction to Catholic social teaching. There are two sections in the chapter. In the first section I hope to show that in one sense his position was by no means a radical one, nor did it represent any major departure from the direction set by earlier popes, especially by Pius XII. In the second section I shall suggest that, despite what has just been said, Pope John had, in another sense, a major role to play in turning the Catholic Church in quite a different direction on social issues.

## SECTION ONE:
## A SUPPORTER OF THE STATUS QUO?

There was an extraordinary freshness about Pope John XXIII, both in his manner and in his two major encyclicals on social issues — *Mater et Magistra*[1] and *Pacem in Terris*.[2] Those who like to categorise everybody as either a liberal or a conservative have little difficulty in seeing 'good Pope John' as a liberal, in sharp contrast to his predecessor. This is of course an oversimplification but as a journalistic generalisation it contains a good deal of truth, especially in so far as it refers to the *style* of the pope; for it is in his teaching that one can find much more continuity with Pius XII. The trouble with these labels is not so much their inaccuracy as the assumption that between them they are exhaustive. In fact, however, there is room for at least one other label — 'the radical' — which cannot be reduced to either 'liberal' or 'conservative'. The word 'radical' has been given a remarkably wide variety of meanings in history;[3] but as used here it refers to the readiness to work for a fundamental change in the structures of society. The radical may be liberal on some issues, conservative on others; but in many cases the radical has an entirely different outlook, one which shows up just how much the liberal and the conservative have in common.

On social issues Pope John was *not* a radical. In regard to the fundamental re-structuring of society his approach was not very different from that of Pius XII; and in some ways Pius XI was more radical than either of them. The similarities and the differences between Pius XII and John XXIII can be found in a significant passage near the end of *Pacem in Terris*, written shortly before John died:

> There are, indeed, generous souls who . . . burn with desire to put everything right and are carried away by such an ungovernable zeal that their reform becomes a sort of revolution.

> To such people we would suggest that it is in the nature of things for growth to be gradual and that therefore in human institutions no improvement can be looked for which does not proceed step by step and from within. The point was well put by Our predecessor Pius XII: 'Prosperity and justice lie not in completely overthrowing the old order but in well planned progress. Uncontrolled passionate zeal always destroys everything and builds nothing. . .'[4]

Pope John's remarks lack the acerbity of his predecessor's. He shows understanding and sympathy for the 'generous souls' who are not satisfied with a step-by-step reform. But, despite this, he in fact reaffirms the gradualist approach of Pius XII. This is no mere verbal acceptance made in the interests of assuring a kind of doctrinal continuity. Pope John really believed that the necessary improvements could come 'step by step and from within', without any radical disruption of the system. He was an optimist.[5]

*Optimism about the World*

This optimism of John XXIII has to be teased out, so as to disentangle various elements in it. First of all it represents a new theology of the world. It would perhaps be more accurate to speak of a new spirituality of commitment to the world, a spirituality that contains the seed of a new theology. During the Second Vatican Council this seed sprouted very rapidly indeed. The new spirituality can be detected mostly as a difference of tone; to document it, one would have to note what John omits more than what he says. What comes through is the fact that he is not afraid that commitment to the world and its values will cause people to neglect the highest spiritual values. One significant point in *Mater et Magistra* is the way in which the pope speaks about human work[6] and especially about agricultural work.[7] Two years later, in *Pacem in Terris*, the new approach is rather more explicit, especially in the pope's call for a 'synthesis' between scientific and spiritual values,[8] an 'interior unity' between religious faith and action in the temporal sphere.[9]

One important element in Pope John's conception of the world is his understanding of how people work together for the common good and how this process is to be facilitated by the civil authorities. On this point there is a clear doctrinal continuity between what he says and the teaching of Leo XIII; but nevertheless there is a difference of tone which has important practical implications. Like his predecessors, John XXIII insists that human authority is derived from God. But, significantly, he immediately adds a text from St John Chrysostom which shows that it is not that a particular ruler is appointed by God but rather that the authority exercised is from God.[10] So already in this first paragraph of his teaching on the question, Pope John is distinguishing between authority and the office-holder. In the next paragraph he insists that human authorities are subject to a higher authority.[11] He goes on to say that civil authorities can impose an obligation in conscience only in so far as their authority is intrinsically linked to the authority of God.[12] If civil authorities make demands contrary to the moral order, or fail to acknowledge human rights, their authority no longer exists and so the citizen is not bound to obey.[13] The whole purpose of political authority is the promotion of the common good.[14] The denial by a government of the right of the individual to an area of personal freedom is branded by Pope John as 'a radical inversion of the order of human society'.[15] These statements indicate that he is emphasising a very different aspect of authority from that stressed by Leo XIII. The latter was afraid of anarchism so he put the emphasis on the right of human authorities to make demands on citizens with the authority of God himself; only reluctantly and minimally did he take note of the cases where human authorities forfeited the right to unquestioned obedience. John XXIII, like Pius XII, was more concerned lest individual freedom be stifled by authoritarian rulers or bureaucracies. So he paid more attention to the duty of authorities to fulfil their proper role, the service of the common good; human authority ceases to be real authority when it fails in this regard. Quite clearly this approach leaves much greater scope for the individual to assess whether those in power are in fact exercising a lawful authority; and there is a wider gap where dissent may enter. Pope John is not of course encouraging political dissent, still less any kind of organised resistance. But evidently his conception of human society is that of a community of persons who voluntarily submit to civil authority in order to attain the common good. He does not hold that democracy is the only valid form of government[16] but the values he promotes are those to which democracy at its best is committed and which it should embody.

The general optimism of Pope John about the world finds expression in his teaching about political organisation and authority. He believes people can cooperate successfully not only at the local and national levels but also at the international level.[17] The whole presupposition of his two great social encyclicals was that people needed only to be encouraged and animated to cooperate more fruitfully. He presumes not merely the ability to cooperate but the fundamental willingness of people and nations to cooperate even at the cost of personal, sectional, or national sacrifice. This presupposition might easily be overlooked. But it is important to note it. For it explains why John XXIII addressed himself mainly to the question, *what* improvements are needed in economic, social, and political affairs in order that people may live with greater human dignity. He did not concentrate on another question which may be equally or more important: *how* can these changes be brought about, especially where many of those who hold power are reluctant to accept reforms that would curb their power.

*Optimism about the Modern World*

John XXIII was not just optimistic about the world in general. His optimism and hopefulness were directed specifically to the *modern* world — meaning the kind of society that had emerged in the Western world as a result of rapid economic growth. Here his tone is notably different from that of Pius XII. He speaks with ringing hope and challenge of this age of the atom and of the conquest of space as 'an era in which the human family has already entered on its new advance toward limitless horizons'.[18] He asks whether the modern developments in social relationships will entangle people in a maze of restrictions so that human freedom and responsibility will be eliminated; and his answer is a firm 'no'.[19] The 'modernisation' of society can, he believes, have more advantages than disadvantages, if it is properly controlled and directed.[20]

In a moving passage in *Mater et Magistra* the pope expresses his distress about the plight of poverty-stricken workers of many lands and whole continents. He adds that one of the reasons for this poverty is the fact that these areas are still underdeveloped in terms of modern industrial techniques. [21] In a later paragraph he says that usually an underdeveloped or primitive state of economic development is the fundamental or enduring cause of poverty and hunger.[22] Clearly he has no serious doubts about the need for 'modernisation' and 'development' as the way in which the world must make progress. He is of course aware that this kind of 'development' can create social problems[23] and even economic difficulties.[24] He also realises that the modern situation offers opportunities for a new kind of elitism. So he warns against abuses of power by the new class of managers of large-scale enterprises — and he makes the important point that such abuses can occur both in private business and in public bodies.[25] Furthermore he notes two causes of poverty which are particularly important in this modern world — the arms race[26] and the squandering of money by governments on prestige projects.[27] But all of this he would see as an argument for control and balance, not a reason for questioning the whole direction of modern 'development'.

## Optimism about Capitalism

We have seen that Pope John's optimism is not just about the world but about the modern world, including the processes of 'modernisation' and 'development'. Now it must be added that the optimism extends even further — to the capitalist system which is most conspicuously associated with 'modernisation'. (Of course Communist countries are also dedicated to economic development; but the West, including the Vatican, has tended to assume that the link between capitalism and 'development' is more natural and more successful.)[28] There are indications that Pope John took a rather optimistic view of what might be expected from capitalist society in the future. Not that he ignored its deficiencies and abuses, or repudiated the condemnations of capitalism by Leo XIII and Pius XI. But he seemed to believe that before too long and without too much trouble the system could be effectively humanised.

One of the more significant and controversial paragraphs in *Pacem in Terris* draws a distinction between 'false philosophical theories' and the 'historical movements' which are inspired by these theories.[29] It is commonly and correctly assumed that Pope John was referring here primarily to those left-wing movements which, historically at least, draw their inspiration from Marx.[30] But the pope would no doubt also apply the distinction to capitalism: the capitalist ideology remains incompatible with Catholic social teaching; but capitalist society in its actual historical development can be viewed rather more optimistically by Pope John.

Already in his 1959 encyclical *Ad Petri Cathedram* the pope had remarked that class distinctions were less pronounced than before.[31] He went on to say: 'Anyone who is diligent and capable has the opportunity to rise to higher levels of society.'[32] This statement shows the extent to which he accepted one aspect of the free enterprise ideology, namely, the assumption that it gives most people a reasonably equal chance of 'getting on', i.e. of moving upwards in society. The implication of this belief is that, by and large, the rich and powerful have 'earned' their privileged place in society, while the weak and the poor are in some sense responsible for their 'failure'. Needless to say, the pope did not accept this implication. But there are indications that he did not question the free enterprise ideology very thoroughly.

One such indication is to be found in an important paragraph of *Mater et Magistra* where Pope John insists on the need for a wider distribution of property of various kinds.[33] Like his predecessors, John XXIII was aware of the tendency of capitalism to concentrate wealth in the hands of the few. What is significant from our present point of view is that the pope maintains that now is a particularly suitable time for countries to adjust their social and economic structures so as to facilitate a wider distribution of ownership. Why *now*? Because, says Pope John, it is a time when an increasing number of countries are experiencing rapid economic development. This statement suggests that John accepted the common assumption that rapid economic growth offers the easiest way to overcome the problem of the unequal distribution of wealth. No wonder; for, on the face of it, this approach seems almost self-evidently correct. Instead of having to face the difficult task of taking wealth from the rich to re-distribute it to the poor, why not create sufficient *new* wealth to enable the poor to become reasonably well-off? But despite its apparent obviousness this line of thinking can in practice play a part in bringing about the very opposite to what it aims at. This is what in fact has happened in large parts of the world. So it will be useful to look more closely at the process.

How best can rapid economic growth be promoted in a society which follows the 'free enterprise' approach? Both the theorists and the real-life capitalists claim that the only effective way is to allow the entrepreneurs and investors an adequate return for their contribution. What it means in practice is that this group must be allowed a major share of the new wealth in the form of profits and inducements. The argument is that the 'national cake' must first be enlarged even at the cost of some delay in redistributing the shares of the 'cake'. So a lower priority is given to equitable distribution of wealth than to creation of wealth. Once that pattern is established it becomes exceptionally difficult to change it. There never comes a time which seems right for a more fair distribution. Various 'compelling' objections disguise the fact that those with wealth have the power to retain it. Their power is exercised both politically and through the moulding of opinion in society. Consequently the best hope left to the poorer and less powerful people is that growth will be so great that they will become better off in absolute terms, even though the gap between them and the rich continues to widen. This is what happened in many Western countries during the 1950s and 1960s. But in a world of limited resources it is increasingly unrealistic to expect that *all* countries can attain such a degree of growth.

The belief that the best way to solve social problems is to speed up economic growth is not confined to Western counries. Most, but not quite all, Third World countries are convinced that their best hope of eliminating poverty lies in rapid growth. And Communist nations also put great emphasis on rapid growth; indeed their leaders have at times imposed almost intolerable sacrifices on the people in order to achieve 'growth'. But there is an important difference between socialist and capitalist societies on this question. In a centrally planned economy increased growth and equitable distribution are not incompatible goals. When failures occur they are mostly due to authoritarianism, or bureaucracy, or to a pandering to some power elite. In a capitalist society, however, the relationship between growth and equitable distribution is complex and particularly interesting:

— First, capitalism is committed to growth not merely for practical reasons but also ideologically. At a practical level an ever-increasing demand seems to be necessary if the whole system is not to collapse. Hence the need for an ideology of growth; this is promoted in various ways, notably by the advertising industry. The belief is fostered that there is no foreseeable limit either to human needs or to the ability of a free enterprise system to meet these ever-expanding 'needs'.

— Secondly, the growth that actually takes place tends, as we have seen, to concentrate wealth in the hands of a minority rather than leading to a more equitable distribution.

— But, thirdly, another part of the ideology of capitalism masks this lack of equity. It promotes an image of free enterprise where all have a fair opportunity to use their talents

94

profitably. Hard work and initiative are correlated with success and prosperity. The implication is that poor distribution of wealth is to be explained more in terms of the laziness and lack of ability of some rather than any lack of opportunity imposed by the system.[34] Furthermore, the idea is fostered that the new wealth will soon 'trickle down' from the richer to the poorer sectors of society. These beliefs are illusions which protect the interests of a particular group by hiding the truth.

Needless to say, Pope John did not set out to promote such misleading ideas. But they must have had some effect on him. This is shown by his statement (quoted above) that anybody who is diligent and careful can rise to higher levels in society. The fact that the pope uncritically accepted this belief suggests that there was a certain blind spot in his outlook. This blind spot becomes more evident when one adverts to the gap between the end he was hoping for and the means he proposed to achieve it. The end-result he wanted was a wider distribution of property.[35] The means by which he hoped this would come about was a gradual reform of the existing structures and the introduction of controls designed to reverse the tendency of capitalism to concentrate wealth in the hands of a few. But Pope John seems to have been unduly optimistic in thinking that this could be brought about fairly easily. Perhaps he was unrealistic in seeing the current time of rapid growth as the best occasion for a relatively painless reversal of this 'normal' pattern. Tampering with the system is never easy — and, ironically, it may be especially difficult when the system is working smoothly as it was at the time *Mater et Magistra* was written.

But surely the pope was correct when he supported his case by noting the progress towards wider ownership made in some economically developed countries?[36] His facts were correct but it is doubtful whether they should be used as the basis for a generalisation. Undoubtedly the years between 1945 and 1961 saw a considerable growth in prosperity for most workers in Western countries. But this was part of a wider reality — the increased wealth of Western nations as a whole vis-à-vis the Third World. This imbalance was in turn related to the extravagant use by industrialised countries of energy and raw materials, much of which came from poorer countries at a very cheap price. So whatever improvement occurred within the Western countries must be seen in the context of an increasingly lop-sided distribution of wealth on the international (or intercontinental) level.

Furthermore, there is a certain ambiguity in the pope's call, at this point in the encyclical, for a wider distribution of ownership of property. What exactly is the end-result that he is looking for here? Is he asking that whatever wealth is available should be distributed more equally? Or is he merely asking that more people (especially those who are poor) should become owners of property? This second position would be compatible with a widening of the gap between rich and poor. It is quite likely that John XXIII did not advert to this possibility. It would seem that he was simply following in the footsteps of Leo XIII by insisting on the importance of more people becoming owners of property (the first position) — and tacitly assuming that this would involve a narrowing of the gap between rich and poor (the second position). But the history of Western countries since World War II shows that this assumption is not justified. There is reason to believe that the gap between the richer and the poorer sectors of Western society has widened during the very period when more and more ordinary workers were becoming owners of the kind of property mentioned by the pope (e.g. a house and garden). Is this the situation that the pope is setting up as a model for the rest of the world? The answer should be, 'no', because in two earlier paragraphs of the encyclical he had insisted very strongly on the central importance of equitable distribution of wealth.[37] Following Pius XII, he even went so far as to say: 'the economic prosperity of any people is to be measured less by the total *amount* of goods and riches they own than by the extent to which these are *distributed* according to the norms of justice.'[38]

One must conclude that, in terms of his own principles, Pope John was not entitled to present as a 'success story' those 'nations with developed social and economic systems' where ownership has become more widespread.[39] These Western countries can certainly be cited as proof that in certain circumstances rapid economic growth under a free enterprise system is compatible with, and perhaps even gives rise to, wider ownership of possessions. But they should not be cited as proof that it is possible in practice to reverse the inherent tendency of capitalism towards an inequitable distribution of wealth and power. This is not to say that John XXIII was wrong when he said that private ownership had increased in some 'developed' countries. But what he said could leave one with a wrong impression, namely, that the present free enterprise system of the Western world requires only gradual and moderate reform in order to become a system that would bring social justice on a world scale.

*The Welfare State*

This issue of whether Western countries serve as a model for a humanised version of capitalism is vitally important. So it is appropriate to say something here about the Welfare State approach adopted in several Western European countries in the years after World War II. It is true that the expanding social services that were offered could scarcely have been provided without the rapid economic growth of those years. (And as growth has slowed down in recent years the social services have come under strain partly through shortage of funds and partly for ideological reasons.) But it would appear that the determination to cope with poverty through national social welfare programmes came *prior* to most of the economic growth. It is arguable that the fundamental change in structures and attitudes involved in the Welfare State owes more to the chaos at the end of the war than to the success of a revived capitalism. Workers were determined never again to face the deprivations of the depression years; and the breaking of the moulds that came during and after the war offered the chance to give political expression to this determination. The point is that basic changes in social structures are more likely to be associated with the *failure* than with the 'success' of a growth-oriented free enterprise model of society. This suggests that it is illusory to expect raw capitalism to develop naturally, organically, and painlessly into a system characterised by equitable distribution of wealth and effective care for the weaker sectors of society.

It is well to note also the limited aims of the Welfare State approach. It did not set out overtly to bridge the gap in *ownership* between rich and poor by wholesale nationalisation or redistribution of capital goods; in other words it is not to be equated with a full programme of socialism. Rather it presupposed the continuance of a free enterprise economy with its inherent tendency towards imbalance and concentration of wealth. It sought to cope with the resultant poverty and deprivation i.e. with the effects rather than the causes. In some European countries the Welfare State approach was combined with a limited type of socialism which set out to redistribute ownership through the imposition of very high levels of taxation on income and profits. But in other countries it was not linked to any serious effort to redistribute ownership. So the Welfare State approach is not necessarily socialistic. In fact its comparative success was due largely to the fact that it was supported also by people who were opposed to socialism. Not that it was universally accepted; there were many champions of a rugged free enterprise philosophy who fought against any build-up of a comprehensive programme of state welfare. But, faced with the ideological struggle between left and right, the majority of voters in Western Europe settled for the Welfare State as a kind of compromise — a way of combining social compassion with the efficiency and respect for initiative of the free enterprise system. The Welfare State was seen by many as a way of giving 'a human face' to a society built on a capitalist economy.

Twenty years ago this approach seemed to be working well. It seemed to offer a direction which could be taken further in the future, not merely in Europe but in the wider world. So the scenario for the future envisaged by many concerned people, including, most probably, Pope John and at least some of the drafters of *Mater et Magistra*, would have been along the following lines: a healthy ever-expanding economy, primarily free enterprise in character but including some degree of State capitalism, combined with expanding public welfare programmes (supplemented by the welfare programmes of voluntary agencies, especially the Churches) to mitigate the deficiencies and cope with the casualties of such an economic system. The intervening years have made this scenario increasingly problematical. First, an indefinite period of rapid economic growth can no longer be presumed: there are severe limits to the amount of cheap energy and raw materials that are available to make this possible; and furthermore the inherent problems of a capitalist order (problems of prediction, credibility, cycles, protectionism, etc.) have proved far more intractable than expected. Secondly, it is now more evident that the 'development' of the West depended on the availability of cheap resources from the Third World so it cannot be seen as a model which can be repeated all over the world. Thirdly, the Welfare State approach has itself run into serious difficulties in Western Europe: the expansion of the 'national cake' has slowed down but the demands of the stronger groups in society have increased; the result is that there is less left for the poorer segment of society, which in some Western countries now comprises about a quarter of the population. Finally, government efforts to stimulate the economy are costing the tax-payer a great deal; the heavy tax burden offers a convenient opportunity for opponents of State welfare to renew their ideological attack on the social services as wasteful and as an encouragement to idleness and parasitism. And in such an atmosphere it becomes quite unrealistic to hope that something analogous to the Welfare State will emerge at the *international* level, with the rich nations providing adequate help for the poor ones.

The conclusion that emerges from what has been said is that Pope John, like many of his contemporaries, including notable economists and social scientists, showed a rather uncritical optimism in relation to Western-style democratic capitalist society. Most of the scholars and religious leaders of more recent times (including Pope John Paul II) would be far more cautious; they would be slow to assume that national and international social justice can come about through a gradual and relatively painless reform of the capitalist order of society.[40]

### Option for the Poor?

Pope John's social encyclicals played a major part in bringing the Catholic Church into a more open relationship with modern society. But was this at the cost of an acceptance of the Western *status quo*, subject only to gradual and relatively minor reforms? Did his openness to existing Western society imply a playing down of the Church's challenge to the world? More specifically, did it involve a failure to make an effective option for the poor? These questions call for a carefully nuanced response.

The first thing to note is that Pope John himself clearly did not see himself as having to choose between on the one hand an option for the poor and on the other hand an acceptance of capitalist society. He believed that the latter could be tempered and adapted in such a way as to ensure that the poor really were looked after. His encyclicals appeared at a time when the Western economic model seemed to be working well and seemed to be amenable to the kind of reforms he was looking for. It was not a time when many Church leaders or scholars saw the issue in terms of a clash between capitalism and social justice. To present the issue in terms of such a stark choice is to see it more as it was seen thirty years earlier (at the time of Pius XI's *Quadragesimo Anno*) or as it is seen by a significant number of Church leaders today, twenty-two years after the appearance of *Mater et Magistra*.

Another important point to note is the fact that John XXIII consistently adopted the 'spoonful of honey' approach, avoiding condemnations as far as possible, praising what he could, and inviting people to make improvements. The fact that he is less critical than his predecessors in matters of social injustice is no indication that he had abandoned their concern about the exploitation of the poor. Nor does it prove that he had become an enthusiastic convert to the capitalist system. There seems to be a considerable degree of over-statement in the conclusion of the scholar Camp that Pope John saw capitalism 'as a positive good'.[41]

Nevertheless, John XXIII differed from the popes who went before him in so far as he seems to have approved of the general direction in which the world was moving. Camp is broadly correct in judging that Pope John 'did not want a change of institutions. Rather, he frankly admired what was already being done and wished an expansion of its benefits to more people.'[42] The pope did, however, want *some* changes. He thought gradual reforms could make the world a more just and humane community of people and peoples. But in proposing such gradual reform he was at the same time implicitly giving a considerable measure of endorsement to the existing free enterprise system. From the point of view of their formal teaching the social encyclicals of John XXIII show no very radical departure from the tradition of social teaching of his predecessors. But there are subtle differences in tone and emphasis which give these encyclicals a different effect when seen as interventions by the pope at this particular time. Pope John did not demand a radical reconstruction of society such as Pius XI had proposed. It is significant that the summary of *Quadragesimo Anno* given in *Mater et Magistra* omits all reference to Pius XI's account of Italian corporatism.[43] It also preserves a careful vagueness in the way it uses such terms as 'vocational groups' and 'intermediate bodies'.[44] So, despite the continuity with the past from a 'doctrinal' point of view, the net effect of the social teaching of Pope John was rather different from that of Pius XI. It was to give a certain approval and legitimation to the Western economic approach, provided this is taken in conjunction with the democratic reformist and socially conscious currents of the thought of that period.

Whether John XXIII's position is considered to be an improvement on that of Pius XI depends of course on the stance of the person making the judgment. A fairly typical evaluation of *Mater et Magistra* is that which was given by John F. Cronin who was assistant director of the Social Action Department of the conference of U.S. bishops. He held that the encyclical was 'realistic, moderate, and progressive'.[45] Obviously he saw this as high praise. It is a useful exercise to 'translate' his words into more descriptive and neutral language:

— 'Realistic' means that the encyclical does not call in question in any radical way the economic order existing in Western society and dominating most of the world.
— 'Moderate' means that the reforms it calls for would not seriously disrupt this order either in their extent or by the speed with which they are to be introduced.
— 'Progressive' means that the encyclical fits comfortably into the more 'enlightened' strand of Western thinking, sharing the values of the liberals — provided one has in mind not the hard economic liberalism of the nineteenth century but the socially conscious liberal thinking of more recent times. Understood in this way, Cronin's words can be applied not only to *Mater et Magistra* but to Pope John's social teaching taken as a whole.

In the light of the clarifications just given, it is now possible to offer a fairly brief answer to the question whether John

XXIII failed to make an effective option for the poor. He was deeply concerned about the plight of different categories of poor people; and he proposed a variety of measures designed not merely to provide relief but to prevent imbalances in society.[46] Nevertheless he did not commit the Catholic Church to an option for the poor if one takes that in the very specific sense in which it is frequently used today — namely, a radical challenge to the capitalistic structures that prevail in Western countries and largely determine the international economic order. On the contrary, the effect of his interventions in social issues was to give a certain sanction and support to these structures, provided they are supplemented and restrained in ways that limit their harmful social effects.

## SECTION TWO:
## A NEW DIRECTION

It would be misleading and unjust to stop at this point in the evaluation of the effect of Pope John's encyclicals. For there is a sense in which his teaching made a major contribution towards putting the Church on the side of the poor. More accurately, one might say he removed from the rich and the powerful an exceptionally important weapon which they could use to maintain injustice in society. To explain how he did so it is necessary to look closely at his teaching about 'socialisation'.

### Socialisation

Probably the most important single passage in *Mater et Magistra* is the following:

> One of the main features which seem to be characteristic of our time is undoubtedly an increase in the number of social relationships. Day by day people become more interdependent and this introduces into their lives various kinds of associations which are generally recognised in contractual or public law. . . . These developments in social life are both a sign and a cause of an increasing degree of State intervention in matters of considerable importance and risk since they have to do with the intimate life of the person.[47]

102

The first English translation of this passage followed the
Italian version in using the word 'socialisation' where the
Latin text speaks of an increase in social relationships. [48]
But the more widely used English versions avoid this word
very deliberately,[49] either for the purely linguistic reason
that it is not used in the Latin text or on the grounds that its
omission from the Latin was a significant correction of the
original unofficial working text in Italian.[50] It was felt by
some that to use the word 'socialisation' in the English translation might give the impression that Pope John had abandoned
the papal tradition of being opposed to socialism. In fact some
sectors of the media did interpret the encyclical as proposing
some version of socialism. Consequently, Church spokes-
persons were kept busy explaining that as used in the working
text 'socialisation' did not really mean the introduction of
socialism — and that it didn't even mean what Pius XII meant
when he used the word. (For him it meant, mostly, nationalisation.)[51] They explained that the word was being used in a
technical sense to describe a recent development in Western
industrialised society. The main features of this development
may be described as follows:

> People are now more closely inserted in a web of relation-
> ships where the actions of each individual affect many
> others. This gives rise to the need for greater control.
> Many aspects of daily living which used to be seen as
> personal or family matters are now organised or at least
> regulated on a larger scale. So the individual and the
> family have to rely more on, and use the services of, large
> institutions. Some of these are, technically, private in-
> stitutions — trade unions, for instance, or non-State
> insurance schemes. But many are new organs of the
> public authorities — from local councils up to national
> governments and even international agencies.

The originality of John XXIII lies not so much in his
noting of this fact of modern life as in his response to it. He
holds that it would be not merely pointless but positively
wrong if the Christian were just to bemoan and resist this
development, pining for the simple life of the past.[52] Of
course the pope admits the dangers it poses — especially the
risk of excessive interference with personal responsibilities [53]

and an undue degree of bureaucratisation. In this he was taking account of the preoccupations of Pius XII. But Pope John evidently considers the positive aspects of the process to be more important: it promotes the personal welfare of individuals in many ways; and it can also enable people to live, work, and play more as a community.[54] So he believes that the process is not inherently destructive of humanity.[55] But on the other hand it is not to be seen as automatically beneficial either. In fact it is not a process whose outcome is pre-determined at all.[56] Everything depends on the people involved; it is they who are responsible for the direction it takes.[57]

So much for John XXIII's account of 'socialisation'. But what is so significant about his approach? In order to answer this question it is necessary first of all to look closely at the accident of history which makes of resistance to 'socialisation' a policy associated with 'traditional conservatism'. Twentieth-century conservatives in Europe and America see themselves as standing in defence of the *traditional* independence of the individual against the encroachments of society in the form of the State. But how traditional is it for the individual to have a high degree of independence from society? It is not a tradition that goes back very far. It finds its high point in America at about the time the United States came into existence; and the U.S. constitution enshrines and defends various rights of the individual. But the notion of the independence of the individual as a traditional value is largely a myth. In fact traditional societies tend to leave very little room for individual independence; most of a person's behaviour is prescribed and enforced by the community (though not by written laws and regulations of the modern type). So there is a certain irony in the fact that conservatism should be associated with rugged individualism. The more normal type of conservatism would be that which resists individualism in favour of socially determined behaviour.

So the important thing to note is that the 'socialisation' of which Pope John is speaking is a feature of modern Western society, to be understood in the light of *Western* history. It would appear that one of the early effects of Western modernisation and urbanisation was to weaken many traditional social relationships and the obligations attached to them. The result was greater independence for individuals. There was a period when the more fortunate and more ruthless of the new generation seemed to have the best of two worlds. On the one hand they had a high degree of freedom from social constraints, allowing them a wide scope for initiative (and at times for opportunism and even exploitation). On the other hand they could still rely on patterns of obedience, respect, and cooperation inherited from the past. The less fortunate people at the bottom of the social ladder had, correspondingly, the worst of two worlds. The decline in social restraints left them open to new forms of oppression. But their efforts to protect themselves were resisted by the rich who justified themselves by invoking a myth they had built around the values of untrammelled freedom and rugged individualism.

Whatever about the myth of independence for the individual, the reality was that before long there emerged an obvious need for new and different forms of social institutions and restraints. Society could no longer 'free-wheel' on the traditionally ingrained patterns of cooperation. There had to be new social systems to look after security, welfare, public health, education, economic development, etc. And as society became more concentrated in urban areas, less centred on small community units, these needs expanded. No wonder then that Pope John felt it was pointless and wrong to resist the expansion of such social institutions. Rather they should be intelligently planned and controlled. The aim should be to retain as much as possible of the values of personal freedom while protecting the common welfare. But neither was it any wonder that there should be strong resistance to the new restraints. Precisely because they are needed to prevent the exploitation of the weak by the strong, they are experienced by the powerful as unwarranted limits to their freedom. And one of the most powerful weapons used to resist these restraints is the invocation of the myths of the defence of the 'traditional values' of personal initiative and freedom, and old-fashioned rugged independence.

## The Newness of Mater et Magistra

Against this background one can understand the position of John XXIII and the reaction to it. It is a carefully nuanced position. Pope John preserves a clear continuity with his predecessors in his teaching about the values that are to be preserved and the means of doing so. Like them he stresses the principle of subsidiarity.[58] Following them he insists on the importance of vocational groupings and similar intermediate organisations which are not organs of the State itself.[59] He maintains that intervention by government or other public authorities should be limited to those cases where it is really necessary.[60]

On the other hand, John XXIII differs from Pius XI and Pius XII in his judgment about where *in fact* such State intervention is required. It is here that the newness of *Mater et Magistra* becomes very evident. Retaining continuity with previous social teaching from a 'doctrinal' point of view, it is startlingly different in its net effect. For in fact it proposes a programme of action that might well have been borrowed from the manifesto of a moderate socialist political party! The real issue then is not whether the *word* 'socialisation' is the correct translation of the Latin text. Rather the issue is whether the pope is moving the Catholic Church away from its suspicion of such 'socialistic' notions as that of the Welfare State. When one provides a literal translation of the Latin text of the encyclical one loses not only the word 'socialisation' but also its overtones; and these overtones might have conveyed more accurately what Pope John was referring to. Nobody is likely to object to 'an increase in social relationships'. But the problems begin when one starts to spell out the implications. So it is opportune to look at some of these implications as envisaged in the encyclical.

Pope John develops and extends the teaching of Pius XI, [61] and bypasses the reservations of Pius XII,[62] when he says that in some circumstances employees may be entitled to a share in the companies where they work[63] and to a say in management both at the level of the individual firm[64] and in determining policy at various levels, even on a national scale.[65] Again, the State must exercise strict control over managers/directors of large businesses.[66] An increased amount of State ownership is justified by the needs of the common good in the modern situation.[67] It must also be recognised, says the pope, that in fact the State and public authorities have taken on a greatly expanded role in coping with social problems.[68] Indeed Pope John proposes just such a role for them in dealing with the special difficulties of those working in agriculture[69] — and he goes into considerable detail in regard to tax assessment,[70] credit facilities,[71], insurance, [72] social security,[73] price support[74] and price regulation,[75] and even the directing of industry into rural areas.[76] All this is necessary because in modern Western life human inter-dependence is possible only by going beyond one-to-one relationships and those of the small community; life is lived on a scale that requires the massive apparatus of the State to be actively involved in directing and controlling the economic and social life of the people. Even when a nation keeps this State involvement as low as possible by respecting the principle of subsidiarity (as Pope John asks), still the common good nowadays requires far more State 'interference' than was needed in the past. *Mater et Magistra* gives a mandate for this extra involvement by the State; and the result begins to look like an encouragement to 'socialisation' in the popular sense of the word.

Now one can see why some right-wing American Catholics reacted to the encyclical by saying '*Mater si, Magistra no*'. Their opposition is a confirmation of the fact that there really is a distinct change of emphasis in Pope John's social teaching — even when one makes allowance on the one hand for exaggerations of its socialising tendency and on the other hand for its considerable degree of continuity with the teaching of Pius XII. One is hardly likely to find socially conservative Catholics objecting to the teaching of Pius XII — even though there are echoes of that teaching in even the most 'advanced' parts of *Mater et Magistra*.[77] Probably the most important effect of the encyclical, seen as an intervention in the continuing debate about social issues, was that it began the process of breaking the long alliance between Roman Catholicism and socially conservative forces.

With the issuing of Pope John's encyclical in 1961 it began to seem credible, for the first time in the modern era, that Catholicism might have more in common with 'the left' than with 'the right'. There is a certain irony in the fact that *Mater et Magistra* should in this sense be more radical than even *Quadragesimo Anno*. For, as pointed out above, Pope John was no radical. He was looking for moderate and gradual

107

reforms in the capitalist order, while Pius XI was asking for a much more fundamental restructuring of society. But the corporatist ideals of Pius XI were somewhat right-wing, at least in their background and overtones: some strands of corporatism were drawn from a conservative nostalgia for the guilds of the past; others were drawn from aspects of the fascist model of society. Corporatism was strongly opposed to socialism; and Pius XI rejected even a mitigated form of socialism. Pope John, on the other hand, while continuing to insist on the importance of private initiative,[78] private property,[79] and intermediate non-State vocational groupings,[80] put forward an ensemble of practical proposals that was far more congenial to 'the left' than to 'the right'. He seems to have realised that the Church's traditional defence of private initiative and private property had come to be used in an ideological way; and he was determined to put an end to this.

A whole body of social teaching had evolved as a vindication of the dignity of the individual against a totalitarian type of collectivism or socialism. But this teaching had come to be seen as a support for a rather individualistic type of free enterprise, and for the private interests of individuals or groups over against the public interest. It is important to see how this had come about. There was no time at which the Church's social teaching could seriously be accused of giving sanction to capitalism in the form of ruthless big business. But capitalism has another face, a more attractive one. It is what might be called 'frontier free enterprise', typified in the small-town entrepreneurs who use local resources and their own initiative and skill to meet local needs and provide employment in the area. Different popes wanted to encourage this kind of initiative and to protect it against bureaucracy. And their defence of the latter could be used as giving a measure of support to capitalism in all its forms.

Public opinion in Western countries — and especially in the U.S.A. — is subject to the same confusion. The idealised image of free enterprise is used to give respectability to capitalism in its less acceptable forms. Frequently this takes place unconsciously, simply because people have not had the opportunity or education to make the necessary distinctions. But it is not at all uncommon to have a deliberate manipulation, a campaign to justify capitalism in its more unacceptable forms through a glamorisation of the ideal of free enterprise. One feature of this campaign is the reduction of all the various possible options to just two. People are presented with a stark choice between two alternatives: on the one hand is free enterprise with its respect for personal initiative and responsibility; on the other is a massively bureaucratic State socialism which is centralised, inflexible, and inefficient. (The books and television programmes of Milton Friedman provide examples of this kind of over-simplification.)

This background helps one to understand what is meant by the claim that the Church's social teaching had come to be used in an ideological way to defend sectional interests. In most cases this was not the result of some sinister plot but an unfortunate accident of history. In the political sphere Catholics were among the strongest opponents of socialism. So it is quite understandable that a lot of emphasis was put on those parts of papal teaching most strongly opposed to socialist tendencies. Meanwhile papal reservations about capitalism were rather under-played — except for the relatively short period when the corporatist proposals of *Quadragesimo Anno* were taken seriously as providing a workable alternative model of society.

In the social sphere there was a similar process. As 'modern' life patterns came more and more to replace the traditional ones there was an ever-increasing loss of the former support-systems for the individual and the family. The anonymity of modern urban-style living did not lend itself easily to the development of new *voluntary* support systems to replace the extended family and the local community. So there was a great need for the State or other public authorities to provide the individual and the family with supports in social, cultural, and economic affairs. Without a great increase in public welfare programmes of all kinds — and the taxes to pay for them — only the very wealthy could live a dignified human life in this 'modern' world which had emerged. But Catholic social teaching had not taken sufficient account of this new situation. Church authorities tended to be opposed to socialised health care programmes. They were also opposed to giving the State a monopoly in the area of education and culture. Traditional papal teaching was that the State should not intrude itself unduly into the economic sphere; therefore nationalisation of industry or of the economic services such as banking should never go beyond what was proved to be strictly necessary.

The effect of all this was that almost by accident the Church came to be allied with certain sectional interests. It seemed to be more concerned with the defence of the rights of private groups than with the public interest and especially the needs of the poorer classes of society. That was not its intention nor its ideal. The principles proposed in the Church's social teaching were put forward as a defence of people against bureaucracy and totalitarianism. But the way in which they were being applied in practice was now causing the Church to be allied to the opponents of welfare programmes badly needed by the poor. Similarly, the Church's defence of private property — intended to protect the dignity of the person — was now invoked to justify resistance to land reform. Even the payment of the heavy taxes needed to support social welfare programmes for the poor could be opposed on the grounds that they were an undue interference in private ownership and a step towards socialism.

The link between sectional interests and Catholic social teaching was further strengthened by the fact that dioceses and religious congregations were themselves the 'private' owners of many schools, colleges, hospitals, and other property. They felt themselves threatened by anything that seemed like a move towards nationalisation or a State monopoly of such services. This gave them a certain common interest with the more privileged groups in society. For instance, in many Western countries the medical profession jealously guards its privileged position and resists the expansion of public health schemes designed to help the poor. It is all too easy to find situations where Catholic social teaching was invoked to justify such stances and where the Church found itself allied to a conservative group resisting the kind of changes that would make for a more just society. In the sphere of education the situation was rather similar. There were some Catholic schools designed specifically for the wealthy; so it was not surprising that they should find common cause with other 'elitist' institutions. But more interesting is the situation of the great majority of Church-run schools where it was the policy to charge very low fees so as to be available to the less well-off. Nevertheless those who sent their children to such schools tended to be middle-class people or people with middle-class aspirations. Consequently these schools were inclined to propagate middle-class values. The school authorities were not usually seen as favouring the type of change in educational structures that would lessen the inequalities in society.

The general image of the Church was therefore that of a socially conservative force giving ideological and 'political' support to those who were opposed to left-wing changes. All this happened despite the fact that the original purpose of most of the educational and medical institutions of the Church was to serve the poor. It even happened when these institutions continued to be at the service of poor people. For they worked *within* the existing system. Originally they had represented a challenge to the current structures of society. But as time went on they became incorporated as parts of the system. In so far as these institutions required a legitimation for their existence this was provided by Catholic social teaching. And so, the social teaching of the Church seemed in practice to be offering support for the *status quo* rather than calling prophetically for structural changes in the interests of the poor.

What has been outlined so far is an unfortunate but almost accidental process by which Catholic social teaching came to justify conservative social stances, as against efforts to minimise the gap between the different sectors of society. But at times this process has been taken further by a *deliberate* harnessing of the social teaching of the Church to make it serve a political function. This may have taken place in some of the American campaigns against anything that could be labelled 'communist' or even 'socialist'. But the most obvious and blatant example is the way in which right-wing authorities in Latin America seek in the Catholic faith an ideological support for their attitudes. They resist land reform and a more equal division of wealth, in the name of the sacrosanctness of private property. They also invoke Church teaching about obedience to authority and about non-violence as support for their resistance to the changes demanded by social justice. The social teaching of Pope John is a major step towards the prevention of such an ideological use of

111

Church teaching and towards the recovery of its original purpose.

## A Shift to the Left

There are two passages in *Pacem in Terris* which express a key insight of John XXIII:

> One of the fundamental duties of civil authorities . . . is so to co-ordinate and regulate social relations that the exercise of one man's right does not threaten others in the exercise of their own rights. . .[81]
> The common good requires that civil authorities maintain a careful balance between co-ordinating and protecting the rights of the citizens on the one hand, and promoting them, on the other. It should not happen that certain individuals or social groups derive special advantage from the fact that their rights have received preferential protection.[82]

There is of course nothing very startling in these as general statements. But the pope seems to have had in mind actual situations where the entrenched rights of some were the main obstacle to the exercise of the rights of others — especially of the poor. In the modern situation social justice required the recognition of new rights for the people at the lower end of the social scale. But the recognition and promotion of these rights was being hindered, either deliberately or uncritically, by the invocation of Catholic social teaching on the right to private property and the right to personal initiative. This amounted to an ideological use of this teaching, i.e. its use as a cover and legitimation for resistance to the changes needed to promote social justice. So the passages just quoted were intended to prevent such an abuse.

Already in *Mater et Magistra* Pope John had set out to lessen the chances that such things could happen. By means of that encyclical he had publicly and clearly put the weight of the Church on the side of a policy of social reforms in favour of the poor and deprived, both within each country and at the international level. *Mater et Magistra* advocated a considerable degree of control by public authorities over the activity of individuals and groups. It also recommended certain initiatives to be undertaken by the State to help those

112

who are disadvantaged in society. The traditional and philosophical basis for such State control and initiative can be found in this passage: 'Our predecessors have constantly taught that inherent in the right to have private property there lies a social role and responsibility.'[83] Leo XIII can certainly be cited as insisting on the importance of property owners using their wealth responsibly.[84] Pius XI insisted that 'the right to own private property has been given to man . . . both in order that individuals may be able to provide for their own needs and those of their families, and also that by means of it the goods which the Creator has destined for the whole human race may truly serve this purpose.'[85] Pius XII gave priority to the universal purpose of the goods of the earth and saw the institution of private property as a means for the attainment of this purpose.[86] Quite evidently there is a pattern here: each of these popes in turn lays greater stress than his predecessor on the social obligations attaching to private property. In *Mater et Magistra* John XXIII built on the foundation laid down just twenty years earlier by Pius XII. John's own contribution consisted mainly in drawing the obvious practical conclusions. He saw clearly that quite often private ownership was not in fact serving the purpose for which Pius XII had said it had been instituted. So he proposed a variety of measures to ensure that its social function should be attained. By the very fact of owning property a person incurs social responsibilities. Pope John was not content with encouraging property owners to take these responsibilities seriously; he envisaged that they should be compelled by law to do so.

As we have seen, Pope John was not looking for a radical restructuring of the present order of Western society. Given that order, he accepted the need for State intervention in social and economic affairs to an extent well beyond what would have been advocated by Catholic leaders in the past. Perhaps even more important was the fact that he eliminated a good deal of the suspicion of State control and State initiatives, a suspicion which had been a central feature of the Catholic social outlook. In this sense it is not inaccurate to see in *Mater et Magistra* a certain 'opening to the left' (*apertura a sinistra*) in the socio-economic sphere. How closely that was related to an opening towards the left in the political

113

sphere remains open to debate. Certainly, *Pacem in Terris*, issued two years after *Mater et Magistra*, contains a very significant passage referred to earlier.[87] In it the pope distinguished between false philosophical theories and the historical movements that are inspired by such theories; the latter, says the encyclical, can change profoundly and may contain positive and praiseworthy elements. This statement provided a justification for a significant change in the attitude of the Vatican in the political field. It was an irenic gesture directed mainly towards left-wing movements at the national and international level. It left the door open for practical political cooperation between the Catholic Church and communist governments and parties. But it is important not to focus attention on the political question to an extent that plays down the significance of the move towards the left that had already taken place on social and economic matters in *Mater et Magistra*. Perhaps the most accurate way to sum up the effect of that encyclical, and of Pope John's social teaching in general, would be to call it not so much an opening to the left as a decisive move away from the right.

This helps one to understand why *Mater et Magistra* contains detailed directives on such specific matters as the two kinds of insurance needed by farmers.[88] The pope scarcely imagined that his proposals were so original and compelling that governments would immediately adopt them! Rather it must be presumed that John is speaking not to governments or political parties or civil servants as such but to those to whom the encyclical is officially addressed — 'the ... bishops, clergy and faithful of the Catholic world'.[89] He feels the need to go into specific details because the approach he is advocating is quite different from the prevailing interpretation of Catholic social teaching, especially as regards its practical applications. One may show, as Bolté does quite effectively,[90] that there is considerable continuity between Pope John's teaching and that of his predecessors. One can conclude quite correctly that he was within a developing tradition. But this continuity applies at the level of 'doctrine' and general principles. In the application of the principles and in the practical implications for the stance of the Christian on social questions the discontinuity is more obvious. It would be wrong to exaggerate this discontinuity, to speak as though

114

Pope John were advocating socialism. But it must be said that *Mater et Magistra* stands as a turning-point in Catholic social teaching.

The extent to which the encyclical was a turning-point has emerged more clearly in recent years. It stands at the source of two important developments whose full implications could hardly have been foreseen at the time. The first of these is in the area of theory, though it has many practical effects. *Mater et Magistra* opened up cracks in what had been a rather monolithic body of social teaching. It raised doubts about attitudes that had not previously been questions – for instance the attitude of suspicion about State intervention and a conviction that it ought to be kept to a minimum. Before long there was considerable questioning of many other parts of the traditional social outlook. Furthermore, the encyclical was controversial and was subject to a variety of interpretations. This gave rise to fragmentation at the practical level: there was no longer a clear, universally accepted Catholic 'line' on many socio-economic issues. It was not long before the very concept of a 'social doctrine' was called into question.[91]

The second development was that the encyclical began the process by which the Catholic Church got new allies and new opponents. This was perhaps the most important effect of the encyclical – at least for those who recognise that social teaching arises from, and relates back to, social praxis. The speed at which this development has occurred varies from place to place and even from continent to continent. Latin America is the region where one can see most clearly what may be involved. The 'option for the poor' which the Church is making in many parts of that continent could never have taken place unless the Church had ceased to be an ally of the rich and powerful. The refusal to provide a legitimation for the privileges of the 'elite' was a major factor in enabling the Church to opt for solidarity with the poor and oppressed. The Church of course sees itself as having a message for all of humanity and every sector of society. But many Latin American Church leaders became convinced that they must at times give a specific answer to the question: 'Whose side are you on?' In regard to basic issues of social justice they felt that they could not plead neutrality. So they committed the Church to making what came to be called 'a preferential, but not exclusive, option for the poor'. For the ability to see the need for such an option, the Church owes much to John XXIII and especially to the social teaching of *Mater et Magistra*.

# 6

# Vatican II: Another Agenda

This study of Vatican social teaching is concerned mainly with what the popes had to say. On what grounds should it include a study of any documents issued by the Second Vatican Council? Firstly, these are official Vatican documents. Secondly, it would be a mistake to make too sharp a contrast between papal teaching and the teaching of the Council. It is true that the documents of Vatican II represent much more than the views of John XXIII and Paul VI, the two popes who presided over the Council. Indeed there is little doubt that they contain things that these popes would not have said had there never been a Council. But these two popes played a major part in the genesis of the Council documents. Indeed Paul VI helped to formulate the Council statements; and he signed them, promulgated them, and set up the procedures required to implement them. The documents of the Council represent not merely the consensus of the bishops from all over the world but also the consensus of these bishops with the Vatican, above all with the pope. There can be no doubt of the entire commitment of Pope Paul to the teaching of Vatican II. It is evident, then, that it would be a serious mistake to study papal teaching without making a close examination of the teaching of Vatican II.[1]

## The Liberal Agenda

Just nine days after Vatican II began, the Council Fathers issued a short but significant 'Message to Humanity'. In it they noted two issues of special urgency which they saw facing them — peace and social justice.[2] However, before long the bishops and their 'experts' became engrossed in other issues. So there was an interval of more than three years before the

117

Council issued any formal teaching on these two topics which they had singled out in their first message. It is true, of course, that during that interval work was going ahead on successive drafts of the document which eventually became *Gaudium et Spes*, the Pastoral Constitution on the Church in the Modern World. But until quite near the end of the Council there was considerable doubt as to whether this document would be issued at all. And when it did eventually come, the parts of it dealing with peace and social justice were comparatively short; and in places they showed signs of having been drafted with undue haste.

What happened? Why were these 'urgent issues' left so late in the Council? The standard answer is that the participants in Vatican II had first to work through certain urgent 'internal' theological and pastoral issues such as the sources of faith, the nature of the Church itself and its public worship, as well as the nature of the ministry and the Church's authority structure. Only then could they deal satisfactorily with the 'external' issues of the Church's relationship with the world, notably in regard to questions about peace and social justice. This answer is correct as far as it goes but it is not a complete answer. What has to be added is that at an early stage of the Council, 'the liberal agenda' came to dominate both the discussions and the documents of the Council. Among the items on that agenda were: the use of the vernacular in the liturgy, the collegiality of bishops, the renewal of religious life, the role of the Bible in revelation, the Church's openness to other Christian Churches and to other faiths, and the issue of religious freedom. The main drama of the Council was the struggle between liberals and conservatives on these issues. This polarisation applied also in the area of the theology of marriage and sexuality; so it affected one of the major topics dealt with in the second and more practical part of *Gaudium et Spes*. The issues of social justice and peace did not split the participants in the Council along the same lines. For instance, one of the champions of the conservative line, Cardinal Ottaviani, spoke out strongly in favour of what was called a 'progressive' stance in regard to war and peace.[3] On the other hand some of the more 'progressive' bishops took a much more cautious stance when it came to speaking out against the holding of nuclear weapons. This indicates that

118

the usual categories of 'liberal' and 'conservative' did not apply very well to the views of the bishops and theologians on some socio-political issues. In the case of matters of peace and social justice the issue is to what extent the Church is prepared to take a radical or prophetic stance that challenges the current values of society. A desire that the Church should take up a prophetic posture is compatible with either conservative or liberal tendencies — though the radical-conservative combination has quite a different character from the radical-liberal one. Perhaps the most significant thing from our point of view is that at the Council the struggle between liberals and conservatives on internal Church matters tended to obscure the other issue, namely, the extent to which the Church should mount a radical or prophetic challenge to the world on socio-political questions.

But why did 'the liberal agenda' take over in the Council? Because, by and large, it represented the concerns and priorities of the Northern European theologians — and through them of the majority of European and North American bishops — as against those of the Roman establishment. It is important to note that on the whole the bishops from the Third World (indigenous and expatriate), though they were very numerous,[4] were not very involved or very significant in the polarisation between liberals and conservatives. As Vatican II progressed, there came to be a growing realisation that the Church is not just Western and Eastern but also Asian, Latin American, and African — and therefore that the Council documents would have to take serious account of the Third World. A fully elaborated Third World theology did not emerge at the Council to challenge the liberal and conservative approaches, both of which were quite Western in their concerns. But at least some of the major questions that were of interest for the Third World came to be given a rather higher priority than in the past. The drafters of *Gaudium et Spes* tried to take account of these questions. But the final result was that some of its paragraphs read as though statements about the situation in 'developing countries' had been 'patched in' to passages drafted originally with the Western world in mind.[5] Some of the drafting committees included people from the Third World — and it is doubtful whether a fuller representation would have led to any great improvement in the text.[6] What was missing was a coherent Third World theology and a body of 'experts' to articulate such a theology. In the absence of these it is not surprising to find that even Third World problems are looked at to some extent from a First World perspective. This is very evident in the treatment of 'development' and in the chapter on culture.[7] Nevertheless, *Gaudium et Spes* represents a considerable advance on earlier Church documents — even those of John XXIII — in so far as it begins to recognise more clearly that Third World countries have their own history, traditions, and social structures, as well as their own problems; and that none of these are to be treated as though they were no more than adjuncts to those of the West.[8]

## The Contribution of Gaudium et Spes

What contribution does *Gaudium et Spes* make to the Church's social teaching? Before one looks at the more significant points in its content it should be noted that the importance of this document lies not only in what it says but also in the process that produced it. *Gaudium et Spes* expresses the consensus that emerged after three years of private and public dialogue, debate, and even controversy. It crowns a three-year process of thorough and intense exploration by experts in the various matters it deals with, as well as a process of education of the bishops and of the millions of people who followed the progress of the Council. So, even where it merely repeats the teaching of Pope John or earlier popes, it does so with a greatly increased degree of authority and credibility.[9]

*Gaudium et Spes* repeats important themes from the two social encyclicals of John XXIII.[10] In general it tends to temper the extraordinary optimism of Pope John's documents. It does so, not by toning down his Christian hope and his high ideals, but by adopting a more dialectical approach: the ideal is contrasted with reality — a reality marred by social evil.[11] Another important contribution of Vatican II to socio-political questions is the attempt to offer a solid theological basis for its practical directives. Among the more successful instances of this are the Council's statements on religious liberty,[12] on peace,[13] on human work,[14] on the nature of and need for human authority,[15] and on the

120

relationship of the Church to the world.[16] Rather less successful efforts in this direction are the Council statements on 'development'[17] and on culture.[18] In presenting a theology of these different realities a positive effort was made to ensure that a Scriptural basis was given as well as a more philosophical component. In some cases there is quite a good integration of the two.[19] Elsewhere the integration is not so good.[20] In those passages of *Gaudium et Spes* which are more philosophical in tone the drafters distance themselves somewhat from the neo-scholastic approach of earlier documents: the text incorporates what is best in the natural law tradition and integrates it with a more existential idiom.

Pope John's determination to issue an encyclical on peace before he died led him to up-stage the Council document on this question. Nevertheless, those who were drafting *Gaudium et Spes* succeeded in making one major contribution on this issue. The document proposes a conception of peace which provides a philosophical-theological basis for its more practical statements where it follows in the same general direction as Pope John. Peace is presented as not merely an absence of war. It is an ordering of society; but real peace is built not just on any order but on one which is to be brought into existence by the thirst of people for an ever more perfect justice.[21] There are three important points here:

— First, peace does not just happen. Though in one sense it is a God-given gift to society,[22] still it has to be brought about by human commitment and effort.

— Secondly, it is not attained once for all but has to be constantly defended,[23] renewed,[24] and brought nearer to the ideal.

— Thirdly, and most importantly, peace is firmly linked to justice; and it is the passionate desire ('thirst') for justice that motivates people to work for peace.

The justice of which the document speaks is not simply the putting right of 'political' grievances. It extends to the whole *economic* order. That is why this chapter goes on to treat of international cooperation in the economic field.[25] In this way the Council Fathers reacted against the tendency, common among statesmen in the more 'developed' countries, to think that a more peaceful world can be brought about without too much tampering with the present inequitable economic world order. The Council document helps to make it clear that there are not two distinct international questions, one about peace and one about economics. The two are the same question.

This firm determination to present the problems of the less 'developed' countries in terms of justice marks a subtle but significant development in the social teaching of the Church. It is not entirely original; for Pius XII and John XXIII had both spoken of these problems in terms of the principle that the goods of the world are destined for the people of the world; and the latter had said that it is a matter of justice that the goods of the earth be better distributed.[26] On the other hand the Council statement is not as specific and detailed as later papal documents. So, what one finds is a gradual process by which justice comes to be presented as the heart of the issue. *Gaudium et Spes* represents an important stage in that process.

For anybody concerned with the theme of the Church's 'option for the poor' the following passage will be seen as one of the most significant statements of the Vatican Council:

> God destined the earth and all that it contains for the use all men and all peoples . . . Furthermore, the right to have a share of earthly goods sufficient for oneself and one's family belongs to everyone.
>
> . . . If a person is in extreme necessity, he has the right to take from the riches of others what he himself needs. Since there are so many people in this world weighed down by hunger, this sacred Council urges all, both individuals and governments, to remember the saying of the Fathers: 'Feed the person dying of hunger, because if you have not fed him you have killed him.' According to their ability, let all individuals and governments undertake a genuine sharing of their goods . . .[27]

The train of thought in this passage is exceptionally interesting. The words 'and all peoples' were deliberately added into the first sentence after some discussion, precisely in order to indicate that the Council had in mind the problem of poor countries, not just poor individuals.[28] By going on to speak within the same passage of the person in extreme necessity the document seems to be suggesting that to be in such extreme need is the plight not just of occasional isolated and desperate individuals but of whole peoples. This impression is confirmed by the fact that the very next sentence speaks of so many people in the world weighed down by hunger.

In strict logic one might have expected that the document would go on to conclude that the masses of hungry people have the right to *take* what they need from the rich peoples of the world. Instead, however, the Council Fathers make an earnest appeal to individuals and governments to share what they have with the poor. Why this rather weak conclusion? Could it be that the hungry masses are not considered by the Council Fathers to be in 'extreme necessity'? That is most unlikely, since there would then have been no point in referring to the person in extreme necessity. Or could it be that the drafters of the document were drawing back from the obvious conclusion of their statements, namely, that these poor people have the right to take what they need? That is not to be assumed, because there is a more likely explanation. It is that the readers are being allowed to draw the conclusion for themselves precisely because it is so obvious. If the passage is understood in this way then the exhortation to the rich to share what they have must be seen as a combination of a timely warning and a moral threat. It means: if you do not share willingly, then the poorer peoples will in any case take what they need — and they will be justified in doing so. In this way the Council document succeeds in taking a very strong stance on the issue of international social justice, without lapsing into fruitless condemnations. The difficulty of course is that not everybody will see or accept the full implications of what the Council is saying. But it is doubtful whether harsh words of condemnation would be any more effective than the nuanced approach adopted in the document, in bringing about the fundamental changes that are called for.

What are the changes that are required? The answer given by *Gaudium et Spes* is rather vague. This is not surprising because there was a new factor in the discussions about social justice, a concept of 'development' whose full implications had not yet been worked out. This notion of 'development' gave rise to a good deal of optimism about solving the problems of poverty. Many, if not most, of the bishops and experts at the Council probably believed that the best way to attain international social justice and overcome poverty was for Western-style 'development' and democracy to be adopted as quickly and painlessly as possible by the rest of the world. The question then becomes, what changes are required to facilitate such a process? And the kind of changes envisaged, while they may be fairly comprehensive, are not of the type that would involve a radical replacement of the present notion of 'development'. The assumption behind this whole approach is that Western-style 'development' can be generalised; other countries can follow the path along which the Western industrialised countries have passed during the last two centuries.

Granted this context, *Gaudium et Spes* was quite advanced for its time. It insists that there is need for profound changes in the way international trade is carried out.[29] It calls for the establishment of 'a truly universal economic order'[30] – a phrase that seems to anticipate the 'New International Economic Order' ('NIEO') which was called for, some years later at the United Nations. *Gaudium et Spes* recognises that a major source of injustice in international trade is the inequality in *power* between trading partners; to compensate for this the document calls for the setting up of institutions to promote and regulate international trade.[31] This is precisely the kind of thing that the NIEO requires: a major expansion and strengthening of international bodies to regulate the supply and price of Third World products; these agencies could ensure that over-production and erratic supply do not lead to exploitation of the producers of such products. If such bodies really had effective power, and if they were not dominated by the wealthy nations, this in itself would constitute a fundamental change in the existing economic order. If they were gradually extended to cover the whole range of goods and services exchanged in international trade, then the cooperating nations would in effect have built up, piecemeal, the basic economic elements of a world government. And this embryonic world government for economic affairs would have adopted as its basic principle, not the capitalistic principle of the 'law' of supply and demand, but a commitment to the common good of all, as envisaged by *Gaudium et Spes.*[32] So in fact the full implications of the changes proposed in the Council document are more far-reaching than would appear at first sight – possibly more radical than the Council Fathers themselves fully realised.

From what has just been said it is clear that the Council favoured a reform of the world's economic structures. Indeed *Gaudium et Spes* explicitly says that there is need not merely for a conversion in the mentality and attitudes of people but also for 'many reforms' in socio-economic life itself, that is, in its structures.[33] But, apart from the fairly brief points noted in the previous paragraph, the document does not go into much detail in specifying what these reforms should be.[34] In one very carefully phrased passage the Council says that 'in many situations there is urgent need for a reassessment of economic and social structures'.[35] The choice of the word 'reassessment' is noteworthy. Some of the modern language translations speak here of reforming or recasting the structures.[36] But this is to miss the nuance of the Latin version. By choosing the word 'reassessment' the drafters suggest that the Council is not identifying itself with those who glibly assume that the solution to all social problems is the overthrowing of existing structures. But what is significant is that the Council Fathers did not flinch from calling for a reassessment; they did not start with the presumption that any fundamental restructuring is unnecessary; nor did they rule it out on the grounds that it might be a threat to stability. They did, however, add that there is need for caution lest some of the priceless heritage of non-Western cultures be lost by the hasty imposition of 'technical solutions . . . especially ones that offer people material advantages while being inimical to the spiritual character of the human person'.[37]

## The Reasons for Change

It is not sufficient to say *what* changes are called for. Two further questions need to be answered: *why* such changes ought to be made and *how* they are to be brought about. In this section an attempt will be made to see what answer the Council gives to the first of these questions; then in a subsequent section we can consider the answer to the question about how change is to be brought about. The first thing that must be said is that *Gaudium et Spes* is not entirely clear in the answers it gives to the question why changes are needed.

125

Is it simply in order that no significant group of people will be left starving or totally unable to look after themselves? In other words, is it to overcome *absolute* poverty? Or is it necessary to go beyond the overcoming of absolute poverty and bring about changes with the purpose of tackling the problem of *relative* poverty as well, i.e. to ensure a more even distribution of the goods of the earth, even in situations where the poorer groups are not in extreme necessity? As noted above, the Council document suggests that whole nations may be living in a state of extreme necessity — and it points out that this imposes on rich people and the governments of the wealthier countries a serious and pressing moral obligation to make the changes required to meet their needs. [38] But, clearly, social justice involves something more than that. If the basic principle is that the goods of the earth are destined for all people of the earth, this calls for equity in their distribution. But what does equity mean in practice? It can hardly be some utopian attempt to divide the goods of the earth in exactly equal shares. That would be quite unrealistic, even as an ideal. Indeed various popes over the previous seventy years had insisted that it is of the nature of human society that its people have a diversity of wealth and status; and Vatican II certainly did not explicitly repudiate this teaching. But it undoubtedly went much further in the direction of equality than did the papal teaching of fifty years earlier:

> Excessive economic and social inequalities within the one human family, between individuals or between peoples, give rise to scandal, and are contrary to social justice, to equity, and to the dignity of the human person, as well as to peace within society and at the international level.[39]

However, the Council gives very little by way of guidelines that could enable one to decide at what point the inequalities can be considered so great as to be inequitable or unjust.

There is one text that could be significant in this regard. It is the passage in which the Council declares that in certain circumstances it may be right to expropriate and divide up the *'latifundia'* i.e. those large estates which are so common in the Third World, especially in parts of Latin America. What would justify the confiscation of such properties? Is it the mere fact that such huge estates exist in areas where there are so many poor, powerless, and exploited people? The Council does not say so, at least not explicitly. It seems rather to suggest that the key point is precisely the failure by the owners of these estates to make proper use of the land.[40] Presumably the argument would be that the owner who fails to use the land productively is failing to ensure that the goods of the earth are used for the benefit of all — and this justifies expropriation. The implication of this line of argument would be that if an owner uses the land productively then it would be wrong to confiscate the land. But whatever about the strict logic of the argument, the text seems to recognise that there is a very close connection in practice between the possession of huge land-holdings and the blatant exploitation of the local population. This exploitation is at least a contributory factor, if not the primary basis for the call for expropriation. In theory the exploitation could be remedied in other ways than by confiscation of the land; but in practice the two are almost inextricably linked. The Council document remains rather vague about the precise basis for expropriation. This may well have been deliberate. For many of the bishops would have been reluctant to make any statement that seemed to restrict unduly the right to private property.[41]

However, in the Council document the traditional emphasis by the Church on the rights of private property owners had to be balanced against the equally traditional protest of the Church against leaving workers in a totally powerless and vulnerable position, with no property of their own to provide them with a minimum of security. What seems to be original in this statement on expropriation is the willingness of the bishops to accept that in very many actual cases the balance tips in favour of the poor and powerless: in the concrete, the right to private property has to yield to the cry of the poor — and therefore expropriation becomes justifiable. The Council Fathers would not have made the statement at all unless they believed it had a fairly widespread application. In his commentary on this section of *Gaudium et Spes*, L.J. Lebret (who himself played an important role in helping to draft the text) raises important questions about the basis on which compensation ought to be calculated in the case of expropriation of land. This issue arises especially, as Lebret notes, in cases where the market value of the land has greatly increased because of such extrinsic factors as the decision to utilise it for housing or for some public purpose.[42] The Council document itself refrains from entering into such detailed questions and is therefore able to retain a certain vagueness about the fundamental moral principles that lie behind its call for social change.

## Obligation to Help the Poor

An important light is thrown on the attitude of the Council Fathers by a late addition which they made to one passage in *Gaudium et Spes*. The text is the one in which we are reminded that the Fathers and Doctors of the Church taught that people are 'obliged to come to the relief of the poor *and to do so not merely* out of their superfluous goods'.[43] The italicised words were added at a fairly late stage in the drafting of the document;[44] and evidently this involved a major change in the meaning of the statement. It also involved a correction of Leo XIII's statement in *Rerum Novarum* that people are obliged to give to the poor out of what remains over when they have provided for their own needs and for what is appropriate to their station in life.[45] Pius XI had repeated this teaching in *Quadragesimo Anno* but had added that the use of superfluous wealth to provide work for others is an excellent act of liberality, particularly appropriate to our time.[46] A closer look at the effects of the teaching of these two popes will help to show why a different line was taken at Vatican II.

Pope Leo XIII said that one is obliged to give to the poor out of one's '*superflua*'. This gave rise to a rather distasteful type of casuistry – an attempt to measure what amount of wealth is appropriate to the status of different classes of people, the remainder of the person's income being seen as 'superfluous'. This kind of casuistry allowed the rich to calculate that they had no obligation to give to the poor until the normal status symbols of wealthy people had been acquired.[47] The basic intention of Pope Leo's statement thus became perverted and even contradicted: instead of imposing a heavy obligation on the rich to help the poor, it offered a kind of justification for turning a deaf ear to the cry of the poor, on the grounds that one has to live up to

128

one's social standing. No wonder then that Vatican II decided to assert a much more urgent obligation to help the poor. The Council was able to do so by appealing to an even more ancient and honourable tradition than that invoked in *Rerum Novarum*. Pope Leo had referred to St Thomas Aquinas in support of his position; the Council document by contrast refers to Basil, Lactantius, Augustine; Gregory the Great, Bonaventure, and Albert the Great.[48]

Pius XI introduced a certain modification into the position of his predecessor by trying to take account of the modern economic situation. This is one where wealth cannot be divided simply into that which is used up on consumer goods and that which is hoarded; a third category has to be added, namely, wealth that is invested productively. Given this situation, Pius XI was correct in saying that productive investment can help others by giving employment. But his way of expressing it has a certain air of unreality: it could give the impression that such investment is an act of generosity, whereas in fact it is generally motivated by self-interest.[49] Vatican II, like Pius XI, was in favour of investment.[50] Nevertheless, *Gaudium et Spes* does not refer at this point to what had been said by Pius XI. One may surmise that this was because the drafters of the document did not wish to give the impression that the Council Fathers saw capitalist investors as great benefactors of humanity.

When compared with the teaching of Leo XIII and Pius XI, the text of *Gaudium et Spes* represents a notable change of emphasis. There is a shift away from the undue stress which had been laid on the rights of property owners. These rights have been relativised by the Council document, not merely in principle — as Pius XII had already done[51] — but in the practical applications of the principle to the world of the time. There are two grounds for this change of emphasis, both of them aspects of social justice. The first is the defence of those who find themselves in extreme need — in *absolute* poverty. The second is the obligation to work for an equitable distribution of wealth and power; this concerns the *relative* poverty of some when compared to others.

It is clear that *prima facie* the obligation to overcome relative poverty is a much broader and more demanding one than the duty to overcome absolute poverty: the call is not merely to meet the basic needs of those in dire want but also to ensure that power and wealth are distributed fairly; it would therefore seem to require more radical change. Nevertheless, it does not always work out like this in practice. In fact the plight of those who are in absolute poverty can give rise to a more complete commitment and even to a more radical and far-reaching challenge to the existing economic structures of society. To understand how this happens it is useful to look briefly at the typical attitudes of concerned people in relation to the different kinds of poverty. Consider first the viewpoint of the majority of good people, including Church leaders, who would like to see a more equitable distribution of goods. Very often such people assume that existing political-economic structures can be adjusted without too much disruption, to give a fair deal to all. The changes they envisage would not turn poor countries into rich ones overnight; but the poor nations would be helped to follow the path of 'development' already trodden by the West; and this might eventually lead to an equalisation, or at least to a considerable amount of 'catching up' by the poor countries. Such an ideal was probably that envisaged by most of those who voted in favour of *Gaudium et Spes* at the Council. It may be summed up as being an attitude of 'optimistic gradualism'. Contrast this with the outlook of people who take their starting-point from situations of absolute poverty. They begin by trying to alleviate the plight of the millions who lack the basic necessities of life and human dignity. But those who take the time to examine the fundamental causes of poverty very often come to realise that the existing economic structures of the world are consolidating that poverty, and even at times *causing* much of it. So it may easily come about that genuine commitment to the overcoming of absolute poverty gives rise to a truly radical questioning of the kind of society we have developed. Because it is grounded in a realistic assessment of the facts, this attitude is not so easily modified by the theory I have called 'optimistic gradualism'.

Because of their general optimism about the possibility of 'development' for poorer countries most of the bishops and even of the experts at the Council did not see themselves as having to choose between a reformist approach and a more radical challenge to the whole system. It would be incorrect to claim that they opted definitively for one of these approaches rather than the other. All that can be said is that the Council showed itself to be deeply concerned about poverty at the international level. It issued a strong challenge to rich people and rich nations to take action on this matter. And it accepted the need for major changes in the economic structures of the world.

## The Process of Change: Violent and Non-violent

*How* are the necessary changes to be brought about? Who are to be the agents of change? Vatican II seems to presume that the required action will have to be taken by the rich and powerful. It directs a strong appeal to them to make changes — both for altruistic or moral reasons[52] and also in their own self-interest, since injustices give rise to discord and war.[53] The Council does not have anything very inspiring to say specifically to those who are poor and powerless. Indeed it seems to speak more *about* the poor than directly *to* them. Its strongest statement is the one in which it affirms the right of those in extreme need to take what is necessary;[54] and to this statement a cautious footnote was appended pointing out that in applying this principle all the moral conditions must be fulfilled. The Council did not really address itself to the question of what could be accepted as a legitimate way of 'taking what is necessary'. The crucial issue here, of course, is whether violence could be justified; could it even be that a war of liberation might be justified on these grounds?

At Vatican II the debate about violence and war seems to have been dominated by the kind of moral issues that were mainly the concern of people in the First World. A major question was whether modern atomic, bacteriological, and chemical weapons had caused the traditional just war teaching to be no longer applicable to actual situations. The Council forcefully condemned total war,[55] but refused to rule out entirely the possibility of a justified war of defence.[56] But unfortunately the text of *Gaudium et Spes* does not deal specifically with the question of war in the form in which it arises for much of the Third World, namely, whether or in what circumstances a 'war of liberation' might be justified. This omission by the Council merely reflects the lacuna in theological thinking at that time. Typical of the state of theological reflection and interest of this period is a book entitled *International Morality* published shortly before the Council. The author gives a fairly extensive treatment of issues relating to the morality of war between states. But he devotes only a minimum of space to wars of liberation by oppressed peoples. Even more significant is the fact that what he does have to say about such wars is not concerned with whether or in what circumstances a people may be entitled to resist colonial or neo-colonial oppression; rather he considers the question from the point of view of those *against* whom such a war of liberation would be directed. He asks such questions as whether it is permissible to engage in psychological warfare against revolutionary forces – an issue that was very real in France but was not the most urgent question facing Christians of the Third World.[57]

It is interesting to note that at one stage in the preparation of drafts for the Council document a text was proposed recognising the legitimacy of active resistance to oppression, parallel to the legitimacy of a just war between states. But in the debate many bishops intervened to say that this was too hasty an answer to a very delicate question. To nuance the text adequately would require much work, so it was decided to drop the statement entirely.[58] The failure of the Council to take the time and trouble needed to clarify the issue may be seen as an indication that the Third World agenda was not given a very high priority at Vatican II. The effect is that there is something of a gap in the teaching of the Council in relation to war and the use of violence. It should be added, however, that the fact that the Council omitted the proposed statement does not imply that it rejected the view that it is possible to have a legitimate rebellion or 'war of liberation'.[59]

High on the agenda for the Third World comes the question of *non-violent* resistance to oppressive governments. Does the Council have anything to say which would be of help to a people who are the victims of colonial or racialist governments, or of a neo-colonial system operating through repressive governments controlled by privileged minorities? In the course of a fine general statement about peace the Council Fathers express their admiration for those who renounce the use of violence to vindicate their rights, relying instead on the kinds of defence that are available to those who do not have power.[60] But when it comes to saying something more specific on the question of non-violence, the Council addresses itself to an issue that was mainly of interest for the First World: it speaks of conscientious objection and in a carefully worded passage gives it guarded support.[61] But *Gaudium et Spes* does not examine the kind of question about non-violence that would be of particular relevance and urgency in the Third World. The major question there would be, what does it mean in practice to make use of 'the kinds of defence that are available to those who do not have power'?[62] Does such a defence include the use of political strikes, civil disobedience, mass marches (even when such marches are prohibited by the government), sabotage of government property, and so on? The Council does not give an answer, or any clear guidelines that would enable people suffering gross oppression to work out an answer.

A treatment of such questions, in order to be really helpful, would have to be placed within a wider context, in which the right of a people to resist the government would be considered. The Council document does not offer such an examination; but it takes one important step towards it by giving a clear account of the nature and limits of human authority.[63] Towards the end of this account the conclusion emerges that people are entitled to defend their own rights and those of their fellow citizens against the abuses of an oppressive government. There are, however, two provisos: (1) the limits laid down by the natural law and the Gospel must be observed; and (2) people should not refuse to obey in those matters objectively required by the common good.[64] Each of these two conditions raises more questions than it solves. There is considerable doubt about what are the limits laid down by natural law and the Gospel — especially on the question of violent resistance, or even of any kind of resistance prohibited by law. And the difficulty about the second proviso is that it is so vague as to be practically meaningless. At first sight it seems quite specific: it appears to be saying that people should resist only on the particular points where there is an abuse of rights by those in authority. But could it not be that the common good would best be served by an attitude of total non-cooperation with an extremely oppressive government? This is what took place during most successful wars of liberation. Such action seems to be compatible with the *Gaudium et Spes* statement, for the text adopts the common good as the criterion. But at that point the meaning of the passage has become so all-embracing that it has little or no content!

### Some Inadequacies

There is not much point in combing the text of *Gaudium et Spes* for guidelines about liberation struggles, violent or non-violent, when in fact the Council was working to a different agenda, set mainly by the First World. As the previous paragraphs should have made clear, one problem about such an agenda is that it does not give a sufficiently high priority to the burning issues of the Third World. But a further problem is that when Third World issues are given consideration they are looked at mainly from the perspective of the First World. To bring out this point we may note some serious deficiencies in the manner in which the notions of authority and poverty are treated in *Gaudium et Spes*.

Let us look first at the question of authority. At a fairly early stage in the Council document there is a deeply moving passage about the human life of Jesus Christ. It contains one statement which could be unremarkable to somebody living in a well-run Western democracy but might pose problems for somebody living under an oppressive Third World government: 'Jesus Christ . . . willingly obeyed the laws of his country.'[65] This statement seems to foster a spirituality of unquestioning obedience to civil authorities that may be quite inappropriate for millions of Christians who are victims of injustice. There seem to have been few theologians to speak on behalf of these people at the Vatican Council. Did nobody think of questioning the accuracy of the statement that Christ willingly obeyed the laws of his country, or at least seek to clarify which set of laws was in question? Was there anybody there to point out some of the important things about Christ that the passage fails to say — for instance, his challenge to the religious authorities of his time; and his judicial murder through an alliance between local religious leaders and the colonial power? Such facts about Jesus Christ could be just as relevant as his obedience, to Christians in the Third World.

134

The treatment by Vatican II of the question of poverty is also deficient; a reason for this is that the perspective is not that of the masses of the world's poor. In the original 'Message to Humanity' from the Council Fathers in the early days of Vatican II there is deep compassion for the poor but no clear indication of solidarity with them. For instance the Fathers say they 'want to fix a steady gaze' on the poor; it is as though they are looking at the poor from outside.[66] The Council document on the renewal of the religious life, when treating of the vow of poverty makes only passing reference to the poor.[67] This contrasts very sharply with a follow-up document issued a few years later, in which religious are exhorted to hear 'the cry of the poor' and to see the links between that cry and social injustice.[68] It was only in the few years *after* the Council that this new spirituality of the poor came to the fore.

Perhaps one reason why the Council was unable to propose any very rich spirituality of poverty is that during those years bishops and theologians were in the process of disengaging from an older spirituality. As we saw in a previous chapter, some popes had in the past espoused a rather 'escapist' spirituality, where poverty was to be endured in the hope of future reward. The new 'worldly' theology associated with the Council — and especially with *Gaudium et Spes* — found little place for such an approach. So, poverty is considered from a very practical point of view. *Gaudium et Spes* presents it as an urgent problem, a problem which is to be overcome mainly by 'development'.[69] In one place Christians are exhorted to have their whole lives 'permeated with the spirit of the beatitudes, especially with the spirit of poverty'.[70] But the point is not developed. Indeed, the manner in which the document emphasised full human development left little opening for an integration of a spirit of poverty as a major element in the spirituality it was proposing or presupposing.

Within a decade it became evident that a notable lacuna had been left in Chrstian spirituality. If a fatalistic spirituality of poverty is to be replaced, there is need for something powerful to take its place. It is not enough to be *for* the poor; one must discover what it means to be *with* the poor. Only then can one experience what it is like to be humanly weak and powerless, but still to be powerful in the awareness that

God is on one's side. Out of such an experience can come a spirituality that is not passive and escapist but active and 'worldly' — though nevertheless open to the transcendent. This will be a spirituality which does not allow itself to be used ideologically by people at either end of the political spectrum; by extreme conservatives, opposed to social change and social justice; or by those revolutionaries whose vision is narrowly materialistic. *Gaudium et Spes* does not propose a fully rounded spirituality of this kind. It was drafted and approved at a period when the leaders of the Catholic Church were so concerned with offering a positive theology of the world that they were as yet unable to discern sufficiently which aspects of the world ought to be challenged. One might say that the document is so taken up with the liberal agenda that it does not deal adequately with the radical agenda.

## A Starting-point

Despite its shortcomings *Gaudium et Spes* must be judged to be a major achievement. This judgment applies not merely to the document in general but also to its contribution in the area of social justice. For it offers a theology and spirituality of the world which provides a solid foundation for a Christian approach to the question of poverty — an approach which can avoid lapsing into escapism or secularism. In the face of issues of social justice, the liberal agenda can lead on naturally to a more radical one. The liberal seeks to be open to the world, accepts the pluralism of modern society, seeks dialogue with those who have a different outlook, all in the interests of making the world a more human place in which to live. One danger facing the liberal is that openness may come to mean that one stands for nothing in particular. Related to this is the danger that service of the world may come to mean simply conforming to the existing situation, accepting the dominant values of society. The radical approach offers a corrective for this. It seeks to be of service to the world precisely by challenging some of its dominant values. The world to which the radical is committed is not the present world but the future — or the present in so far as it is open to a very different and better future. It is not the world of the rich and the powerful, or, more accurately, not the world as structured to favour this privileged group. It is primarily the world of the dominated, the oppressed, the poor — a world in need of liberation.

In regard to the role of the Church in society, *Gaudium et Spes* offers many instances of what I have been calling the liberal agenda. It seeks to make Christians aware that, living in a pluralist world, they must try to understand and engage in dialogue with people of other outlooks — and this applies even in the case of atheists.[71] This theme of understanding and dialogue is very evident in the second last paragraph of the document which points out the need for dialogue within the Church itself, with other Christians, with people of other religious traditions, with humanists, and even with those who oppose and persecute the Church.[72] The basic principle that is being applied is respect for others, a respect that allows for their freedom; and that is what the word 'liberal' means. All this is quite central to Christianity. Nevertheless it is not the only thing that is central to Christianity. There is a danger that having discovered the principle of liberty (or having restored it to its central place) Christians might stop there. If that were to happen the Church would have become liberal but would have ceased to be prophetic. It would be an exaggeration to suggest that this is what happened during the course of the Vatican Council, and that it has become evident in *Gaudium et Spes*. But it does not seem unfair to say that on certain matters related to justice, poverty, and 'development', the liberal dimension of this document is stronger than its prophetic dimension.

Nevertheless, *Gaudium et Spes* provides a solid basis for the step from the liberal to the radical or prophetic agenda. It does so especially in the chapter in which the role of the Church in the modern world is treated formally and explicitly.[73] There the Council Fathers see the role of the Church as making the human family more truly human.[74] Among the ways in which this is to be done are the proclamation and the fostering of human rights,[75] the establishing and building up of the human community; and the initiation of action for the service of all, and especially of the poor.[76] (This reference to service of the poor is especially significant; but it is weakened by the addition of the phrase 'such as works of mercy and similar undertakings'; had these instances

137

not been given the text could more easily be taken as referring to a structural reform of society for the benefit of the poor.) Furthermore, it is precisely in its commitment to freedom — to the liberal agenda in the best sense — that the Council took what may well be its most important step towards the adoption of a prophetic role on matters of social justice. There is one section of *Gaudium et Spes* which treats of 'The Political Community and the Church'. In it there is a paragraph which can be seen as a new charter, or at least a new mandate, for the relationship between the Church and political authorities.[77] A key passage states:

> The Church ... does not rest its hopes on privileges offered to it by civil authorities; indeed it will even give up the exercise of certain legitimately acquired rights in situations where it has been established that their use calls in question the sincerity of its witness or where new circumstances require a different arrangement.[78]

The relinquishing of privilege in order to retain freedom of witness, of judgment and of action is central to the liberal outlook. But it is precisely because the Church in Latin America has taken this seriously that it has gained the freedom to adopt a prophetic role. So long as Church authorities sought patronage, protection and privileges from the State they remained dependent on those who held power in civil society. This dependence inhibited the Church from offering an effective challenge to oppressive governments and unjust social and economic structures. It even allowed the rich and powerful to 'use' the Church by giving an aura of religious legitimation to the existing structures of society and a certain approval to those who held power. The passage just quoted from *Gaudium et Spes* was accepted by much of the Church in Latin America as an invitation to adopt a very different posture — to disengage itself from the embrace of the privileged elites and to challenge structural injustice. In this sense it was *Gaudium et Spes* that provided the foundation on which was built, three years later at Medellín, the Latin American Church's formal commitment to taking 'an option for the poor'.

# 7

# Paul VI on the Progress of Peoples

As we have seen, three major documents on social questions were issued by the Catholic Church's highest authorities at two-year intervals in the first half of the 1960s — *Mater et Magistra* in 1961, *Pacem in Terris* in 1963, and *Gaudium et Spes* in 1965. One might have expected Pope Paul VI to pause for a while before writing another social encyclical. That he did not wait is a good indication of his deep commitment to the issue of international social justice and his sense of urgency about it. Barely sixteen months after the publication of the Council document he issued *Populorum Progressio* ('On the Development of Peoples'), a major encyclical both in terms of its length and its importance. It can be said that it does at the global level what Leo XIII's *Rerum Novarum* did at the level of the nation.[1] Its concern is primarily with the relationship between rich and poor nations rather than rich and poor individuals or classes. This is made clear in the very first section where the pope states baldly: 'Today the principal fact we must all recognise is that the social question has become worldwide.'[2]

*Interest in the Causes of Poverty*

Pope Paul does not rush in with solutions to the problem of poverty without taking the trouble to seek its basic causes. This is one respect in which *Populorum Progressio* represents a notable advance on earlier Church documents. It analyses the global situation and sets out to understand why there is such an imbalance between rich and poor countries. Among the causes of poverty and injustice mentioned in the encyclical are: the evil effects left as a legacy by colonialism in the past, the present neo-colonial situation which has largely replaced the older form of colonialism, and the imbalance of power between nations — an imbalance that gives rise to injustices in trade relations between them.[3] It may be argued that on the first two of these issues the analysis does not go far enough and that the judgments made are rather too lenient. For instance the account of the effects of colonialism seeks to balance the good against the evil.[4] It underestimates the extent to which the colonial powers shattered not only the political and economic structures of the colonised peoples, but also the social, cultural, and religious framework which gave order and meaning to their lives.[5] Perhaps too it overestimates the extent to which Western science, technology, and culture have been of real and lasting benefit to most of the Third World; for what has to be considered is not the wonderful advantages that might have been derived through the interaction of Western learning with the cultures of these other countries, but rather the actual effects of the imposition of Western-type schooling in the so-called 'developing countries'.[6] But in one paragraph the pope does note the way in which past colonial history has left an enduring bad effect on the economy of many poor countries by leaving them dependent on a single export crop which is subject to price fluctuations.[7] For all its caution the encyclical succeeds in ways like this in challenging the view widely held in the West — and promoted by the West in the Third World — that the former colonies have in the long run benefited from their colonial history by being brought into the mainstream of modern civilisation.

Pope Paul is equally cautious but firm in the way in which he speaks of neo-colonialism. He refers to it more as a suspicion or possibility than as a fact; but it is left to the readers to judge whether there is justification for such suspicion of 'political pressure and economic domination, aimed at maintaining or acquiring control for a few'.[8] The pope adverts in different places to the two features that are characteristic of a neo-colonial situation: economic domination at the international level and both political and economic domination at the national level. At the national level, he refers to regimes where a small privileged elite hold a monopoly of wealth and power.[9] And his treatment of the international issue is perhaps the most trenchant part of the whole encyclical: he challenges the present system of international trading relations, [10] pointing out that they are such that 'poor nations become poorer while the rich ones become still richer'.[11] It is clear then that the pope does not simply assume that poverty and underdevelopment arise from purely natural causes or the laziness of the people living in the poorer parts of the world.[12]

There is a pressing urgency in the way in which Pope Paul calls for change.[13] If injustices are to be overcome peacefully there must, he says, be 'bold transformations in which the present order of things will be entirely renewed or rebuilt'.[14] What he is calling for is evidently a change in the *structures*. That is shown not merely by the words he uses here but also by the kind of changes he proposes throughout the encyclical and the basic principle which inspires them. This principle is that 'the rule of free trade, taken by itself, is no longer able to govern international relations'; and therefore 'the fundamental principle of liberalism, as the rule for commercial exchange' is called in question.[15] The basic reason for this is that international trade is unjust at present because there is a gross inequality between the trading partners. So what is called 'free trade' must be severely restricted.[16] Competition should not be entirely eliminated;[17] but the same kind of support system which is now given *within* wealthy countries to the weaker sectors of the economy should be introduced on a *global* scale, between rich and poor countries.[18]

This proposal for a planned approach on a world scale, aimed at the protection of the weak and the stabilisation of markets, is very close to the demands made a few years later for a 'New International Economic Order' (NIEO). This NIEO, sought by the so-called developing countries in the North-South dialogue, seeks the same goals and proposes the same means as are outlined in the encyclical. As Barbara Ward remarked: 'Many of the ideas of this New Order have such firm roots in *Populorum Progressio* that the Encyclical might almost have been its founding document.'[19]

*Comparison with* Quadragesimo Anno

In his study of the notion of Catholic 'social doctrine' M.-D. Chenu discerns a general pattern: the early social encyclicals tend to be 'moralistic' in tone, while the more recent ones recognise that a change of attitudes is not sufficient —

141

there must be reform of the *structures*. So he holds that Paul VI, while still retaining elements of 'moralism', is looking for structural change in society.[20] There is a good deal of truth in this view of Chenu; but the pattern is rather more complex than Chenu suggests. If one compares Leo XIII's *Rerum Novarum* with Pius XI's *Quadragesimo Anno*, one finds that while the former is primarily moralistic in tone the latter calls for *both* attitudinal and structural change. Each of these encyclicals focuses the reader's attention mainly on the economic situation within the typical industrialised country of the West. The two major social encyclicals of Pope John in the early 1960s show that there has been a shift towards an outlook that is more international or global. The solutions put forward by John XXIII for these global problems tend once again to be rather 'moralistic' in tone, although he recognises the need for new institutions or structures. In Pope Paul's *Populorum Progressio*, by contrast, there is a much clearer analysis of the problems of the world economic order — and a recognition that they arise largely as a result of the way the existing structures work. Nevertheless, Paul VI remains convinced that attitudinal change is of major importance; and he does not oppose this to structural change.[21] What emerges from the comparison, then, is a fairly close parallel between *Quadragesimo Anno* and *Populorum Progressio*, with each of them calling for changes both in attitudes and in structures. In particular there is a similarity between the outspoken rejection in each of the two encyclicals of the liberalism that underlies capitalism. Pope Paul himself recalls the strictures of Pius XI:

> . . . the baseless theory has emerged which considers material gain the key motive for economic progress, competition as the supreme law of economics, and private ownership of the means of production as an absolute right that has no limits . . . This unchecked liberalism led to dictatorship rightly denounced by Pius XI as producing 'the international imperialism of money'. One cannot condemn such abuses too strongly, because . . . the economy should be at the service of man.[22]

Despite the similarities, there are also significant differences in approach between the two popes. In the first place, as already noted, the international economic order is the principal focus of concern for Paul VI, whereas for Pius XI the individual nation was still central. Secondly, Pope Paul, while making proposals for major changes in the economic system, does not give quite the same impression as Pius XI of having a ready-made alternative to the present capitalist system. This is partly a difference in style: Pope Paul is more concerned to shun anything that would smack of triumphalism. But the difference is also one of theology: Paul VI is far more reluctant than his predecessor to imply that there is a specific 'Catholic answer' to social and economic problems.

One of the more interesting things that is revealed by a close study of the two encyclicals is that neither of them is quite what it seems. At first sight *Quadragesimo Anno* appears to reject capitalism outright and to propose a corporatist alternative; but what its author actually wanted was a free enterprise system which would be more or less equivalent to capitalism without its abuses and without its ideology. On the other hand Paul VI's condemnations of capitalism are more subdued; but the changes he proposes in the international order would impose such limitations on international capitalism that if they were properly implemented they would transform it entirely.

Does this mean that Pope Paul in *Populorum Progressio* is really rejecting capitalism outright? The reply must be: it depends on what one means by 'capitalism'. Paul VI, like Pius XI before him, condemns the injustices perpetrated by unchecked capitalistic trading.[23] Like Pius he insists that a just economic order cannot be built on the principles and ideology of liberalistic capitalism.[24] He proposes instead the guiding principles of *solidarity* of rich and poor,[25] and of *dialogue*,[26] leading to *planning* on a global scale.[27] But he does not favour a totally planned international economic order in which there would be no room for competition and free enterprise — a kind of world socialism. He says explicitly that 'the competitive market' should not be abolished entirely in international trading but that it should be kept within the limits of what is just.[28]

Pope Paul carefully refrains from going into specific detail about how the international economic order should operate. But it is reasonably clear that he would want to apply on a *global* level the same kind of guidelines as he lays down for national development:

> It pertains to the public authorities to choose, and even to impose, the objectives to be pursued, the ends to be achieved, and the means by which these are to be achieved; and it is for them to stimulate all the forces required for this common activity. But they should see to it that private initiative and intermediate institutions are involved in this undertaking. In this way they will avoid an absolute community of goods and the danger of arbitrary planning which, by denying liberty would prevent the exercise of the fundamental rights of the human person.[29]

This is a remarkably traditional statement, defending the values with which Catholic social teaching had all along been concerned. But the point I wish to emphasise here is the role that is assigned to 'the public authorities' in ensuring that society is organised in this way. If these guidelines were applied on an international scale there would need to be some kind of world authority to play this role. So one can see why Pope Paul favours a move in this direction.[30] Until such time as such a world government can emerge, the role of 'public authority' at the global level can be played, at least to some extent, by international agencies, by a concerted plan agreed to by the different nations, and by a collaboration on a world-wide scale resulting in a common fund to help all, especially the poorer nations.[31]

One reason why Paul VI stresses the need to move towards a world authority is that he sees the close link that exists between the economic order and the political order. A good deal of the encyclical is concerned with the disparity in *power* between the rich and the poor.[32] The crucial issue is not simply who are the owners of wealth and resources but what individuals or groups or nations have the power to impose their will on others. It is power that enables the rich to become richer by forcing the weak to make trading agreements that are unjust.[33] Conversely, the deprivation of power, of opportunity to determine one's conditions of living and working, is itself a kind of poverty.[34] Individuals and peoples are entitled to become 'the agents of their own destiny' and to assume responsibility for their world.[35] This is one of the

central points in Pope Paul's conception of human development — that individuals and peoples should be enabled to have
the prime responsibility for their own development.[36] In
the light of this understanding it is only natural that the
encyclical should address itself to the issue of power. But
when the question of power is raised, one is led to ask a
rather awkward question: who has the power to bring about
the kind of changes the encyclical proposes? From this a further question arises: are those who have this power likely to
exercise it, or is the encyclical just another instance of wish-
ful thinking?

## Could a Revolution be Justified?

Quite obviously the pope himself cannot enforce a new international order. He can appeal to statesmen,[37] to scholars,[38]
to all people of good will[39] — and especially to Christians and
other believers.[40] Above all he can appeal to the members of
his own Church, especially the laity, to bring about the basic
change in mentality and structures that are called for.[41] In
addition to a moral appeal made in the name of justice he can
offer strong arguments based on the self-interest of those who
could bring about the changes required. He does this by noting that what is at stake is not merely the life of poor nations
and civil peace in the developing countries but also world
peace.[42] He argues that the rich themselves will be the first
to benefit as a result of sharing their superfluous wealth with
the needy. And here his argument is based on a threefold
threat facing those who fail to respond to the needs of the
poor:
— they place their own highest values in jeopardy by yielding
to greed;
— they call down on themselves the judgment of God;
— and they also call on themselves the wrath of the poor.[43]
This is a very interesting juxtaposition of arguments since the
pope does not limit himself to moral and religious arguments
for change; he adds to them a *warning* that the oppressed may
themselves take violent action to bring about change.

What is the teaching of the pope about such violent action
by the poor and oppressed? It is mainly pragmatic rather than
moral in character. His attention is not focused principally on
whether or not such violence would be justified but on the

145

fact that it is in everybody's interest not to allow such a desperate situation to develop. He warns the complacent of the risks they run:

> When whole populations destitute of necessities live in a state of subjection barring them from all initiative and responsibility, and from all opportunity to advance culturally and to share in social and political life, men are easily led to have recourse to violence as a means to right these wrongs to human dignity.[44]

At once the pope goes on to point out that a revolutionary uprising produces new injustices, imbalances, and disasters.[45] So he argues that to fight the present evils in this way only produces greater misery. Of course this does not mean that such evil is to be endured without any resistance. The whole tenor of the pope's teaching is that the situation is to be changed. In the very next sentence he does not hesitate to use militant language: injustices are to be fought against and overcome.[46] What Pope Paul is opposed to is not radical change itself but violent revolution as a means of bringing it about.

This rejection of revolution is not absolute. The pope inserts a qualifying parenthesis into the passage where he argues against a violent insurrection:

> . . . a revolutionary uprising — unless there is question of flagrant and long-standing tyranny which would violate the fundamental rights of the human person and inflict grave injury on the common good of the State — produces new injustices . . . and provokes people to further destructive outrage.[47]

The syntax of this sentence is not very satisfactory. The parenthesis is clearly meant to suggest that in certain extreme situations a revolution might be justified. But it does not say this explicitly. For the sentence does not express a moral judgment but rather points out a fact — that revolution leads to further injustices. One must assume that the element of vagueness in the passage is deliberate. Indeed there is considerable subtlety in the way the whole sentence is phrased, a subtlety which enables the pope to achieve a number of purposes at the same time:

— Firstly, and most obviously, the main thrust is to show that violent rebellion is a futile way to seek to overcome injustice, because it tends to bring about the very evils that it sets out to overcome. This fact already constitutes a strong moral argument against insurrection — as the final sentence of the paragraph points out: 'A present evil should not be fought against at the cost of greater misery.'[48]

— Secondly, Paul VI faces up to the question of the possibility of a justified revolution, a question that had been shelved by Vatican II. Apparently he recognised that, in spite of the very strong arguments against revolution, it would be flying in the face of a strong Catholic tradition to rule it out entirely. His parenthesis enabled him to take account of this tradition.

— Thirdly, even in this brief parenthesis, the pope succeeds in specifying the kind of conditions in which a revolution might be justified: he speaks of flagrant and long-standing violations of human rights and grave injury to the common good of the State. His language here combines a traditional Catholic element (the common good) with a usage more familiar to the modern secular world (violations of human rights).

— Fourthly, while taking account of the possibility that a revolution *might* be justifed, the pope very carefully refrains from saying explicitly that it *would* be justified in such circumstances. Had he done so, it might seem that he was inviting oppressed peoples or groups to use what he said as a criterion for measuring the severity of their oppression; and this could in some cases amount almost to an incitement to revolution. This thought must have weighed heavily on Pope Paul and on those who helped to draft the text of the encyclical. Their solution to the difficulty was the parenthesis quoted above — a statement which is nuanced to the point of being rather tortuous in its phrasing. The passage as it stands does not encourage people to use violent means to overcome injustices, even in extreme circumstances.

Nevertheless, if the passage was to have any relevance, it had to indicate that the pope was taking some stance or making some judgment, however carefully nuanced, in relation to the possibility of revolution being morally justified. Simply by adverting to violent insurrection and refraining from condemning it absolutely, the encyclical implies that there are situations in our world today where revolution might be permissible. This point was not lost either on those who looked to the Church for support in maintaining an unjust *status quo*, or on those who wished to enlist the Church in their struggle for liberation.[49] So, despite its brevity and careful phrasing, this passage had, and still has, considerable importance. It serves to clarify the official stance of the Church on an issue which is quite central to the meaning of the notion of an 'option for the poor'.

This is not to say that 'option for the poor' necessarily means approval for violent resistance to oppression; but it could mean refusal to make a blanket condemnation of all such resistance; and that is what we find in *Populorum Progressio*. It is clear that, faced with the same ultimate choice as that which faced Leo XIII, Pope Paul refused to take the same position. Leo XIII had said that in the last resort Christians must endure injustices rather than rebel.[50] Paul VI implies that this is not so. Although the difference between the position of the two popes arises in relation to an extreme situation on which Church authorities might not have to make any pronouncement in practice, nevertheless the effect extends much more widely. For the question has to be asked whether the Church is only bluffing when it claims to be on the side of the oppressed. What happens when the bluff is called? Where does the Church stand when flagrant injustice mounts to a point where violent resistance is the only realistic means of bringing about change — as could be seen not long ago in Nicaragua and Zimbabwe? Does the Church automatically take the side of the 'law and order' of the established power? Or may it at least tacitly condone the violent resistance of the 'freedom fighters'? The stance taken in such situations is a test for the credibility of the Church's claim to be committed to social justice. If Church authorities balk at this test under the guise of standing for non-violence and the rule of law, then one must conclude that social stability has been given a higher priority than social justice. What is at stake is a major issue involving the definition by Church authorities of the nature and values of the Church. Is commitment to justice in the world so central to the mission of the Church that this value cannot be compromised without denying or damaging the identity and meaning of the Church?

148

As we shall see later, this question was formally answered in a document issued by the Synod of bishops four years after Pope Paul issued his encyclical. And there can be little doubt that what the pope said in this passage contributed significantly to the strong stand taken by the Synod on the indispensability of justice in the Christian message.

It should be noted that even in extreme situations Church authorities are not usually faced with just a straight choice between two alternatives, namely, that of condemning revolutionary action or of supporting it. Of course people on both sides would wish to restrict the choices in this way; but in fact a whole range of options is open to Church leaders in these circumstances. For instance it may be that a strategic silence is the best service that they can give: the common good and the credibility of the Church itself may best be served by diligent efforts to promote peace without any explicit public judgments on whether or not the 'freedom fighters' are justified in taking up arms. In fact it does not at all follow that when Church leaders make an option for the poor and oppressed they must therefore give unqualified support to those who rebel even against intolerable injustice. A more urgent need may be for them to speak out against atrocities committed by the forces on either side; for it can easily happen in a struggle of this kind that, from the point of view of the means employed, *both* sides are wrong. However, the crucial point to be noted here is that a blanket condemnation of *all* violent resistance to a grossly unjust regime could only be interpreted as tacit support for the *status quo*. It is precisely this kind of unqualified condemnation which Pope Paul refuses to give in *Populorum Progressio*. This refusal represents a very important option by the official Church for the cause of the poor and the oppressed. As we have seen, Pope Paul calls for radical changes in the structures of society. But he believes that violent revolution is not the way to bring them about. What then are the alternatives?

*Models of Change*

The encyclical makes helpful suggestions about various means that could be used. For instance it proposes the following measures:

— a world fund to relieve the destitute;[51]

— more foreign aid in the form of money, goods, and skilled people;[52]
— limits on international competitive trading, so as to restore some equality between the trading partners;[53]
— a concerted international plan to promote development;[54]
— and moves towards the establishment of an effective world authority.[55]

But these are all instrumental means. However, the issue I wish to raise here is different: if violence is unacceptable, what does Paul VI consider to be a morally acceptable way of inspiring or compelling individuals, groups, and nations to make use of the appropriate instrumental means?

A first step towards answering this question is to find out what model of change the pope has in mind. Two very different models might be used; and it is also possible that elements from both could be combined. On the one hand there is the confrontation model. In this, the principal means for bringing about change is pressure or threat. It is presumed that those who have wealth or power will yield it up only reluctantly and in the face of some pressure that they dare not ignore. On the other hand there is a consensus model which lies at the opposite pole from the confrontationist approach. Here change is envisaged as coming about by the willing agreement of all parties; and the agreement is based on rational argument, emotional appeal, and moral pressure from the various partners in the dialogue. The presupposition in this case is that all the parties have sufficient goodwill and commitment to justice to move them to make concessions; they are prepared to sacrifice immediate self-interest in order to bring about long-term harmony and promote the common welfare of all.

There are many indications in *Populorum Progressio* that it was the consensus model of social change that Paul VI had mostly in mind. This is quite evident where he expresses the hope that 'a more deeply felt need for collaboration and a heightened sense of unity will finally triumph over misunderstandings and selfishness.'[56] It underlies his commitment to a 'dialogue between those who contribute wealth and those who benefit from it'.[57] Its justification is his conviction that the world, despite all its failures, is in fact moving towards greater

150

brotherhood and an increase in humanity.[58] It is true that, as noted earlier, the pope invokes some element of warning and threat when he speaks of the danger that the wrath of the poor may be provoked by the greed of the rich,[59] and when he refers to the temptation to seek solutions to problems of injustice through violence;[60] as also when he notes that lack of cooperation between rich and poor nations is a threat to the peace of the whole world.[61] These remarks show that Pope Paul was prepared to strengthen his case for dialogue and collaboration by reminding the rich and powerful that if they do not make concessions willingly they may eventually be forced to do so — and may in fact lose their wealth and power entirely. But all of this can form part of the rational argumentation involved in using the consensus model. There is very little indication in the encyclical that Paul VI favoured a confrontational approach in the effort to overcome injustice and oppression.

If one were using a confrontation model for social change then it would make sense to encourage the poor and oppressed to *demand* their rights — and to organise themselves in such a way that this demand would have to be heard. This could be done at two levels — within any given country, and at the international level of relationships between rich and poor countries. Conspicuously absent from *Populorum Progressio* is any direct and explicit proposal by the pope to the poorer groups or classes within each country that they should mobilise themselves politically and engage in strong, though non-violent, action in pursuit of justice. Perhaps this was not to be expected in any case, since the main subject of the encyclical is poverty at the global rather than the national level. What then does the pope have to say to the poorer nations? Does he encourage a confrontational approach? Undoubtedly he supports the concept of regional cooperation among the poorer countries.[62] But this cooperation is to facilitate planning, investment, distribution, and trade; there is no suggestion that it is for the purpose of confronting the rich countries more effectively. Pope Paul's attitude is summed up in this statement: 'The younger or weaker nations ask to assume their active part in the construction of a better world . . . This is a legitimate appeal; everyone should hear and respond to it.'[63] Their asking is an appeal rather than a demand. They ought to be heard; but if they are not, there is no suggestion about what they might do about it.

*Agents of Change*

Having considered the question of the model of change being used by Pope Paul, the next step in finding out how change may be brought about is to ask, *who* are to be the major agents of change. This has to be answered at different levels. In the first place the encyclical has as a central theme the idea that every person and all peoples are entitled to be the shapers of their own destiny.[64] This is one of the most important contributions of *Populorum Progressio* to the understanding of development: it is not possible to develop people; development is something people have to do for themselves.[65] It is for this reason that the encyclical stresses the importance of basic education and literacy. These are seen as the key that enables people to assume responsibility for themselves, their lives, and their world: 'To be able to read and write, and to get training for a profession, is to regain confidence in oneself . . .'[66]

To say that every person and all peoples are called to be agents of change and directors of their own development, though very important, is not enough. For the question arises whether some are called to play a more central role than others. From the encyclical it would appear that this is the case. The kind of change envisaged by the pope seems to be mainly 'from the top down'. Those who are considered to have the most important role in bringing about change are nearly all people or institutions that exercise considerable influence in society as it is at present. At the international level these are the rich countries and their leaders,[67] as well as international agencies such as FAO and the UN.[68] Within wealthy states the emphasis is put on the roles of statesmen, journalists, educators and learned people.[69] As regards the poorer countries, special mention is made of those 'elite' who are studying in the 'more advanced countries'.[70] Another group who get special mention are the 'experts' and development workers who go from the rich countries to help in the development of the poor ones.[71]

What role is assigned to the Church in transforming the structures of society? The pope asserts that 'the Church has never failed to foster the human progress of the nations'.[72] But in the past, he implies, this was done mainly through 'local and individual undertakings', and these 'are no longer enough'.[73] In the new situation, where concerted action on a global scale is required, the role of the Church is to offer 'a global vision of the human person and human affairs'.[74] It is in this context that the pope proposes a conception of integral human development, a development of the whole person and of all persons and peoples.[75] In addition to this, Church leaders — and especially the pope himself — can make appeals, offer arguments, and issue warnings, of the kind noted above. Laity also have a role to play: without waiting passively for directives they should 'infuse a Christian spirit into the mentality, customs, laws and structures of the community in which they live'; and they should commit themselves to bringing about the basic reforms that are indispensable.[76] Special reference is made to the role of Catholics in 'the more favoured nations' in bringing into being 'an international morality based on justice and equity.'[77] Here again it appears that the more important agents of change are those who already have wealth, power, or influence.

There is a close connection between the model of change one is using and the kind of agents to whom one assigns a major role in transforming the structures of society. Since Pope Paul envisages change as coming mainly through consensus, it is understandable that he gives special importance to those who now hold economic and political power; for they must agree to the crucial decisions. Similarly, another very important group are those who can mould the opinions of society — educators, journalists, and in general those who are well educated and privileged. On the other hand, those who think it more likely that radical changes will come only through some kind of confrontation may hold that those at or near the bottom of society could become major agents of social change. For this to happen the poor would have to become aware of the possibilities open to them and would need to harness their anger and become organised to exercise real power.

The consensus approach and the confrontational one are not entirely incompatible. They begin to converge once stress is laid on literacy and education for the poor. But this applies only if the education is one that enables people to become aware of their dignity and rights, an education that facilitates them in taking responsibility for changing society. What is the position of the encyclical on this issue? It contains a short but glowing statement on the importance of fundamental education and literacy: '. . . basic education is the primary object of any plan of development . . . and . . . literacy is . . . "a privileged instrument of economic progress and of development."'[78] In these words there may well be an echo of the views of the great Brazilian educator, Paulo Freire.[79] But if so, there is also a significant omission: unlike Freire, the pope does not clearly and explicitly link literacy and basic education with the awakening of a critical and combative political consciousness. The statement in *Populorum Progressio* could give the impression that learning to read and write, together with the training for a meaningful type of work in society which is made possible by becoming literate, is the way in which otherwise marginal people are enabled to take control of their lives.[80] But there are certain kinds of literacy programmes which aim only to insert the participants into an unjust and oppressive society; and in this case the literacy training is for the purpose of domesticating people rather than giving them real responsibility. For instance when the Brazilian military government found that Freire's literacy programme was awakening people to demand their rights, they replaced it with one that seemed to be politically neutral. This meant in fact that the alternative programme provided an implicit endorsement of the *status quo*. The encyclical does not bring out in any very explicit way the fact that certain political options underlie any adult education programme, or indeed any kind of education. This omission weakens what it has to say — without however depriving it of all value, for in modern society literacy has generally become a *sine qua non* for anybody who wants to exercise real responsibility.

The fact that the encyclical does not make a clear link between basic education and the heightening of political awareness is quite significant. It lends support to the view that the pope thought changes in society should be brought about mainly by those 'at the top'. It leaves one with the impression that he was not particularly anxious to encourage

154

any great groundswell of pressure for change 'from below' — that is, from the masses of the poor and oppressed. In so far as the encyclical adverts at all to any such movement this seems to be thought of as a threat, leading to the danger of violence and perhaps revolution.[81] It is certainly not presented as a potentially positive force, which can be harnessed and become a powerful lever for bringing about non-violent change, something which the Church might therefore encourage and become involved in.

This can be understood in the light of the pope's commitment to an approach based on consensus. Consensus can be valued so highly that one fears to risk it by encouraging confrontation. So long as the positive value of confrontation is overlooked it is almost inevitable that there will be a failure to take sufficient account of the role that the poor and oppressed can play as agents of change for the better. In *Populorum Progressio* there is no indication that the poor are seen as specially called by God to transform society. That was a theological insight that had not yet come into prominence.

As noted earlier, *Populorum Progressio* does not offer any strong encouragement to the poor and oppressed to organise themselves politically. Perhaps one reason for this is that the pope, like many other Christians, was a little slow to acknowledge — and perhaps even to recognise — that confrontation may at times be compatible with Christian faith, and even demanded by it. It is not uncommon to associate confrontation with angry disagreement, leading on quite easily to violence. That is undoubtedly what happens in many cases, and it is always a risk. But it may be a risk that is worth taking. For, properly handled, confrontation may provide a better basis for a healthy consensus; the powerful ones may need to be shaken out of their complacency. Furthermore, the act of confronting those in power may give to those who feel powerless a sense of their own dignity and their rights, as well as a belief in their ability to bring about change, with or without the willing cooperation of those whom they are confronting.

The conclusion that emerges from this examination of *Populorum Progressio* is that it contributes very significantly towards committing the official Church to a realistic option for the poor; but that this is somewhat weakened by the fact that it shies away from confrontation. Being on the side of the poor in their cry for justice must surely involve encouraging them to find effective ways of ensuring that their voice is really heard. The encyclical lays so much stress on the value of collaboration of rich and poor, and on the duty of those 'at the top' to initiate this, that it does not pay enough attention to what the poor can and should do. However, it would be a mistake to make too much of this point. For even though the pope did not explicitly encourage the poor to take the initiative, still the overall effect of the encyclical would be to inspire them to do so. By pointing out the injustices of the world and the obligation of the rich and powerful to remedy them, Paul VI was necessarily making the poor more aware of their rights and in some sense encouraging them to seek these rights actively. The pope may not have set out to stir up the poor and to provoke strife; but no doubt he would accept that his words might well have that effect in certain situations.

# 8

# Medellín and *Octogesima Adveniens*

One part of the world where the teaching of Vatican II on the role of the Church in the modern world was taken very seriously was Latin America. Many Church leaders and committed Christians in that area also took to heart and applied to their own situation what Paul VI said in *Populorum Progressio*. This was part of an extraordinary change that was taking place there during the late 1960s. It was something that affected every level of Church life, from the grassroots communities to the bishops and leaders of religious orders. Of course many people, and even whole areas, remained largely untouched by the new approach. But the movement for change was sufficiently widespread and influential to find expression in various local conventions of Church leaders — and eventually to become the dominant force at a major gathering of Church leaders from all over Latin America, which took place at Medellín in Colombia in 1968. In the first section of this chapter we shall consider fairly briefly the documents that were issued by the Medellín Conference. This will lead on to the second section where we shall examine at more length the teaching of the apostolic letter *Octogesima Adveniens*, a document that may be understood at least partly as a response by Pope Paul to all that Medellín came to stand for.

## SECTION I
## THE DOCUMENTS OF MEDELLÍN

It is not my purpose here to study the changes that were taking place in the Latin American Church, in terms of their causes and their effects. But it is necessary to devote a few pages to a study of some of the documents in which the new approach was given classical expression; for otherwise we would be ignoring something that had a profound influence on Pope Paul VI during the latter half of his pontificate. In August 1968 the second general conference of Latin American bishops took place at Medellín. For some time before that meeting it had been clear that it would be a most important one. This was recognised by Pope Paul who travelled to South America to address the gathering. But it is doubtful whether anybody could have guessed beforehand the extent to which Medellín was to be a turning point in the life of the Latin American Church — and indeed of the Catholic Church as a whole. The documents that were issued by the conference[1] have an extraordinary freshness, clarity, and power. They became the charter for those who were working for a radical renewal of the Church in Latin America. But their influence did not stop there. Medellín gave inspiration to committed Christians all over the world. The Vatican itself was deeply affected by Medellín and its aftermath. The major documents concerned with social justice issued by Rome in the following decade have to be understood as being at least partly a reaction to all that is represented by Medellín — a reaction that is at times welcoming and at other times worried.

There are a number of topics that are particularly important in the Medellín documents from our point of view. These can be summed up under four main headings: (1) Structural Injustice; (2) A Poor Church; (3) Conscientisation; (4) The Struggle for Liberation. We shall consider each of these in turn.

*(1) Structural Injustice*: Time and time again the Medellín documents speak of the Latin American situation as being marked by structural injustice.[2] These unjust structures uphold and foster dependency and poverty. This is carried to a point where 'in many instances Latin America finds itself faced with a situation of injustice that can be called institutionalised violence'.[3] Poverty, then, is not just something that happens; it is caused largely by human action of a kind that does violence to great masses of people. And this is not

158

just particular actions but a pattern of behaviour that has over many years created a situation of 'internal colonialism' and 'external neo-colonialism'.[4]

*(2) A Poor Church*: Church leaders hear the 'deafening cry' for liberation[5] that rises from the millions of poor people who are the victims of this situation. What is their response? In the Medellín document on the poverty of the Church a distinction is made between different meanings of poverty:

— Material poverty is seen as an evil, caused mainly by injustice.
— Spiritual poverty is described as 'the attitude of opening up to God'.
— Poverty as a commitment is a way in which 'one assumes voluntarily and lovingly the condition of the needy of this world in order to bear witness to the evil which it represents and to spiritual liberty . . .' after Christ's example.[6]

The bishops then outline the role they see for 'a poor Church'. A Church that is poor denounces material poverty caused by injustice and sin; it preaches and lives spiritual poverty; and it is itself bound to material poverty as a commitment.[7] The Latin American bishops then go on to recognise that their obligation to evangelise the poor should lead them to redistribute resources and personnel within the Church itself, so as to give effective 'preference to the poorest and most needy sectors'.[8] This preference is one important element in what has come to be called the 'option for the poor'. But such an option cannot be confined to what happens within the organisation of the Church. Another aspect, equally or more important, is the stance of the Church vis-à-vis society. In the Medellín document the bishops accept that they have a duty of being in solidarity with those who are poor. This solidarity is made concrete through criticism of injustice and oppression. But it is not enough to do that from outside. The bishops say that solidarity with the poor 'means that we make ours their problems and their struggles'.[9] It is against this conception of solidarity with the poor and commitment to their struggle against injustice that one must locate the 'conscientising' role of the Church.

159

*(3) Conscientisation*: The Medellín document on peace points out that people become responsible for injustice by remaining passive, by failing to take courageous and effective action, for fear of the sacrifice and personal risk involved in doing so. So the document favours a process for inspiring and organising 'the popular sectors', that is, the masses of ordinary people. It says that justice, and therefore peace, can prevail 'by means of a dynamic action of awakening (*concientización*) and organisation of the popular sectors which are capable of pressing public officials who are often impotent in their social projects without popular support.'[10] This statement is especially important because it recognises the need to stimulate action for justice from the grassroots. What is envisaged is that the ordinary people should be helped to put pressure on the authorities in order to attain social justice. In the last line of the passage just quoted, the writers tactfully imply that this pressure is a service to the authorities, enabling them to put into practice their plans for reform. The document does not mention the fact that if there had been no pressure from below the people in authority would often be quite happy to allow such reforms to remain empty promises!

This account of what is involved in 'conscientisation' helps one to appreciate the significance of the undertaking made by the Latin American bishops at Medellín to commit the Church 'without counting the cost' to the basic education of illiterate and marginal people.[11] The bishops were well aware of what they were taking on, and of the possible cost. Their statement makes it clear that the type of basic education they have in mind is one that is not limited to teaching these people merely to read and write; rather it aims at enabling them to become the conscious agents of their own integral development.[12] The commitment is undertaken in the knowledge that this kind of basic education will increase the recognition by oppressed people of the fact that they are oppressed, with a consequent increase in tension and a risk to peace.[13] It is significant that it is in the document on peace that there is insistence on the awakening of the masses to political consciousness. This indicates that Medellín is committed to the view that there can be no genuine peace that is not based on social justice. So it may happen that an apparent peace, built on oppression, has to be put at risk in the effort to attain true peace and liberty.

*(4) Struggle for Liberation*: The word 'liberation' is used quite frequently in the documents of Medellín.[14] It does not evoke the cautious and even fearful reaction produced in some Church leaders by the word. 'Liberation' has a very positive connotation and it is closely linked to 'humanisation'.[15] The bishops leave one in no doubt that they want to help the poor and oppressed to attain liberation. But what does it mean in practice for them to be in solidarity with the victims of injustice and to support them in a struggle for liberty? How far should Church leaders go? Are they to give approval to revolutionary movements using violent means to overthrow unjust structures and oppressive regimes? The Medellín document on peace addresses itself to this question, making use of the statement on this topic in paragraph 31 of *Populorum Progressio*. The text of this statement by Pope Paul was quoted in the previous chapter. There we noted that it contains two elements. The main one is that a revolution is an unacceptable remedy for injustice because it gives rise to worse evils. The second point is the parenthesis in which the pope indicates that there might be certain rare exceptions to this general guideline.

The Medellín document quotes from both parts of Pope Paul's statement — but it does so in reverse order, putting first the point that revolutionary insurrection can sometimes be legitimate, and then the point that it generally gives rise to new injustices.[16] The document then goes on to state the judgment of the conference on the situation in Latin America:

> If we consider then, the totality of the circumstances of our countries, and if we take into account the Christian preference for peace, the enormous difficulty of a civil war, the logic of violence, the atrocities it engenders, the risk of provoking foreign intervention, illegitimate as it may be, the difficulty of building a regime of justice and freedom while participating in a process of violence, we earnestly desire that the dynamism of the awakened and organised community be put to the service of justice and peace.[17]

Nobody could claim that this powerful statement of Medellín distorts the meaning of the passage in *Populorum Progressio* to which it refers. Yet there are important nuances to be noted. It is already a significant difference that what was a parenthesis for Pope Paul has now been moved to a more central position. This means that the words are given an added weight. They become the basis for a detailed and careful evaluation of the Latin American situation. There is an obvious comprehensiveness and balance in the passage just quoted. It shows that the bishops at Medellín have carefully weighed up the case for and against violent revolution. On balance, because of the convergence of all the factors listed, they suggest that Christians should commit themselves to peace rather than violence. The implication must be that if there were to be a change in some of the key circumstances, then the balance might well tip in the other direction. Indeed, even in regard to the situation depicted in the document, there is a certain reserve in the way in which the bishops express their moral evaluation. What they present is not so much a firm and explicit moral judgment that revolution would be wrong but rather an exhortation — 'we earnestly desire . . .'. Once again this is not really contrary to what the pope had said in his encyclical. But it seems to push his words a little further, and to draw out implications which he had perhaps deliberately left vague. Confronted with the starkness of poverty and the harshness of oppression in Latin America, and the urgency of the pressure to take a stand on one side or the other, the bishops at Medellín felt they could not take refuge in vagueness. Perhaps more than anything else it is the clarity with which they present the options facing the Church that is most significant in the Medellín documents. They sharpen the issues related to social justice and option for the poor and thereby pose a serious challenge to the whole Church.

## SECTION II
## OCTOGESIMA ADVENIENS: A SHIFT TO POLITICS

Less than three years after the Medellín conference, Pope Paul issued another major document on social issues. This was *Octogesima Adveniens*, issued in May 1971 to commemorate the eightieth anniversary of Leo XIII's *Rerum Novarum*. [18] Although this apostolic letter of the pope contains several references to *Populorum Progressio*, nevertheless it has a distinctly different tone and perspective. This difference may be partly expressed by saying that in this new social document 'development' no longer plays such a central role as it did in the earlier one.

When 'development' is taken as the overall integrating concept for the treatment of social issues there is a tendency to see difficulties such as poverty, apathy, and poor distribution of resources as problems which have *not yet* been solved. The half-hidden assumption here is that in general the world is 'developing', but that in some areas or spheres this process is still at an early stage — and that is why the problems remain as yet unsolved. *Octogesima Adveniens* disengages itself to a considerable extent from this almost mythic conception of development, by questioning the notion of 'progress' as 'an omnipresent ideology'.[19] Once one adverts to the fact that the gap between rich and poor areas is not due simply to the fact that the latter have *not yet* become developed, then it becomes more evident how deceptive can be the image that likens the poor to those at the bottom of a ladder which all can climb. The sad truth is that some nations or groups are poor not just because they have so far failed to climb the ladder but because they have been *prevented* by others from doing so — or have even been thrown down the ladder! When poverty is seen in this perspective the solution that comes to mind might be described more properly as 'liberation' rather than 'development'.

The word 'development' conjures up the image of a nation harnessing natural forces more effectively and becoming more organised and scientific in agriculture and industry. The word 'liberation' on the other hand suggests the shaking off of an oppression imposed by other people — whether this be the domination of a rich and powerful minority within the country or the dependency and poverty created in 'the South' by an unjust international economic order and maintained by the wealthy nations of 'the North'. It follows that the use of the word 'liberation' indicates a perspective in which political action is central. When one speaks of development the emphasis tends to be rather more on economic issues; and this applies even when the word 'development' is used in the very broad and rich sense which Pope Paul gives it in *Populorum Progressio*.

Medellín uses the word 'liberation' freely and in a positive sense. *Octogesima Adveniens* does not follow it in this respect; it uses the word only rarely and in contexts that do not suggest that it could be an alternative to 'development'.[20] This is scarcely an accident. Presumably the pope was reluctant to use the word, on the grounds that it might be taken to mean violent revolution. Nevertheless, the tone and content of this apostolic letter indicate that Pope Paul was concerned about the kind of issues for which 'liberation' is proposed as the solution. Indeed, one of the more significant features of *Octogesima Adveniens* is that the major issues with which it deals are not purely economic ones. The focus has shifted from economics to politics.

In the few years after *Populorum Progressio* was issued it began to dawn on more and more people — inside and outside the Church — that underlying most economic difficulties are political problems. This became especially evident in Latin America. The 'Alliance for Progress' between the U.S. and Latin America was to have ensured the 'development' of the latter during the first development decade, the 1960s. But the economic development that took place in countries like Brazil did not solve the problems of poverty; instead the gap between rich and poor became even wider. The problems were political; for even the choice of a particular model of development is itself a political rather than an economic decision. The Latin American bishops and their experts at Medellín were aware of this; so the Medellín documents were notably political in their perspective. No doubt this encouraged Pope Paul to shift his focus of interest to the underlying political questions.

A well-known expert on Catholic social teaching, Philip Land, holds that Pope Paul is 'in notable contrast to papal tradition' when he recognises 'that most social problems are at bottom political problems'.[21] This statement is true in one sense but it requires some qualification. Many of the proposals made in earlier social documents of the popes refer to the political sphere. In fact most of the remedies proposed for socio-economic problems are obviously political — ranging from the espousal by Pius XI of a corporative type of system within the State, to Pope Paul's insistence in *Populorum Progressio* on the need for new international institutions leading towards a world government. However, it is one thing to propose political solutions to economic and social problems but quite a different thing to recognise clearly that designing and bringing into effect such solutions brings one into the sphere of political activity. The novelty of *Octogesima Adveniens* lies largely in the extent to which it consciously addresses itself to some of the political problems involved in choosing and implementing an equitable order in society.

Although at one point in the document the change of perspective is made quite explicit, one could easily overlook its significance. It seems better, then, when quoting the passage to quote also some important sentences from the preceding and following paragraphs. This will help to show the kind of issues that come to the fore when the focus shifts from economics to politics. It will be noted that certain key words or phrases are prominent — 'liberation', 'model of society', 'structures', and 'share in . . . decision-making':

*Para. 45.* People today long to be freed from need and dependence. But this liberation starts with the interior freedom that people must find again with regard to their goods and their powers . . . Nowadays many are questioning the existing model of society. The ambition of many nations . . . blocks the setting up of structures which would put some limits on the drive for advancement, in order to ensure greater justice . . .

*Para. 46.* Is it not here that there appears a radical limitation to economics? Economic activity is necessary and, if it is at the service of people, it can be 'a source of brotherhood and a sign of Providence'. . . . Though it is often a field of confrontation and domination, it can give rise to dialogue and foster cooperation. Yet it runs the risk of unduly absorbing human energies and limiting people's freedom. This is why the need is felt to pass from economics to politics. It is true that in the term 'politics' many confusions are possible and must be clarified, but each person feels that in the social and economic field, both national and international, the ultimate decision rests with political power. . . .

*Para. 47.* The passing to the political dimension also expresses a demand made by people today for a greater share

165

in the exercise of authority and in consultation for decision-making.[22]

It is from this political perspective that Pope Paul calls for a revision of the relationships between nations in the economic sphere and questions the models of growth that operate within the rich nations.[23] He then goes on to express concern about the growing and uncontrolled power of multinational corporations;[24] these too create economic problems that have to be controlled by political action. In an earlier paragraph he had spoken of the power exercised by the mass media and the need for political control to prevent abuses of this power.[25]

But how is political control to be exercised in practice over economic activity? *Octogesima Adveniens* calls for the devising of new forms of democracy, of a type that will not merely make it possible for all to be informed and to express themselves, but will also involve everybody in a shared responsibility.[26] Pope Paul sees himself as going beyond John XXIII in this regard: the latter called for a sharing of responsibility in economic life, especially within each company or business; but Paul VI extends the demand to the social and political sphere.[27] However, he does not have much to say here about the means by which this can come about. He adverts rather briefly to the role that should be played by trade unions[28] and by the media[29] and he makes some general but very important remarks about the role of 'cultural and religious groupings'[30] − of which of course the Church is the one that most concerns him.

*Basis and Guidelines for Political Action*

Economic questions have to be subsumed within the wider sphere of the political; that is made quite clear in *Octogesima Adveniens*, as we have seen. But that has to be balanced against another very important point, namely, that politics is not an ultimate either. Political activity has to be based on an adequate concept or model of society and this in turn derives from an integral conception of what the human vocation is, and of the wide variety of ways in which that vocation is realised in society.[31] The component elements in this concept of society are convictions about the nature, the origin, and the purpose of the human person and of society. It is the role of cultural and religious groupings to promote such

166

convictions — and in doing so they are obliged not to impose their views on people but to respect human freedom. It is not for the State or political parties to compel people to accept certain teachings. If they did so it would lead to a dictatorship over the human spirit. It would be the imposition of an ideology in which the State or a political party make themselves out to be the total or ultimate human reality, refusing to recognise any values that transcend the political order.

Pope Paul goes on to point out the inadequacies of social ideologies in general, noting especially the danger that an ideology can become 'a new idol' — an ultimate explanation of, and justification for, action and even for violence. Ideologies, he holds, tend to have a totalitarian character and can impose slavery on people in the name of liberation.[32] He develops this point further by examining in some depth the relationship between socialist or Marxist-inspired movements and Marxist ideology. He begins by recalling the very important distinction made by Pope John XXIII in 1963 between false philosophies and the historical movements that have sprung from such philosophies.[33] What follows might be described as a commentary on Pope John's statement in so far as it refers to Marxism. Pope Paul notes certain distinctions that have been made between four different meanings or levels of Marxism.[34] The most attenuated of these versions of Marxism is one which would like to see it merely as a scientific method for analysing society. But the account the pope gives of it leaves one in no doubt that he finds even this limited Marxism quite unacceptable. He sees it as offering a false objectivity and an unjustified certainty, based on a selective and biased interpretation of the facts. In the following paragraph Pope Paul goes on to say that it would be 'illusory and dangerous' to forget that the various aspects of Marxism are intimately linked and radically bound together. In particular he notes two dangers:

— that of accepting a Marxist type of analysis of society without adverting to how this is related to ideology:
— that of becoming involved in class struggle and the Marxist interpretation of it, without adverting to the totalitarian and violent kind of society to which this activity gradually leads.[35]

167

It is clear then that for Paul VI, Marxism as such — at least in any of the versions or aspects he describes — is not compatible with a Christian approach. Furthermore, he is very hesitant even in the way in which he speaks of socialist movments. He recognises in a vague and general way the possibility that Christians might in some circumstances be entitled to play a part within such movements.[36] But he lays far more stress on the danger that Christians may idealise socialism and be misled in their practical activity by purely abstract and theoretical distinctions between the ideal of a just society, the historical movements that propose to bring about such a society, and the ideology that still influences these movements — an ideology that is incompatible with the Christian faith.[37]

All this seems to indicate that for Pope Paul the distinction made by his predecessor between movements and philosophies, though valid in theory, ought not to be used in present circumstances as a basis for a *rapprochement* between Catholicism and socialism — or at least only with extreme caution. Perhaps the pope felt that such caution was the appropriate response from Rome at a time when many Catholics all over the world — and not least in Italy, and even in Rome itself — were attracted by the prospect of 'an opening to the left'. But despite this reserve of the pope in relation to any such move, *Octogesima Adveniens* still leaves plenty of space for it. This comes not from any enthusiasm of Pope Paul for socialism but rather from the basic approach which he adopts in this document. He takes the view that in the face of 'widely varying situations' it is difficult for him 'to utter a unified message and to put forward a solution which has universal validity'; and he even adds that it is not his ambition to do so.[38] This leaves room for a wide measure of pluralism in relation to options about political activity.

It would appear that there are in fact two different but interacting reasons why a certain pluralism of options is accepted in the document. On the one hand there is the personal discernment that each individual Christian has to make, with the likelihood that not everybody will come to the same conclusion.[39] On the other hand there is also the much more objective diversity of situations arising from differences of region, of culture and of socio-political systems.[40] It is this latter which is of particular concern here since it raises the possibility that Christians in Latin America might be entitled and even obliged to collaborate far more closely with left-wing movements than would be appropriate in Europe or North America. Even the very paragraph in which the pope issues his warnings about socialism also contains references to 'different continents and cultures', to the variety of circumstances that need to be taken into account, and to the need for careful discernment and judgment.[41] The effect is that, in spite of a certain similarity between Pope Paul's reservations about socialism and the judgments of Pius XI forty years earlier,[42] there is in fact a very great difference between the two.

A dramatic departure from the approach of previous papal documents: that is how Philip Land describes the position outlined in *Octogesima Adveniens*.[43] He sees it as the relinquishment by Rome of the practice of 'handing down solutions to specific questions'. Chenu believes there is a truly radical change of approach. Formerly there was a deductive method by which a universally valid 'social doctrine' was applied to changing circumstances. But now there is an inductive method in which the different situations are themselves the primary location from which theology springs, through a discernment of 'the signs of the times'.[44] It is doubtful whether Pope Paul himself would have wished to make such a very sharp distinction between what he said here and the approach adopted in earlier papal teaching. But undoubtedly there is a notable difference of emphasis in his approach; and this has implications both for the role of the pope as a moral teacher and for the nature of theological method:

— As a moral teacher the pope cannot hope to be familiar with situations all over the world; so he must respect the discernment done at local or regional level.

— As regards theological method: Paul VI is far more willing than earlier popes to adopt an inductive approach; that means accepting that if one is to discover universal principles about social morality one must start from the variety of cultural and geographical situations in which moral issues arise.

A discernment of 'the signs of the times' at the regional level is precisely what the Medellín conference set out to offer — and what its documents claim to represent. So one must conclude that *Octogesima Adveniens* really offers very solid support to the Medellín conclusions – not so much because the pope agrees with the details of the evaluation as because he recognises the right and duty to make the kind of moral evaluation which the Latin American bishops undertook there. The caution and misgivings of *Octogesima Adveniens* are to be understood against this background. They ought not to be seen as a rejection of anything in the Medellín conclusions. But they constitute a salutary warning against generalising the Medellín outlook and attitudes without going through the same kind of process. In each area the Church must make its own assessment of the social, economic, cultural, political, and religious situation in order to discern what needs to be done. In this evaluation the points made in *Octogesima Adveniens* about the dangers of socialism – and also of liberalism[45] – ought to be given due weight; they may help local Church people to take a more detached and objective view of their situation.

Given the general approach adopted in this document there are strict limits to the kind of direction it can give. It must of necessity restrict itself to examining general trends[46] and promoting general values such as participation in decision-making,[47] education to a sense of solidarity with others,[48] and preferential respect for the poor.[49] Even within these limits, however, it could have been rather more specific in addressing itself to some of the more political issues left hanging in *Populorum Progressio*. A central one is how the poor and powerless can in fact be facilitated in taking responsibility for their lives. Paul VI makes a very important contribution when he emphasises that the Gospel calls for a 'preferential respect' for the poor; and when he goes on to insist that 'even equality before the law can serve as an alibi for flagrant discrimination, continued exploitation and actual contempt.'[50] But there is a certain incompleteness in the remedy he proposes for the problem. He calls for 'a renewed education in solidarity'.[51] This is certainly needed; but is it enough? It does not seem to take sufficient account of the fact that in some situations those who hold power have no interest in yielding it to the poor. Indeed, as the pope himself is aware, the temptation to resort to violent revolution arises in those areas where those in power remain un-

170

aware of, or insensitive to, the injustices of the present situation and are determined to prolong it.[52]

*Trade Unions and Politics*

*Octogesima Adveniens* does not move to any significant extent beyond the consensus model of social change adopted in *Populorum Progressio*. It does not go as far as Medellín in calling for a conscientisation of the masses. In contrast to the Latin American bishops the pope does not appear to be in favour of encouraging the poorer people of society to demand change.[53] It is not so much that this is directly ruled out; it is simply not mentioned as a major way in which injustices are to be overcome.

There is one passage in *Octogesima Adveniens* which is quite significant in this connection; it is where the pope speaks about the role of trade unions. Having defined the scope of their activity he notes the danger that they may abuse their power. One such misuse is in the economic sphere: they may demand more than society can afford — and the demand may be enforced by calling a strike, or threatening to do so. The second misuse of power is much more important from our present point of view: 'Here and there the temptation can arise . . . to desire to obtain in this way demands of a directly political nature.'[54] What is notable here is the pope's insistence that unions should not be involved in matters that are 'directly political'. Apparently Paul VI wants trade unions to confine their representation of workers to specific economic issues and, presumably, other 'local' grievances. The implication is that unions would be 'trespassing' on the territory of political parties if they were to concern themselves with issues that can be labelled 'directly political'.

It is very difficult to draw a clear line between matters that are 'directly political' and the more limited issues that are only indirectly political or not political at all. Obviously the pope himself was well aware of this, since a central point in *Octogesima Adveniens* was, as we have seen, the need to 'pass from economics to politics'.[55] Nevertheless Pope Paul finds himself forced at this point to make this distinction. It is not difficult to guess why. Trade unions represent workers over against employers. If the unions were

171

to become concerned with issues that are 'directly political' this could lead to a sharp political polarisation of society along *class* lines. The weapons used by both sides would be mainly economic ones — strikes and lockouts. The end result could be an overt class war. This would go against the whole thrust of Church social teaching since the time of Leo XIII. Pope Paul, like his predecessors, has an ideal of fruitful dialogue and collaboration between all groups in society, particularly across class barriers. So he did not wish to have a political division which reflected and reinforced the existing economic and social divisions of society. And certainly he did not want the strike weapon, which was designed to rectify specific economic abuses (mainly local ones), to be employed as a political weapon against governments. Consequently he insists that it is an abuse to call a strike for any 'directly political' purpose. That means he must maintain the existence of a sphere that is 'directly political' and must define the role of unions in such a way that they are not concerned with that sphere of activity.

In fact the pope's account of the role of trade unions is quite vague. The only point at which it becomes rather specific is when it refers to 'lawful collaboration in the economic advance of society'.[56] The pope does not spell out any role that trade unions might play in ensuring that workers have adequate participation in decision-making in a given factory or in a particular industry. To do so would show up just how difficult it is to delineate an area that is directly political; for participation at this level is a political matter in one sense, though not yet 'political' in the fullest sense. The problem becomes much greater when there is an expansion of the traditional role of trade unions so that they come to be accepted as one of 'the social partners' in society, with an acknowledged voice in determining the wider pattern of the economic and social life of the nation — a role that clearly is 'directly political'.

Pope Paul strongly advocates the need for 'a greater sharing in responsibility and decision-making' both 'in economic life' and in 'the social and political sphere'.[57] It is easy for him to make such general proposals for new structures to promote participation in industry and society. But the difficulty for the pope arises when it comes to moving from this

172

desirable end to the *means* that might bring it about in practice. It is not easy to overcome traditional suspicions of trade unions of a certain type, suspicions that may be well grounded because of the history of the trade union movement in continental Europe. It is particularly difficult when he is aware of the strength of class divisions in our world and is reluctant to approve of anything that might exacerbate them further. No wonder then that Pope Paul's treatment of trade unions and of the strike weapon is so limited and cautious. All the indications are that he would be quite reluctant to approve of a general strike designed to put pressure on an unjust regime and perhaps even to bring about its downfall. This would be the clearest instance of the use of an economic weapon in a matter that is 'directly political'.

One can certainly sympathise with the pope's aim in trying to preserve some kind of distinction between economic and political affairs. For it may be of real benefit to society if economic grievances and tensions can be prevented from taking on an overtly political form, and if political divisions do not follow exactly the economic and social divisions in the country. However, the main benefits that come from this approach have to do with the *stability* of society. Stability is a very good thing in a society which is reasonably just. On the other hand stability may not be a good thing in a country that is highly stratified socially and economically, a society built on flagrant social injustice. In this situation radical change may be a higher priority than stability. And for this to take place it may be necessary for economic and social divisions to be reflected in politics. In practice this means that it will be far more difficult for trade unions to avoid playing a political role.

Take a situation where the economic difficulties of workers are due mainly to the grossly unjust structures of the society: if unions are really to promote justice for workers then they must become involved in wider political issues. To claim that, even in such circumstances, trade unions ought not to concern themselves with matters that are 'directly political' would be to condemn them to impotence and futility. Furthermore, to say that the strike-weapon should not be used even in such situations for 'directly political' purposes would be to deprive the poor of the most effective means they have of changing

173

society in a not-too-violent way. It is true that in theory, even in a very unjust society, political grievances could be left to political parties. But in practice a repressive regime will seldom tolerate such overtly political opposition. It is not so easy for a repressive government to eliminate or control the activity of trade unions and their use of strikes in a quasi-political way.

It would seem then that Pope Paul, while acknowledging that it is not possible for him 'to utter a unified message' of 'universal validity',[58] does not take this limitation sufficiently seriously in what he has to say about trade unions and strikes. He is still inclined to generalise from an experience that is too limited, too European. The significance of this goes beyond the particular issue of the role of trade unions. It throws light on why *Octogesima Adveniens*, for all the important advances it makes, still does not face up fully to the major issue left hanging in *Populorum Progressio* — the question of confrontation. The pope has now acknowledged that social and economic progress require political action. But his ideal of politics is a very high one — perhaps so high as to be unrealistic, except in certain situations. It is one in which there is room for political debate and even, presumably, a measure of political confrontation. But this political activity is to remain in some sense partitioned off from other spheres of life by being channelled through political parties (or perhaps by other analogous forms of formal political action). Such a version of democracy has worked reasonably well in most of Western society since the end of World War II. It seems to offer Europe a greater measure of stability than it had in the 1930s when political activity was less insulated from other spheres of life. So one can see why Pope Paul should favour it.

Unfortunately, the presuppositions for such a model of political activity are not always present everywhere in the world. Formal political activity is frequently restricted in places where the gap between rich and poor is very wide; for the rich soon find that they have to exert oppressive political power in order to retain their privileged position; and the poor, if they have sufficient spirit left to resist at all, will do so with little regard for the niceties of the political rules. In such circumstances it is no longer realistic to think that political struggles can be confined to a limited sphere where 'the political game' is played out according to accepted rules. For there no longer exists the fundamental social consensus which provides the underpinning for a contained measure of disagreement and struggle in the narrowly political sphere. To take account of such situations the Church's social teaching would have to face up to the question of a much more radical kind of confrontation in society than that which takes place between the political parties in a democratic state. *Octogesima Adveniens* does not seem to address itself to situations of that kind.

In my examination of *Populorum Progressio* I noted that Pope Paul seemed in danger of overlooking the positive value of confrontation. In general the same must be said of his position as given in *Octogesima Adveniens*: he sets such a high value on consensus that he does not take sufficient account of the fact that genuine dialogue presupposes a degree of equality between the partners; and this equality may be achievable only through a confrontation in which the rich and powerful are compelled to yield some of what they have to the poor. There is, however, one short cryptic statement in *Octogesima Adveniens* which indicates that the pope was aware of this. In saying that relationships based on force do not lead to a true and lasting kind of justice he adds the following qualification: '... even if at certain times the alternation of positions can often make it possible to find easier conditions for dialogue.'[59] This obscure remark could be taken to mean that some confrontation may at times be helpful. But the statement is so vague that it cannot be taken as representing a significant departure from the pope's commitment to a consensus model of political action — particularly in view of the fact that he does not distinguish here between force and confrontation.

Nevertheless there is a sense in which *Octogesima Adveniens* goes much further than previous papal teaching on the question of confrontation as on other issues. It does so not primarily because of what it says directly on the question but because of the basic methodological principle that it lays down. This is that solutions to social problems have to be worked out in the light of local cultures and socio-political systems.[60] This leaves an opening for a more positive appreciation of the role of confrontation of the rich by the poor.

175

The relatively painless consensus model, which worked fairly well in Europe in the time of Pope Paul's papacy, does not have to be taken as the model for the whole world. 'For everything there is a season . . . a time to break down and a time to build up . . . a time go embrace, and a time to refrain from embracing . . .' (*Ecclesiastes* 3:1–5).

# 9

# Two Synods and Pope Paul's Response

A few months after Pope Paul issued *Octogesima Adveniens* the question of social justice came to the fore once again in Rome. The occasion was the Synod of Bishops which took place there in 1971. At the Synod, Church leaders from Latin America had the opportunity to engage in formal dialogue on the theme of justice with bishops from the universal Church and with members of the Vatican Curia. In the first part of this chapter we shall examine the document which expresses the conclusions reached at that meeting. However, the document issued from that Synod opened up much more discussion and controversy on the question of justice and liberation. The topic came up again for discussion at the next Synod of Bishops in Rome three years later. A year afterwards Pope Paul issued the document *Evangelii Nuntiandi* ('Evangelisation in the Modern World'), making use of the Synod materials and giving his own response to the issues which arose there. In this document he said some important things about liberation and the role of the Church in promoting it. The second part of this chapter will be devoted to an examination of the pope's teaching in *Evangelii Nuntiandi*.

## SECTION I
## 'JUSTICE IN THE WORLD' (SYNOD 1971)

Late in 1971 the Synod of Bishops, having met in Rome, issued a document entitled 'Justice in the World'.[1] Though relatively brief, it is one of the most important statements on social justice ever issued by Rome. The document is important not only for its content but also because of its sources.

The Synod brought together bishops from Churches all over the world, leaders encouraged by the renewal initiated at Vatican II, people who were ready now to take further bold steps in the area of the relationship between Church and world. The Latin American bishops and their advisors, who were working hard at that time to implement the directives of Medellín, were a particular source of inspiration at this Synod. The actual text owed very much to a few key people working in or with the Pontifical Commission for Justice and Peace. This Commission had been established by Paul VI in 1967 and by 1971 it was at the height of its power. It had become the focus in Rome for fresh approaches and deep commitment on social justice questions.[2]

The document 'Justice in the World' has 'a quality of concreteness and realism'[3] which is reminiscent of the Medellín documents. Its overall plan is also clearly influenced by the approach adopted at Medellín. A genuine attempt is made to begin from the real situation in the world, in order to discern there 'the signs of the times',[4] the specific ways in which God is speaking to today's world and calling people to respond.

*Structural Injustice and Misdevelopment*

One of the more significant points in the text is the emphasis on structural injustice. The document does not oppose personal conversion to structural reform, nor does it merely juxtapose the two. Instead it indicates how the former is conditioned by the latter, for it speaks of 'the objective obstacles which social structures place in the way of conversion of hearts'.[5] Many bishops at the Synod spoke out strongly about structural injustice at the international level. The document reflects their views. It does not hesitate to say that the conditions left by the colonial domination of the past may evolve into 'a new form of colonialism in which the developing nations will be the victims of the interplay of international economic forces'.[6] This outspoken linking of past imperialism with present structural injustices in the international economic order is much stronger than the position adopted by Paul VI about colonialism and neo-colonialism in *Populorum Progressio*.[7]

In the very same sentence the Synod document insists

that this danger can be avoided only by 'liberation'. So the word 'liberation' is used in a positive sense, in a way that seems to be a definite advance on the usage of Paul VI in *Octogesima Adveniens*. However, there is a significant difference between the way the word is used here and its use at Medellín. 'Justice in the World' speaks of attaining 'liberation through development', a usage that does not appear in the Medellín documents. These latter frequently speak of liberation without any mention of development, and occasionally put the words 'liberation' and 'development' side by side.[8] But this more nuanced usage of the Synod document does not mean that it is less daring than Medellín. Rather it had to take account of a variety of different situations. In Latin America 'development' had already come to be a bad word among many of those who were working for justice. They saw that it had come to be associated with the imposition of a model of economic growth that widened the gap between rich and poor. Therefore it seemed right at Medellín to replace the word 'development' to a considerable extent by the word 'liberation'. In other parts of the Third World, however, and particularly in the newly independent countries of Africa, 'development' was still a very positive word. Leaders, including Church leaders, still believed that the way to overcome poverty was through development. The Synod phrase 'liberation through development' represents an attempt to take account of these different situations and outlooks.

It is to be noted, however, that the authors of the document were well aware of the myths and illusions associated with the concept of development. They insisted on the need to get rid of 'those myths and false convictions which have up to now gone with a thought-pattern subject to a kind of deterministic and automatic notion of progress.'[9] One of the most succinct and striking parts of the document is where the bishops point out that the hope has been in vain that poverty would be overcome through development:

> In the last twenty-five years a hope has spread through the human race that economic growth would bring about such a quantity of goods that it would be possible to feed the hungry at least with the crumbs falling from the

table, but this has proved a vain hope in underdeveloped areas and in pockets of poverty in wealthier areas . . .[10]

The document goes on to list several interrelated reasons for this failure:

— rapid population growth;
— rural stagnation;
— lack of land reform;
— massive migration to the cities;
— costly (high technology) industry that does not give sufficient employment.

On a first reading, the paragraph could give the impression that a variety of unfortunate circumstances (population growth, migration, etc.) have undermined what would otherwise have been a healthy form of development. But the overall tone indicates support for the view that things have gone wrong not so much in spite of 'development' but more *because* of it. The paragraph concludes with a deeply moving sentence — very Latin American in style — which confirms this impression:

These stifling oppressions constantly give rise to great numbers of 'marginal' persons, ill-fed, inhumanly housed, illiterate and deprived of political power as well as of the suitable means of acquiring responsibility and moral dignity.[11]

Taken as a whole, the paragraph amounts to a very radical criticism of the 'development' process that has actually taken place (as distinct from some ideal development which might have occurred). It is not simply that this so-called development has failed to meet the needs of the poor. It is that it has actually increased the numbers of the poor, by creating a whole category of marginal people. In fact, then, this approach makes a far more trenchant criticism of 'development' than appears at first sight.

In the next paragraph the document puts forward an even more serious criticism of the kind of 'development' that has taken place: the environmental costs of the benefits are so heavy that it is simply not possible for all parts of the world to have the kind of 'development' that has occurred in the wealthy countries:

180

Furthermore, such is the demand for resources and energy by the richer nations, whether capitalist or socialist, and such are the effects of dumping by them in the atmosphere and the sea that irreparable damage would be done to the essential elements of life on earth, such as air and water, if their high rates of consumption and pollution, which are constantly on the increase, were extended to the whole of humankind.[12]

This passage, if taken seriously, would on its own completely demolish the myth of development on which rich and poor countries had lived for a generation. Both the wealthy and the deprived had assumed that what had been achieved by some could soon be achieved by others, and eventually by all. The relative poverty of some nations compared with others could be endured by them so long as people thought it was temporary. And the use of the term 'developing countries' to describe what were really very poor countries, sometimes growing still more poor, could help to ease the consciences of the well-off in the face of the absolute and abject poverty of millions of people.

To recognise that what had been called 'development' is available only to a limited number of countries is in effect to accept that it is not true development at all, but rather a kind of exploitation. This is a less obvious type of exploitation than one finds in colonialism or in failure to pay proper prices for Third World products. For what is being directly exploited in this case is not other people but the resources of the earth. But in recent years it has become evident that this also involves an indirect exploitation of other people or peoples. For those countries which were first to get into 'development' have taken far more than their fair share of the available benefits, leaving much less for others. Until quite recently it was assumed that new technologies, inventions, and discoveries could ensure that there would be no limit to growth imposed by shortage of energy or raw materials, while toxic wastes could be dumped and dispersed in the sea or the air. Today however, as the Synod document points out, it is clear that there are severe limits to this destructive type of growth; and this changes the situation entirely. Now that it is recognised that those at the end of the queue for development cannot take as much from the earth as those who came early, it becomes formally unjust and exploitative for the 'developed countries' to refuse to share more fairly the benefits they have received from what was the common heritage of all. The fact that the Synod document takes so seriously this issue of the limits to growth, shows that in speaking of 'liberation through development' the bishops do not imagine that poverty in the world is to be overcome simply by rapid economic growth. What poor countries and poor groups need is a type of development that is not modelled on that of the richer countries and regions. Indeed a major element in the real development of the poor is that the rich should be stopped from imposing misdevelopment on the world. The notion of 'liberation through development' needs then to be complemented by that of 'development through liberation'. Although the Synod document does not use this latter phrase, its teaching about justice amounts to more or less the same thing, though the language is more nuanced and polite.

## The Core of the Problem

According to 'Justice in the World' there is one central issue which lies at the heart of the structural injustices of today's world: lack of participation by people in determining their own destiny. The new industrial and technological order 'favours the concentration of wealth, power and decision-making in the hands of a small public or private group.'[13] The kind of positive action required to reverse this inherent tendency of the system is not being taken in the poorer parts of the world or in the 'pockets of poverty' in wealthier areas; and the result is marginalisation of masses of people.[14] To be in a marginal situation is not simply to be economically deprived but perhaps more basically to be deprived of the political power to change one's situation.[15]

The document refers to 'a set of injustices which constitute the nucleus of today's problems'; to solve them concerned people, including Church leaders, must 'take on new functions and new duties'.[16] The required action is to be 'directed *above all* at those people and nations which because of various forms of oppression and because of the present character of our society are silent, indeed *voiceless* victims of injustice.'[17] This statement implies a definite option in

182

favour of the powerless, the oppressed, the victims of structural injustice. It goes a step beyond what Paul VI had said in *Octogesima Adveniens* about the need to move from economics to politics.[18] For it applies this principle to the action of the Church itself in a way that is reminiscent of the commitment undertaken by the Latin American bishops at Medellín.[19]

Unfortunately, the document seems to lose its thrust for a while at this point. Instead of spelling out at once what such an option for the voiceless would mean, the following paragraphs go into examples, giving lists of various victims of injustice — migrants, refugees, those persecuted for their faith, people whose rights are restricted, etc.[20] No doubt this ensures that the statement does not become too abstract; but it is no longer clear how the various injustices listed spring from a common root, apart from the general tendency of people to victimise the weak. Furthermore, no effort is made at this stage to clarify what is meant by saying that action is to be directed *at* the victims of injustice. The phrase is ambiguous at best. Does it imply simply working *for* such people, or is it supposed to mean real solidarity with them?

There is also a certain lack of clarity in the way the Synod categorises those who are victims of injustice. In the passage quoted above it refers to 'people and nations'. In general the Synod pays a good deal of attention to poor nations, and gives a penetrating account of their plight. But who is being referred to when the document speaks of the 'people' (as distinct from the 'nations') that are victims of injustice? Are these victims the members of the poorer *classes*, oppressed by the upper classes? Like previous Vatican statements this document shows that its authors are reluctant to highlight a class analysis of society. What it does instead is list a variety of categories of victimised people, ranging from migrants to political prisoners, to orphans;[21] and it also refers to regional imbalances.[22] What it has to say is undoubtedly true; but it seems to distract attention from the crucial point made earlier in the document itself, that the present pattern of society and its model of development is itself creating a mass of people who are economically and politically 'marginal' — in effect a whole class of people who are poor and powerless.

183

The Synod bishops are prepared to encourage the poor *nations* to take their future into their own hands through 'a certain responsible nationalism' and by forming 'new political groupings'.[23] But they do not have anything quite so strong and clear to say to the marginal people *within* any given society. Instead, the document has two short and rather platitudinous paragraphs under the heading *The Need for Dialogue*.[24] These contain vague remarks about the need for mediation. But it is not made clear what this means, who is to do it, or at what level (local, national, or international) it is to take place. Once again the issue of confrontation, especially between the rich and the poor classes in society, seems to be evaded. That impression is strengthened by the fact that in a later paragraph the issue of how a Christian should act is posed in over-simplified terms; the choice offered is between conflict on the one hand and love, right, and non-violence on the other hand.[25] This presentation does not pay sufficient attention to the importance of a non-violent kind of confrontation, one that aims ultimately at establishing more equal conditions for dialogue.

There is, however, one section of 'Justice in the World' which goes some distance in the direction taken by Medellín when it called for conscientisation. The heading is *Educating to Justice*. There the Synod document speaks of awakening a critical sense and making consciences aware of the actual situation (of injustice) as a step in the process of transforming the world, enabling people to take in hand their own destiny, and bringing about communities that are truly human.[26] But it is not made clear who is to be the subject of such education. Is it the rich, or the poor, or both? If it is the rich, then the assumption remains that change is to come mainly from the top. If it is the poor, then the question of some measure of confrontation has to be faced. If it is rich and poor alike, then the danger is that a crucial point may be glossed over. This is the fact that Church leaders can hardly escape the need to make a certain option. If they seek to promote change in society, a basic choice has to be made: they can act on the view that those at the top of society are the key agents of change; or they can adopt an approach in line with the view that the poor are more likely to bring about the kind of changes that justice requires. Of course, Church leaders will feel called to avoid exacerbating divisions in society and also to avoid identifying the Church too closely with the interests of any particular group or class. So they will wish to work with all sectors of society. Nevertheless, on certain issues a choice, or a series of choices, will have to be made; and people soon sense where the Church leaders stand in practice — especially in such polarised situations as Latin America or Southern Africa.

That the bishops wanted to show special concern for the poor, and even to affirm their special role in bringing about a just society, is not in doubt. That is made clear once again in the final paragraph of the document which says, 'the Church calls on all, *especially the poor, the oppressed and the afflicted*, to cooperate with God to bring about liberation from every sin and to build a world which will reach the fullness of creation . . .'[27] The doubt that remains concerns the *means* by which all this is to take place. It would appear that the Synod, like Pope Paul himself, hesitated to offer open encouragement to the poorer classes of society to challenge existing structures by demanding change and organising themselves in support of their demands.

## Justice within the Church

The area where the Synod of Bishops seems to take most seriously the option for the poor is the organisation of the Church itself. 'Justice in the World' is strikingly new and encouraging in the way in which it commits its authors to practise justice within the Church. That commitment is given expression in these words:

> While the Church is bound to give witness to justice, she recognises that anyone who ventures to speak to people about justice must first be just in their eyes. Hence we must undertake an examination of the modes of acting and of the possessions and life style found within the Church herself.[28]

In the following paragraphs the document goes on to mention various ways in which the rights of people within the Church have to be respected. These include respect for economic rights (wages), juridical rights, and the right to participate in responsibility and decision-making — with special mention being made of the rights of women (lay and religious) and of the laity in general.[29] This support for the rights of those groups in the Church that are most vulnerable and have at times been left more or less voiceless gives real weight to the Synod in speaking out against the marginalisation of people in civil society.

In the next two paragraphs the bishops address themselves to the question of the image of the Church in the world: 'If . . . the Church appears to be among the rich and the powerful of this world its credibility is diminished.'[30] This leads the bishops to say that the possessions, privileges, and lifestyle of the Church and of its ministers and members must be looked at; they must be judged not simply in terms of efficiency but to see whether they hinder the Church in its proclamation and witness of the Gospel to the poor.[31] This section of the Synod document undoubtedly owes much to the new emphasis of the Latin American Church. Even the crisp simple style in which it is written conveys the same sense of quiet commitment as one finds in the documents of Medellín.

*Theological Aspects*

Only a relatively small part of 'Justice in the World' treats of strictly theological issues. Nevertheless the theological contribution of the document is one of its most important aspects. A real attempt is made to sketch out a scriptural theology which links poverty with justice: God is the liberator of the oppressed and Christ proclaims the intervention of God's justice on behalf of the needy.[32]

The authors of the document emphasise that there is a very close connection between our relationship to God and our relationship to our neighbour.[33] They want to repudiate that kind of dualism which would see Christianity as 'spiritual' and other-worldly in its essential character, so that issues of justice in this world are of secondary or peripheral importance to it. So they insist that the 'present situation of the world, seen in the light of faith, calls us back to the very essence of the Christian message'; and they maintain that the mission of preaching the Gospel now calls Christians to dedicate themselves to human liberation even in this world.[34] For, 'the Gospel message . . . contains a . . . demand for justice in the world, and so the Church, though it does not claim to be the only agency responsible for justice in the world, sees itself as having 'a proper and specific role, which is its task of giving witness before the world of the demand contained in the Gospel message, a demand for love and justice'.[35]

The passage in which this theology was best summed up comes quite near the beginning of the document. It is the most quoted part of 'Justice in the World', the item that has made this document famous and controversial:

> Action on behalf of justice and participation in the transformation of the world fully appear to us as a constitutive dimension of the preaching of the Gospel, or, in other words, of the Church's mission for the redemption of the human race and its liberation from every oppressive situation.[36]

Despite the importance of this passage I have held over any reference to it until my examination of the document is almost finished. The reason is that the full significance of the statement and its controversial character seem to have emerged clearly only after the Synod was over. So a discussion of the passage leads one quickly to the debate at the next Synod, in 1974, and to Pope Paul's Apostolic Exhortation *Evangelii Nuntiandi* which came as a follow-up to that Synod.

It appears that the passage just quoted was not considered unusually new or daring when it was presented in draft form to the Synod. Perhaps it was accepted rather too easily because the time available was short; and because the bishops and the Vatican officials wanted to avoid the kind of divisive debate and polarisation which had characterised the Synod during its earlier stages while the priestly ministry was on the agenda.[37] The one word in the passage around which most of the controversy has focused is the word 'constitutive'. By saying that action for justice is a constitutive dimension or element (*'ratio constitutiva'*) of the preaching of the Gospel the Synod was ensuring that such activity could never be dismissed as being merely incidental to the work of the Church; it would have to be given a central place. Ever since the document was issued, this passage, and this word, have been cited on innumerable occasions to show that the Church officially rejects the view that action to bring about a more just society

187

takes second place to more 'spiritual' or 'religious' matters.[38] In fact the statement has become a kind of manifesto for those who are working for political liberation against oppressive regimes or structures and who want to invoke the Church's support for such activity. For this very reason the statement has come under attack from those Church leaders and theologians who see the evangelising mission of the Church as primarily 'spiritual'. This group would like to see the word 'constitutive' replaced by the word 'integral'. This latter word refers to something that is not absolutely essential to the life of the Church but which pertains to its fullness. Those who reject the word 'constitutive' argue that this word should be used only of something that can never be absent without the Church failing to be itself; whereas in practice, they argue, the Church may find itself in some situations so restricted by political authorities that it is totally prevented from undertaking 'action on behalf of justice' (in a quasi-political sense) — yet it does not for this reason cease to be Church.

This argument about the use of words seems to have become a vehicle for a more fundamental disagreement about the appropriate actions and attitudes for a Church faced with major injustice in society. Should it take an overtly political stand like some of the more 'prophetic' leaders of the Latin American Church? Should Church leaders not merely distance the Church from unjust regimes but also encourage active resistance by those who are oppressed? Should Church workers even help to organise such resistance? Or, on the other hand, should this kind of activity be seen as an excessive politicisation of the Church? In certain influential Church circles there was real distress about the new trends that were emerging, especially in Latin America. It was feared that 'liberation theology' was emptying the Christian faith of its deepest transcendent meaning and reducing it to a religious legitimation for revolutionary activity. The resistance to the use of the word 'constitutive' came to be associated with efforts to ensure that the Church would be less active — or at least less obvious — in giving support to liberation struggles of a political kind.

It may be added that many of those who were worried about liberation theology and the politicisation of the Church were people who also wished to minimise the importance of Synods of Bishops. They emphasised the fact that a Synod has a merely consultative role. Its function is to advise the pope; and the pope remains free to accept or reject what is said by a Synod. For these people the campaign to replace the word 'constitutive' with the word 'integral' had a purpose over and above the immediate issue: by implication it brought out the point that the Synod document was not fully authoritative or binding but could be superseded by a statement of the pope. So the difference of opinion about this one word became a focus and symbol for different views about the exercise of authority in the Church — not about the purely legal authority of the Synod but about the kind of authority and weight that should be given to it in practice. This divergence of approach was of course related to a difference about how much autonomy should be left to Church authorities in a region (e.g. Latin America) and how much control should be exercised by the Church's central administration in Rome.

Our concern here is only peripherally with these questions of Church authority. From our present point of view the main thing is that the controversy about the word 'constitutive' brought to a head two closely related theological issues that arise in relation to the Church's action to promote justice:

— What is the nature of human salvation, and how is it related to political, economic, and cultural liberation?
— What should be the role of the Church in working to further these forms of liberation?

Even those who accepted without reservation the teaching of the Synod document on these issues would have to admit that there was need for a much deeper and more extensive treatment of both questions. Clearly then there was a very good reason for choosing the topic 'evangelisation' as the subject for discussion at the following Synod, that of 1974. This choice of topic offered an ideal opportunity for the bishops to deal with these two questions.

189

The Synod of 1974 was an exciting event with a disappointing ending. Some of the excitement in the discussions came from the contributions made by participants from Africa. What they had to say, and their style of saying it, helped the Synod to take more seriously the whole question of the Church and non-Western cultures. It became clear that other parts of the Third World besides Latin America had challenges to issue, and a contribution to make, to the wider Church. In the short term this helped to ensure that political and economic liberation were not the only important topics discussed; the agenda was broadened considerably. In the long term this paved the way for a wider and more integral conception of human liberation, one that gives a central role to culture, as well as to economics and politics.

The ending of the 1974 Synod was disappointing because the participants failed to agree on the text of a major document which they had hoped to issue. Two draft texts were put forward and there was a failure to work out a compromise acceptable to both sides.[39] The result was that both texts were handed over to the pope along with the other synodal materials, in the expectation that he would issue a document on evangelisation, making use of this material. Procedurally, this was undoubtedly a significant victory for those who wished to play down the importance of Synods in the life of the Church, especially since it established a precedent and set a pattern for subsequent Synods; it gave the pope a completely free hand to pick and choose from the materials presented to him, and also to add new material. It could also be used in support of the argument that Synods were a rather ineffective invention, an innovation that could be divisive and that needed the strong hand of the pope and the Vatican Curia to draw some fruit from them. On the other hand, however, this handing over of the Synod material to the pope ensured that more time was available for a deeper and more nuanced treatment of the issues raised at the Synod.

After an interval of just over a year Pope Paul issued his Apostolic Exhortation *Evangelii Nuntiandi* (called in English 'Evangelisation in the Modern World'), as his response to the request of the Synod for a document based on the fruits of its work.[40] It is an exceptionally valuable document, one that explores in depth several vital theological and pastoral issues that had arisen since the time of Vatican II. Needless to say it builds on the teaching of the Vatican Council, but it does not hesitate to deal with new questions and to offer fresh insights about old questions. One of the most important features of the document is the broad sweep of the vision of evangelisation which it offers. Precisely because of this comprehensive character of the Apostolic Letter, it contains a lot of material that is not of direct concern to us here. It should be noted then that I shall confine my attention to the points directly relevant to our subject, omitting other valuable aspects of the document.

### Good News of the Kingdom

Perhaps the best way to begin is to see how the pope deals in *Evangelii Nuntiandi* with the controversial theological question raised by the document of the 1971 Synod when it said that action on behalf of justice is a *constitutive* dimension of preaching the Gospel. Paul VI does not say overtly that he is taking sides in this controversy. But there can be little doubt that what he says in this new document provides a thorough vindication for the statement of the Synod. To see how he does so we need to look at what the document has to say about three key concepts — Kingdom, evangelisation and liberation. We shall look at each in turn, the first two briefly and the third more extensively.

What *Evangelii Nuntiandi* has to say about the Kingdom, though brief, is vitally important. The central point is summed up in one short passage:

> As the one who proclaims the Gospel, Christ announces above all a kingdom, which is the Kingdom of God; he attributes so much importance to this Kingdom that by comparison with it everything else becomes the 'other things that shall be added unto you'. Therefore the Kingdom of God must be treated as an absolute, to which everything else must be referred.[41]

If Christ's primary concern was the Kingdom, then even the Church must not be seen as an end in itself. Rather it is a

191

community of believers gathered 'in the name of Jesus so that they may together seek the Kingdom, build it up and implement it in their own lives'.[42] Building the Kingdom is not confined to what might be called 'churchy' activities, or even to actions that are religious or 'spiritual' in the usual sense of these terms. It also requires very secular activity such as working to overcome oppressive or inhuman structures in society. It follows, then, that by refusing to make the Church itself the ultimate term of reference and insisting instead on the Kingdom as the only absolute value of the Christian, Pope Paul has taken a major step towards justifying the claim that action for justice is a constitutive aspect of the work of evangelisation.

A second important contribution in this regard is made by the pope in the way in which he clarifies the nature of evangelisation and the means by which it takes place. Some key lines are the following:

> The proclamation [of the Gospel] must take place above all by witness . . . a witness which requires presence, a sharing of life, and solidarity; in the carrying out of evangelisation this witness is an essential part, and often the first one.

> However, even the most perfect witness will be of no avail in the end unless there is a clear unambiguous proclamation of the Lord Jesus, to throw light on and justify the witness . . . and to reveal explicitly its true meaning.[43]

This position represents a notable theological advance on what had been said at Vatican II. There, priority had been given to verbal preaching, while witness was relegated to a secondary place. Pope Paul, by contrast, insists that words and witness are both of fundamental importance — each in a different way. Witness without words may remain ambiguous or opaque; words without witness lack credibility. By refusing to put Christian witness in a secondary place Paul VI is rejecting an older theology which would tend to see worldly activity as just a preparation for the Gospel ('pre-evangelisation') or at best an indirect evangelisation;[44] and so long as that theology was held one could not easily show how action for justice is a constitutive element in evangelisation in the proper sense. However, it is not enough to show that Christian living is as

192

important as verbal preaching. A further step is required: one must show why a privileged place should be given to action for justice, over and above many other kinds of secular work. To do this we must go on to look in some detail at the third important word in *Evangelii Nuntiandi* — the word 'liberation'.

### Salvation and Liberation

'Development', rather than 'liberation' was the key word in the Vatican Council's document *Gaudium et Spes* and in Pope Paul's 1967 encyclical *Populorum Progressio*. Medellín gave sanction to the alternative word 'liberation' in the Latin American Church. Pope Paul in writing *Octogesima Adveniens* in 1971 was very cautious in his use of the word 'liberation'. But at the Synod of Bishops in Rome later that same year the word was coming to be accepted as one that could be relevant for the universal Church. Three years later at the Synod of 1974 there was a lot of talk about 'liberation'. After that Synod Pope Paul apparently decided that there was no longer any point in shying away from the word. It would be better to provide a thorough theological analysis of the concept of liberation. In this way he could take what was of value in the word while correcting inadequate or mistaken ideas about its meaning or implications. This is what *Evangelii Nuntiandi* sets out to do; and that is why the notion of liberation is given a very central role in the document.

One of the more valuable aspects of the treatment of the theme of liberation in the document is the way in which it is rooted in the Gospel. After a few introductory paragraphs explaining the occasion and purpose of the document the pope plunges at once into an account of the liberating mission of Christ. He says that the two words that provide the key to the understanding of the evangelisation of Christ are 'Kingdom' and 'Salvation'.[45] Christ came to bring the Good News of the Kingdom of God, that 'good news to the poor' which was promised in the book of Isaiah.[46] The content of this Good News is summarised by the pope in a striking passage:

> As the main point and the very centre of his Good News, Christ proclaims salvation; this is the great gift of God which is liberation from everything that oppresses people, particularly liberation from sin and the Evil One, together

with the joy experienced when one knows God and is known by Him, when one sees God and entrusts oneself to Him.[47]

The most important thing to note here is that the word liberation is given real theological respectability. But this is done in a very nuanced way that is typical of Pope Paul. The word is used in a manner that extricates it as far as possible from the very restricted meaning it had been given in recent times — for many people 'liberation' had almost come to be equivalent to 'revolution'. The pope speaks of being liberated 'from everything that oppresses people, particularly from sin and the Evil One'. This clearly presses the meaning of the word far beyond political and economic liberation. Furthermore, the word liberation is used in the document in a way that does not allow it to replace the word salvation, or even to be seen as entirely equivalent to it. Instead it is given a more limited role; it becomes one of the everyday words (such as 'gift' and 'joy') that are used to explain the meaning of the more primordial word 'salvation'.

One can see that *Evangelii Nuntiandi* makes a notable contribution towards the development of a coherent and comprehensible use of theological language by helping to locate the word 'liberation' within a network of other theological concepts. This is a step towards the emergence of a scientific theological vocabulary in which the various concepts are defined in terms of their relationship to each other.[48] But the development of theological language was scarcely the primary purpose of the pope in this pastorally oriented document. No doubt he was more concerned to communicate an overall vision of evangelisation, one that transcends any division such as 'religious versus secular' or 'spiritual versus temporal'. The reader of the passage quoted above is offered such a vision; and it is one in which action for justice can be clearly seen to be a constitutive dimension of evangelisation.

Evangelisation literally means bringing good news. The passage quoted above says that the Good News of Jesus involves liberation from everything that oppresses people; and economic and political oppression are among the more obvious of such things. So liberation from these forms of oppression (and from cultural oppression which, though perhaps less obvious, is equally evil) is part of the core of the

Good News of Jesus — and therefore of evangelisation; provided of course that, as the passage suggests, it comes as the gift of God. It is part of the subtlety of the passage that this proviso has to be added, although the pope's statement does not put it in the form of a strict condition. The passage does not entitle one to claim that any and every overcoming of political oppression is automatically a part of that 'salvation' which is the core of Christ's Good News. For 'salvation' is presented as something that is the gift of God. So if it were the case that a particular form of political liberation were contrary to God's will, then it would not be part of 'salvation'. On the other hand one is not entitled to argue that any particular event of political liberation is not part of the gift of salvation merely on the grounds that it was brought about by human activity; for human action and divine gift are by no means mutually exclusive. To sum up: the pope here offers an integral vision to those who are engaged in what the Synod of 1971 called 'action on behalf of justice and participation in the transformation of the world'. It is a vision that enables them to situate their activity within the total creative-redemptive pattern by which God in Christ brings salvation to the world; their action and their struggles contribute to the saving work of God, His gift of salvation. In this sense their activity is part of the Good News, part of evangelisation. It is not of course the whole reality of evangelisation. As noted above, the pope insists that a verbal proclamation is also essential. Indeed one of the strengths of the concept of evangelisation as presented in this document is the insistence that it is a complex reality comprising many elements, no one of which on its own should be taken to be the total reality.[49]

The integral vision of human salvation presented in *Evangelii Nuntiandi* includes, as one would expect, a good deal of synthesising and balancing of various aspects. Like most theologians, the drafter of the document finds it impossible to satisfy those who ask for a simple, either/or answer to the question, 'Is salvation found in this life or in the next?' To this question the answer of the document is that it has its beginning in this life but is fulfilled in eternity.[50] But what is particularly valuable in the document is that it offers terms in which the relationship between the present and the future can be explored more fruitfully. It speaks of 'a hereafter' which is 'both in continuity and in discontinuity with the present situation' and of 'a hidden dimension' of this world, an aspect that will one day be revealed.[51]

By using this kind of language the document is able to avoid that naïve dualism which would equate salvation with spiritual welfare as distinct from merely temporal or material welfare. The contrast offered instead is between on the one hand a purely 'immanent' salvation (including both material and spiritual elements) and on the other hand 'a transcendent and eschatological salvation'.[52] It must be noted at once that this is not a simple contrast between an immanent and a transcendent salvation. Rather the contrast is between one that is *merely* immanent and one that is both immanent and transcendent, that is, a salvation that relates to earthly 'desires, hopes, affairs, and struggles' but which also 'exceeds all these limits'.[53]

## Concern about Misunderstandings

A significant part of the teaching of *Evangelii Nuntiandi* hinges on this vital distinction between a conception of salvation that limits it to this world and one that includes worldly affairs but also transcends them. It provides Pope Paul with a solid basis for using the word liberation quite freely and, at the same time, correcting what he considers to be false or inadequate ways of understanding the word itself and also the core of the Christian message. The main worries expressed by him in regard to incorrect ideas about liberation are to be found in paragraphs 31-38 of the document. His reservations can be grouped under the following five headings: Reductionism, Politicisation, Inherent Limitations, Violence, and Attitudinal Change. As I examine each in turn I shall add some comments on the pope's treatment of these different issues.

*(1) Reductionism*: The first and main concern of Pope Paul is that the liberation heralded by Christ and promoted by the Church might be reduced to a much more limited version of liberation, through a failure to take account of the deepest dimensions of what it means to be human. Speaking of the liberation that is proclaimed and promoted by evangelising activity he insists that:

196

It cannot be limited to any restricted sphere whether it be economic, political, social, or cultural. It must rather take account of the totality of the human person in all its aspects and elements, including the openness of the human person to what is absolute, even to the Absolute that is God.[54]

There appear to be two slightly different emphases in the way in which the reservations of the pope are expressed. The first is found in the passage just quoted. It is the concern that every aspect of the human person be taken seriously, including that of a religious openness to God. A somewhat different expression is found in the very next paragraph. There the pope says that the Church re-affirms the primacy of its spiritual function.[55] This statement goes a step further than the previous one: it suggests that the religious aspect is not only indispensable but is also the *primary* concern of the Church. However, this can best be understood as an insistence that the religious dimension of the human person is what is deepest in humanity and is therefore of particular concern to the Church. There are no solid grounds in *Evangelii Nuntiandi* for claiming that social and political concerns are of secondary importance for the Church.[56]

*(2) Politicisation*: Closely related to the danger of reductionism, and following on from it, is the concern of the pope about an excessive politicisation of the role of the Church. If a narrowing down of the Christian concept of liberation were to take place, then the Church's function would also be reduced. The Church would lose its deepest meaning and its activities would be confined to the purely political or social order. That would deprive the liberating message of the Church of its distinctive character. As a result, the message would be more liable to be distorted by ideological groups and political parties using it for their own purposes.[57] The central point here seems to be that what the Church has to offer is not a specific political or social programme but rather an integral vision of what it means to be human – what the pope calls an anthropology, which includes a theology of redemption.[58] If the more transcendent aspects of this vision are ignored, then Christians precisely as Christians will have nothing specific to add to what political movements have to offer. (One recalls here what Pope Paul had said in

197

*Octogesima Adveniens* about the Church not having a ready-made model for human society.[59]) In that case the main value of the Church would be simply its ability to animate and mobilise people for social and political action through the invocation of powerful religious symbols and the arousing of religious fervour. It is a great boost for the morale of any political movement if its followers are assured that their political beliefs are endorsed by the Church and by God. There can be little doubt that Pope Paul was worried that left-wing revolutionaries in Latin America and elsewhere (even in Italy) might be able to interpret the Church's commitment to liberation as giving support to a Marxist and liberationist ideology; and there was of course a danger that this might happen in some places. However it should also be noted that a much more common danger is that Christianity may be harnessed to serve the purposes of right-wing political movements, for instance those that adopt the ideology of 'National Security'.

*(3) Inherent Limitations*: 'The Church sees the links between human liberation and salvation in Jesus Christ, but does not consider the two to be identical'.[60] This is an important statement which is supported by a variety of reasons in the remainder of the paragraph. One valuable point emerges: not only are the achievement of (earthly) liberation and prosperity not in themselves sufficient to constitute the coming of the Kingdom, but all temporal and political liberation contains within it the seed of failure. This is a point that has been developed more fully in recent theology, especially Third World Theology.[61] The achievement of political liberation in a particular area may truly be seen as a salvific event, as the Exodus was for the Jewish people. Nevertheless this does not mean that salvation has been definitively attained in this liberation. Various inadequacies are there from the beginning; and they tend to grow and to create a widening gap between the ideal salvation that is being reached for and the very limited degree of liberation that has been achieved. Unfortunately, this important point made by the pope tends to become somewhat obscured because in the passage it is confused with another, slightly different, point. This second point is that even people who invoke the Bible in support of their actions may in fact be operating on the basis of a notion

of liberation that is not fully Christian; indeed some understandings of the word 'liberation' are simply incompatible with the Christian view of the human person and of history. No doubt this warning of the pope was needed; but coming here it tends to distract attention from a major theological issue — namely, how the gift of divine salvation is embodied in human history, and in what sense any particular achievement of justice may be called salvific in the proper Christian sense.

(4) Violence: Pope Paul was concerned lest there be any confusion between the Christian conception of liberation and the kind of political liberation sought by revolutionaries. He saw the danger that a certain kind of liberation theology, based largely on the Old Testament, could be invoked to justify violent rebellion against unjust regimes. Of all the objections raised against the word 'liberation', this was the most obvious one. It led many rich and powerful groups, including people with power in the mass media, as well as many Church leaders, to put considerable pressure on the Vatican to come out strongly against liberation theology. Pope Paul, as we have seen, responded not by rejecting the word 'liberation' but by clarifying what it means for the Christian, and by using this as the basis for a criticism of incorrect interpretations. Obviously he felt the need to dissociate the Church unequivocally from violence. He devotes one short paragraph of Evangelii Nuntiandi to this question.[62] What he says is very close to what he had already said in Populorum Progressio: violence is uncontrollable; it provokes further violence and gives rise to new forms of oppression, more serious than before. He adds that sudden or violent structural changes are illusory and are of their very nature ineffective; and furthermore, violence is contrary to the Christian spirit. All these points are made in support of his initial stark statement that the Church cannot accept violence — especially armed violence — or the death of anybody as the way to liberation.[63]

The tone of this whole passage is rather more pacifist than that of the corresponding passage in Populorum Progressio. In this statement, by contrast to the earlier one, there is no reference to exceptional situations in which violence might be justified; nor is there any footnote reference to the earlier statement. Should one draw the conclusion that Pope Paul had changed his mind in the intervening eight years? It would seem to be more correct to see this as a change of emphasis rather than a change of mind. The pope was no doubt aware that any mention of exceptional circumstances justifying violent action could be used by revolutionary groups to provide a justification for armed resistance. Perhaps he was not quite happy with the way Medellín had treated his earlier statement, giving rather more prominence to the exceptional situations than he had. It would appear that on this occasion the pope decided it would be inappropriate to mention such exceptional situations. Presumably this decision reflects his assessment of the world situation at the time of writing the document. And not many Church leaders would have disagreed with his judgment in regard to the trouble spots of the world in 1975; for there did not seem to be any obvious situation where all the various factors required to justify violent rebellion were clearly present. Had the document been written three or four years later, when the struggles in Nicaragua and Zimbabwe had come to a head, it is doubtful whether the pope could have omitted all reference to exceptional situations where violence might conceivably be justified. The point I am making here is that the passage in *Evangelii Nuntiandi* was not really intended to be a comprehensive theological statement covering all eventualities; rather it should be understood as a strong pastoral-inspirational exhortation, urging Christians to choose the way of peace. For it is quite unlikely that Pope Paul intended to commit the Church unconditionally to a pacifist position. Furthermore, he would not have wished his words to give any comfort or support to unjust regimes; elsewhere in the document he spoke out strongly against structural injustice.[64]

(5) *Attitudinal Change*: Pope Paul was concerned that a particular notion of liberation could give the impression that a change of structures alone is sufficient to bring about human liberation. So, like his predecessors, he insists that there is need for attitudinal change as well as reform of the structures of society. He speaks of the need for 'a conversion of the hearts and minds of those who live under these systems and of those who have control of the systems'.[65] This warning was no doubt justified, for left-wing reformers have at

times been guilty of 'dreaming of systems so perfect that no one will need to be good', as T.S. Eliot says. But insistence on the importance of conversion can sometimes be used as a way of playing down the importance of structural change or of suggesting that those who insist constantly on the latter are perhaps a little unbalanced or extremist in their approach. There may be some element of that attitude in this paragraph of the document; certainly the relationship between structural and attitudinal change is not treated very helpfully here. However, another section of the document offers an exceptionally valuable treatment of this topic; and it is to this question that we now turn.

### Structures and Culture

The topic is dealt with in paragraphs 18-20, where Pope Paul explores in some depth what the task of the Church in the world really is. These paragraphs provide some of the most memorable and enlightening passages in the whole document — or indeed in any of the papal writings considered in this study. We begin with the following two statements:

> For the Church, to evangelise is to bring the Good News into all the strata of the human race so that by its power it may permeate the depths of humanity and make it new . . .[66] The various strata of the human race are to be transformed. This means something more than the Church preaching the Gospel in ever-expanding geographical areas or to ever-increasing numbers. It also means affecting the standards by which people make judgments, their prevailing values, their interests and thought-patterns, the things that move them to action, and their models of human living; in so far as any or all of these are inconsistent with the Word of God and the plan of salvation they are to be in some sense turned upside down by the power of the Gospel.[67]

After outlining in this comprehensive way the task of the Church the pope then sums up his teaching by saying:

> It is necessary to evangelise, and to permeate with the Gospel, human culture and cultures. This has to be done, not superficially, as though one were adding a decoration

or applying a coat of paint, but in depth — reaching into and out from the core and the roots of life . . .

. . . The Gospel and the process of evangelisation can penetrate all cultures while being neither subordinate to any of them nor the monopoly of any.[68]

The pope is here taking the word culture in a broad and rich sense. It refers to the shared understanding and attitudes of any group of people who together live in their own particular 'world'. Some of these are common to many such groups, and therefore to many cultures; while others differ from culture to culture (e.g. the status given to old people, to women, to handicapped people, to twins; the value set on cattle, on gold, on cats, on brevity, on burial sites . . .). These shared attitudes might be called structures or patterns of thinking and feeling. They become embodied in traditions and in this way they are passed on from one generation to the next. The pope is saying that the Gospel does not belong solely to any one such culture and is not embodied exclusively in any one set of traditions. Rather, it is compatible with all. Nevertheless, this does not mean that it fits in comfortably into the different cultures. Quite the contrary: it poses a challenge to *every* culture and it calls for basic transformations in the traditions, the thought-patterns, and the value systems of each culture.

The most helpful aspect of this whole account is the way in which it bridges the gap that is usually presumed to exist between attitudinal change and structural change. It is commonly assumed that changing one's attitudes is a matter of personal morality; and this is generally what people have in mind when they speak of 'conversion'. Structural changes, on the other hand, are thought of as belonging to the political order, extrinsic to the person as such, and not a matter of personal morality in the usual sense. This dichotomy is challenged by the pope's statements quoted above. They suggest that perhaps the most important structures in our world are our patterns of thinking and feeling and valuing. These are deeply personal; yet in many respects they transcend the individual. They are social realities that are often our unexamined presuppositions. They are 'within' the person without being private. They are a crucial part of the 'strata' of the human race that are to be evangelised and transformed.

It is against this background that the pope says that the aim of evangelisation is to bring about an *interior* change.[69] To make sure that this is not taken to refer to a purely private and individualistic conversion he adds at once that, in evangelising, the Church is 'seeking to convert the individual and collective conscience of people, as well as their activities, their lives, and their whole environment'.[70] A change in the collective conscience of a people would be a change in their value system; and this would normally find expression in changes of the social, political, and economic structures of their society.

People can be oppressed by structures of the mind — by distorted value-systems and patterns of action, by misguided expectations, and by inherited prejudices and insensitivities. Indeed this kind of imposition is especially serious because it makes a person less human in ways that he or she may be quite unaware of. So there is need for liberation from this oppression of the human spirit. In fact the question may be asked whether there can be any lasting value in a liberation from political oppression which is not linked to this more intimate liberation. When Marxists like Mao Tse Tung insist on the importance of a 'cultural revolution' they are thinking of such a transformation of the structures of human thinking and feeling. For Pope Paul, as for them, such a change is essential because 'even the best structures and the most wisely planned systems soon become dehumanised if the inhuman tendencies of people's hearts are not healed'.[71]

This account of the need for the transformation of culture and cultures deepens one's understanding of the nature of human liberation. But the document does not provide an equally detailed and careful treatment of the other more visible forms of oppressive structures. It would have been particularly helpful if it had given an indication of how economic and political structures relate to cultures. The pope could have shown that oppressive political and economic systems in today's world reflect and express those cultural distortions that are typical of Western society — e.g. excessive competitiveness, consumerism, cultural arrogance, restlessness, and an exploitative attitude towards nature. Conversely, it could be shown how these cultural evils are fostered and intensified by the present social, economic, and political structures. Such an analysis would provide the basis for a treatment of human liberation that would be at once profound and comprehensive. But unfortunately there seems to be a certain imbalance and incompleteness in this regard in *Evangelii Nuntiandi*. Having taken the major step of showing the need for the transformation of cultures, the pope does not go on to draw out the implications as regards changing structures in the economic, social, and political spheres.

Why is it that Pope Paul seems reluctant in this document to examine in any depth the role of the Church in promoting liberation in these more public aspects of human living? Perhaps he felt that his treatment of these questions in earlier documents was sufficient and that what was needed now was an analysis of the underlying cultural issue. Probably also he was reluctant to say anything at this time that could contribute to a further heightening of the polarisation between rich and poor, powerful and powerless, especially in the Latin American Church. He may have felt it would be less divisive to emphasise the cultural issue; for many of the same cultural distortions may be common to rich and poor in a particular area. Pope Paul does not go into the interesting question of what might be called 'the culture of the poor' — a set of thought-patterns and values that contrast sharply at times with those of the rich and powerful; a study of this difference between rich and poor would be essential for a proper understanding of why the Bible presents the poor as privileged and more open to God.

Whatever the reason for the incompleteness in the treatment of the question of liberation, the effect is that the account of the role of the Church remains rather abstract. It does not spell out in any very concrete way the commitment of the Church to the overcoming of the many forms of injustice in society. When the pope devotes a paragraph to poverty, marginalisation, neo-colonialism, and the struggle for liberation, he does it in the context of a reminder that these were the concern of many bishops at the Synod. He agrees with the bishops in saying that the Church has the duty of proclaiming the liberation of the myriads of the poor and oppressed, as well as helping this liberation come to birth, and witnessing and working to ensure that it comes to completion. Then the pope adds curtly: 'All this is in no way foreign to evangelisation.'[72] It would be quite incorrect to suggest that he was half-hearted in his acceptance of these points or reluctant to see such activity as part of evangelisation. But it is as though he were using these points as a launching-pad for something else, which is his main concern; and that is that the Church must affect the strata of humanity at a deeper level, a level that lies behind the political, social, and economic order.

The fact that *Evangelii Nuntiandi* does not have much to say about the economic and political structures of society means that it does not emphasise the particular importance of the poor and oppressed to the Church in its task of evangelisation. An early paragraph, dealing with Christ the evangeliser, mentions that he was sent to bring Good News to the poor.[73] One might therefore have expected that this theme would be given some prominence in the treatment of the evangelising role of the Church. There might have been special emphasis on the place of the poor in the chapter entitled 'The Beneficiaries of Evangelisation', or the one called 'The Methods of Evangelisation'. Furthermore, when the document deals with the question of 'basic communities' it does not pay any particular attention to what many of those who advocate them consider to be a central feature of such groups – the fact that they are normally communities of *poor* people.[74] It would appear that the pope, when dealing with the nature of evangelisation, was reluctant to single out the poor and marginalised as a distinct social class; perhaps he feared that to do so would weaken or compromise his stress on universality and unity, two values which should characterise the preaching of the Gospel.

Despite these elements of incompleteness in the way in which *Evangelii Nuntiandi* treats the issue of liberation and the role of the Church in promoting it, it must be emphasised once again that the document makes a very significant contribution towards a better understanding of this whole question. In fact an interesting contrast can be seen in this regard between this document and the first of the great social encyclicals, issued in 1891 by Leo XIII. *Rerum Novarum* was particularly important, perhaps not so much because of its content as because it represented a decisive intervention by the pope on behalf of the poor. *Evangelii Nuntiandi*, on the other hand, is important in relation to the poor for precisely the opposite reason. It does not give the impression of being a major protest against the plight of the poor, comparable to Leo's encyclical or to Pope Paul's own *Populorum Progressio*. In fact if anything it seems to be urging caution and moderation in the face of the eagerness of the liberation theologians to promote a decisive 'option for the poor' by the Church. But some of the *content* of the document is exceptionally important in enabling Christians to know how the deepest roots of poverty and oppression can be overcome. What the pope says here about the transformation of culture and cultures is central to the question of liberation and the task of the Church in witnessing to and fostering it. Cultural oppression is just as important as economic and political oppression. Liberation calls not only for the transformation of society structures in the sphere of economics and politics but also for radical changes in the patterns and structures that mould the way groups of people think and feel and evaluate.

# 10

# John Paul II: An Integral Humanism

Ten years after the Medellín meeting of 1968 another General Conference of the Latin American bishops was to have taken place. This was postponed when Pope Paul VI died in mid-1978; and the death a few weeks later of his successor, John Paul I, raised further doubts about the meeting. However, the new pope, John Paul II, quickly agreed that the conference should go ahead in Puebla, Mexico, in January of 1979 — and he also announced that he would himself travel to Mexico and address the meeting.

Commentators and journalists revealed, and sometimes exaggerated, the tensions behind the scenes in the preparation for Puebla.[1] There can be little doubt that a determined effort was made by some Church leaders to ensure that both the style and the outcome of Puebla would be quite different to those of Medellín. The preparatory document circulated to participants before the meeting was heavily criticised by the more 'progressive' elements in the Church in Latin America. The main body of Brazilian bishops, who had played a key role in implementing the Medellín programme, were obviously dissatisfied with this document. But they were also concerned about the serious polarisation that was taking place in the Latin American Church. So the Brazilian episcopal conference issued a document of its own, as a contribution towards the preparation for Puebla.[2] In content and style it followed the pattern set by Medellín. But it also attempted to cater for the reservations of those who were afraid that the Church was becoming too political, too identified with the cause of the poor in a sense that turned it against others.[3] From a strategic point of view the most significant thing in this Brazilian document was its suggestion that Pope Paul VI's *Evangelii Nuntiandi* should be the point of reference or model as regards style and approach.[4] This offered a middle ground where most of the Latin American bishops could meet. It is not surprising, then, that the final document of Puebla relies heavily on *Evangelii Nuntiandi*; and in doing so it takes a lead from John Paul II, who in his address to the conference, quoted from the document a good deal – especially, as we shall see, on the controversial issue of liberation.

The major issue facing the Puebla Conference was not really whether it would say something strikingly new and radical. Rather it was whether it would re-affirm the basic thrust of Medellín or whether it would allow the commitments of Medellín to die the death of a thousand qualifications. The most likely way in which the inspiration and direction of Medellín could be clouded at Puebla would be by a combination of conservative statements on the more obviously theological issues and, on the pastoral issues, an emphasis on secularisation and culture rather than on economic and political matters.

The final document that emerged from Puebla was one that could give a good deal of satisfaction to those who wanted to re-affirm the direction set by Medellín. Undoubtedly there were some compromises and disappointments; and the Puebla document is much more uneven than the documents of Medellín. There are sections in which the older style of theology is dominant. In general these are the more doctrinal parts. Perhaps the more socially committed bishops decided that their best strategy would be to concentrate on pastoral matters, leaving the 'high theology' to their opponents. Whatever the reasons, the outcome is that, as Sobrino remarks, 'we are faced with the irony that the Christology and, in particular, the ecclesiology underlying the pastoral documents are more inspiring than the doctrinal presentations of Christ and the Church in themselves.'[5] Despite all this, the Puebla document as a whole re-affirms the direction set by Medellín in regard to the crucial pastoral issues. At first sight this may seem to be a rather minor achievement. But in fact it was of major importance. For it is one thing to propose a programme of engagement in the struggle for justice, as Medellín did; but it is a far more difficult thing to re-affirm commitment to that programme more than a decade later, when the full cost has become apparent – and that is what Puebla did.

## Option for the Poor

I do not propose to offer here a detailed analysis of the Puebla document. For the main achievement of Puebla, unlike that of Medellín, was not the document produced at the Conference. The Medellín documents had a profound effect on the life of the Church, not merely in Latin America but far beyond it; and they evoked a significant response both from Paul VI and from the Synod of Bishops in Rome. The Puebla document could hardly have had the same kind of effect. In fact its main significance is that it shows that, despite political and ecclesiastical pressures, the Church leaders were not prepared to compromise on the central elements of the policies adopted at Medellín.

There is, however, one section of the Puebla document which is important in its own right. This is the chapter entitled 'A Preferential Option for the Poor'.[6] The most notable thing in it is its title. For here the conference is adopting this controversial phrase which has become a powerful summary and symbol of the new approach. The use of this term in recent years has evoked strong opposition both inside and outside the Church. Critics maintain that the Church would be abandoning its universal mission if it were to make such an option: it would no longer be preaching the Gospel to *all* people equally. Some of the more hostile critics go further: they see an 'option for the poor' as more or less equivalent to a Marxist 'class option', implying that the Church is taking sides in a 'class struggle'. On the other hand those who favour the term insist that that is not what they mean by it.[7] They believe that the concept has a firm foundation in the Bible, which, they say, shows that God has a preferential care for the poor and oppressed.[8] For those in favour of the term its main value is that it expresses succinctly and uncompromisingly the practical implication for the Church of committing itself firmly to the promotion of social justice. The presence of the term in the Puebla document is perhaps the clearest indication of the commitment of the conference on this issue.

The Puebla document does not attempt to give a systematic account of what the phrase 'option for the poor' does and does not mean. But in a very practical way it indicates what is involved:

With renewed hope . . . we are going to take up once

again the position of ... Medellín, which adopted a clear and prophetic option expressing preference for, and solidarity with, the poor. ... We affirm the need for conversion on the part of the whole Church to a preferential option for the poor, an option aimed at their integral liberation.

This option, demanded by the scandalous reality of economic imbalances in Latin America, should lead us to establish a dignified, fraternal way of life together as human beings and to construct a just and free society.

We will make every effort to understand and denounce the mechanisms that generate this poverty.[9]

The document makes it clear that what is required is a change in the *structures* of society — but it adds that this must be accompanied by a change in people's 'personal and collective outlook', a change that 'disposes us to undergo conversion'.[10] A very brief response is given to the objection that an 'option for the poor' would mean an abandonment by the Church of an evangelisation of the rich: '. . . the witness of a poor Church can evangelise the rich whose hearts are attached to wealth, thus converting and freeing them from this bondage and their own egotism.'[11]

### The Pope and Puebla

What contribution did Pope John Paul II make to the Puebla Conference and its document? Endless words were written about the position he adopted in his address to the conference itself and in his other Mexican addresses. Intense efforts were made by journalists and theologicans in both the 'conservative' and 'progressive' camps to convince the public that the pope was on their side — that he had condemned liberation theology out of hand or that he had come down in favour of what the liberation theologians stood for. Very little of this material is of any value. Even apart from the special pleading that marks such writing there is the further fact that if one really wishes to understand the outlook of John Paul II the Mexican addresses are by no means the best sources to study. This is not to say that the pope did not express himself clearly or would not stand over what he said;

for in fact he contributed significantly to what was said by the Puebla Conference. But in many respects the Mexican agenda was already set for the pope. He was not in a position to decide his own terms of reference, so his choices were somewhat limited. He was coming into a highly polarised situation; so it was more or less inevitable that his addresses — especially his talk to the Puebla Conference itself — would contain a good deal of, 'on the one hand . . . and on the other'. His opening address to the conference represents a careful balancing exercise in which he warns against dangerous tendencies in regard to the theology of Christ and the Church, while at the same time encouraging the Latin American Church not to back down on the commitments made at Medellín.[12]

In the first major section of his address the pope spoke out strongly against those who 'purport to depict Jesus as a political activist, as a fighter against Roman domination and the authorities, and even as someone involved in the class struggle'.[13] He insisted that Jesus 'unequivocally rejects recourse to violence' and 'opens his message of conversion to all'.[14] He went on to speak out against a conception of the building of the Kingdom 'merely by structural change and sociopolitical involvement' without taking sufficient account of the role of the Church.[15] Having issued these warnings the pope was then in a position to take a strong stand on social and political issues. In the third section of his address he spoke of human dignity and of human rights and their violation. Towards the end of this section he went on to speak of the need for 'a correct Christian conception of liberation'.[16] The most striking thing about this passage is that it relies almost entirely on *Evangelii Nuntiandi*; Pope Paul's document is quoted from or referred to no less than six times. John Paul ends this section with the remark: 'As you see, the whole set of observations on the theme of liberation that were made by *Evangelii Nuntiandi* retain their full validity.' Evidently he had decided that this was not the opportune time to make any major new statement on the subject; instead he was offering the teaching of his predecessor as a middle ground where bishops of different outlook could come to a measure of agreement.

One of the more interesting sentences in the Puebla

address occurs where the pope paraphrases the controversial passage of the 1971 Synod — the one in which the bishops had said that they saw action on behalf of justice as 'a constitutive dimension of the preaching of the Gospel'. In his address the pope said: 'the Church has learned that an indispensable part of its evangelising mission is made up of works on behalf of justice and human promotion'.[17] It will be noted that the disputed word 'constitutive' has been replaced — not, however, with the word 'integral' as its opponents had wanted, but with the word 'indispensable'. In the pope's paraphrase the central meaning of the Synod statement has not been lost; but a certain verbal concession is made to the opponents and at the same time the whole idea is presented more clearly and simply. This sentence might be taken as a typical example of what the pope was doing throughout his Mexican visit — trying to bridge the gap between different viewpoints but without compromising on the central issues.

In regard to the question of 'option for the poor' the pope adopted the same approach. In his address at Puebla he did not use the term. But he found another way of expressing the same idea: he said that the Church 'is prompted by an authentically evangelical commitment which, like that of Christ, is primarily a commitment to those most in need.'[18] On other occasions in Mexico the pope expressed this idea in different words:

— Medellín was a call of hope showing 'preferential yet not exclusive love for the poor'.[19]

— 'I feel solidarity with you because, being poor, you are entitled to my particular concern. I tell you the reason at once: the Pope loves you because you are God's favourites.'[20]

Two of the pope's addresses to Mexican audiences are notable for their outspoken character on justice issues. Speaking in the industrial city of Monterrey he insisted that,

the Latin American peoples rightly demand that there should be returned to them their rightful responsibility over the goods that nature has bestowed on them. . . . Bold and renewing innovations are necessary in order to overcome the serious injustices inherited from the past . . .[21]

Even more explicit were his remarks to poor Mexican Indians. To them he presented himself as one who 'wishes to be your

212

voice, the voice of those who cannot speak or who are silenced'. Then he insisted on the need for 'bold changes, which are deeply innovatory' to be carried out 'without waiting any longer'. Since he was speaking to very poor peasants he went straight to what for them would be the crucial change: he pointed out that there is 'a social mortgage on all private property' so that 'if the common good requires it, there should be no hesitation even at expropriation, carried out in due form.'[22] Turning then to the 'leaders of the peoples' and 'powerful classes', he insisted: 'It is not just, it is not human, it is not Christian to continue with certain situations that are clearly unjust.' He added: 'It is clear that those who must collaborate most in this, are those who are in a position to do most.'[23] This address shows how keenly the pope was aware of the need for social, political, and economic changes. But it also suggests that he was still convinced that the best way for him to promote such changes was to state the need bluntly and to appeal to the consciences of those who hold wealth and power.

The addresses of John Paul II, both in Puebla itself and in other places in Mexico, were of major importance for the Puebla Conference. This is obvious from the fact that his words are quoted very many times in the document issued by the conference. Quotations from his addresses were used as the basis for reaching consensus on divisive issues, notably the questions of liberation, 'option for the poor', and the Church's attitude towards ideologies.[24] The Puebla document is a written proof that the pope succeeded in achieving the main purpose of his visit — to contribute to the unity of the Latin American bishops and to help them find a direction in which they could go forward together.

### Social Doctrine

Towards the end of his opening address to the Puebla Conference, Pope John Paul spoke about the 'social doctrine' of the Church, using this term four times within the space of a few minutes.[25] This usage caused some surprise and unfavourable comment.[26] Did it signal a return to an approach that had been abandoned? The phrase 'social doctrine' as used in the generation prior to Vatican II had suggested a corpus of unchanging teaching on social issues. One

213

of the more trenchant critics of the term is Chenu who associates it with an outlook that is no longer acceptable – one that is deductivist and abstract, insensitive to historical and geographical variations, and particularly inappropriate in the Third World since it imposes Western categories unrelated to local circumstances.[27] Chenu attributes considerable significance to what might have appeared to be minor changes in terminology in the drafting of *Gaudium et Spes* during Vatican II: the phrases 'the social teaching of the Gospel' and 'the Christian doctrine about society' were deliberately substituted for the term 'social doctrine'.[28] For him the gradual abandonment of the older term coincided with a new flexible and inductive approach; and this process reached its culmination in the document *Octogesima Adveniens*, issued by Pope Paul in 1971. Chenu seems quite shocked that John Paul II, in his address at Puebla, should have reintroduced the term and insisted on the importance of the Church's 'social doctrine'.[29]

However, one can interpret the pope's use of the term 'social doctrine' in a more sympathetic light than is done by his critics. John Paul was by no means trying to re-impose on the Latin American Church a body of 'social doctrine' that was to be seen as universal and timeless. He was well aware that the social teaching of the Church had undergone considerable development since the time of Leo XIII. (This became much more evident two and a half years later when he issued the encyclical *Laborem Exercens*; as we shall see, this document combines real continuity with the past with a good deal that is quite new and unusual in Church teaching.) When he uses the term he normally understands it in a rather generic sense.[30] It seems clear that what the pope wanted to do was to 'rescue' the term. On the one hand he wanted to rescue it in the sense of bringing it back into use as a theologically respectable term. But in order to do this he had, on the other hand, to rescue it in another sense – to remove the connotations of an unchanging dogmatism. One way in which he does this is by using it as just one term that is interchangeable with a variety of other phrases that refer to the teaching that the Church has developed over the years on social issues, e.g. 'social morals' or 'social thought of the Church'.[31]

Furthermore, as Heckel points out, John Paul's use of the

term 'social doctrine' is *'discreet* and *relatively rare'*.[32] In the first year of his pontificate he used the term mainly in the context of the Church in Latin America and in Poland. In each case there was a particular reason for doing so. Right-wing governments in South America and left-wing governments in Eastern Europe would like to restrict the activity of the Church to a private, so-called 'religious' domain. When the pope finds himself in confrontation on social issues with such regimes, the use of the term 'social doctrine' gives him a certain advantage; the word 'doctrine' suggests that what is at stake is something on which the Church will not yield to pressures from an authoritarian government since it is fundamental to the nature of the Church; the overtones of something unchanging and timeless strengthen this impression; and the word 'doctrine' is a suitable one to use when the confrontation is with the 'doctrines' of national security or of a rigid Marxism.

In Latin America, the use by the pope of the term 'social doctrine' has a further purpose. It represents his rejection of the view of some extreme exponents of 'liberation' that the Church must at this time identify itself fully with the forces of the left. In the years after Medellín, Latin American Christians found themselves increasingly squeezed between ideologies of the right and of the left, each anxious to legitimise itself by enlisting Christian faith in support of its position. One way of escaping this dilemma was to hold that Christianity offered a 'third way', neither of the left nor of the right. For some people, this 'third way' was to be embodied in the Latin American version of Christian democracy. However, as a realistic political alternative this option became less and less credible during the 1970s. The result was that a number of influential Latin American Christian thinkers strongly rejected the notion of a 'third way' — and became highly sceptical about the notion of a 'Catholic social doctrine' on which it relied so heavily. Some of them said openly that committed Christians could no longer afford the luxury of standing on the side-lines; they ought to throw in their lot with the forces of the left, while working *within* these movements to promote Christian values.

By reinstating the term 'social doctrine' the pope was undoubtedly putting a large question mark over this line of argu-

ment. When he used the term in this context he was not trying to impose on his opponents an immutable body of social
dogma. His aim was rather to encourage them not to submit
themselves and the Church entirely and unconditionally to
an ideology of the left. He wanted them to continue to believe
that the Church has a distinctive contribution to make in
working out solutions to social injustices; and to do so it
should maintain a certain distance from ideologies and all
sectional interests.

This is not to say that the pope was himself endorsing the
notion of the 'third way' in a strictly political sense. But he
would be seen as giving some encouragement to those Church
leaders who felt that the best course of action was for the
Church to distance itself clearly from ideologies of both the
right and the left. This was in fact the stance adopted at the
Puebla Conference. The Puebla documents contain strong
condemnations of three different ideologies — capitalist
liberalism, Marxist collectivism, and 'the so-called doctrine of
national security'. Quoting the pope's address, the text goes
on to state that the Church chooses to maintain its freedom
with regard to the opposing systems. It opts 'solely for the
human being' and 'does not need to have recourse to ideological systems'. It finds its inspiration in the tenets of an
authentic Christian anthropology.[33] This position was very
much what the pope would have wanted; and the 'authentic
Christian anthropology' from which it derives its inspiration
is the basis for — and is indeed more or less equivalent to —
Catholic 'social doctrine' in Pope John Paul's sense of the term.

In speaking of this 'authentic Christian anthropology' the
Puebla text adds the significant words: 'Christians must commit themselves to the elaboration of historical projects that
meet the needs of a given moment and a given culture.'[34] By
inserting this statement the drafters of the text ensured that
there would be no abandonment of the principle laid down
by Paul VI in *Octogesima Adveniens*, that the solutions to
social problems have to be discerned in each particular time,
place, and culture. To accept the term 'social doctrine', as
Puebla did following John Paul II,[35] does *not* mean accepting just one universal and timeless model of how society is
to be organised.[36]

The insistence of Puebla that Christians must commit themselves to particular 'historical projects' is especially significant because it comes soon after quotations from the pope's opening address to the conference. The crucial quotation is to the effect that the Church opts 'solely for the human being'.[37] It would be tempting to conclude from the pope's statement that Christians can somehow opt 'directly' for the human person, without getting involved in awkward political choices. The Puebla statement makes it clear that the pope is not to be understood in this way. Rather the normal way in which Christians, like other people, opt for the human person is through making difficult practical choices between alternative political systems. The Christian cannot remain outside history and therefore cannot normally be 'above' politics, the actual politics of the particular time and place. Puebla is here adding an important point to what the pope had said. It is not exactly a corrective, since there is no reason to think that the pope would disagree with the point. But it was not the point that the pope chose to make at that time, for his concern was to insist that Christians do not have to limit themselves to the unacceptable ideologies of left or right that are proposed to them. This is one case in which Puebla made a significant contribution to the dialogue in the Church about how Christians can best work for justice. It ensured that the pope's statement would not be misunderstood or mis-used.

### Integral Humanism

A few weeks after his return from Mexico to Rome the pope issued his first encyclical, entitled *Redemptor Hominis*, 'The Redeemer of Humankind'.[38] This was followed within two years by his second encyclical, *Dives in Misericordia*, 'Riches in Mercy'.[39] These documents gave him the opportunity to outline a good deal of his vision on his own terms, without the restriction of having to relate it to the demands of a particular local situation. *Redemptor Hominis* is a document of considerable importance, both in its own right and because it provides a background against which one can understand various other statements made by the pope. In this first encyclical he ranges over a very wide area, but there is a unifying thread running through it all. The unifying vision of the pope may perhaps be summed up in two phrases from the encyclical: 'in Christ and through Christ, human persons

217

have acquired full awareness of their dignity';[40] and, 'all routes for the Church are directed towards the human person'.[41] These phrases indicate that, while the encyclical is concerned above all with the mystery of Christ and the activity of the Church, these concerns in no way take the author into a 'spiritual' or 'religious' world unrelated to everyday living. Quite the contrary: the pope's concern is directed precisely towards the human person, human society, and the world we live in. He sets out to show that these 'secular' realities are the very things on which Christ and the Church throw light, the thing about which they give hope:

> Man in the full truth of his existence, of his personal being and also of his community and social being – in the sphere of his own family, in the sphere of society . . ., and in the sphere of the whole of mankind – this man is the primary route that the Church must travel in fulfilling her mission: *he is the primary and fundamental way for the Church*, the way traced out by Christ himself . . .[42]

The encyclical helps one to realise that whenever the pope makes statements emphasising the primacy of the spiritual (as he did at Puebla,[43] and in his address to the United Nations,[44] as well as in the encyclical itself[45]) he is *not* reverting to an old-fashioned dualist theology that would justify an 'escape' by Christians from social and political involvement. What he envisages is just the opposite: it is an integral humanism embracing all dimensions of life, including the economic, the political, the cultural, and the religious. Within this humanistic vision, 'the spiritual' means for him those dimensions and aspects of human life that are deepest.[46] The Christian is called to explore whatever is found to be deepest in human experience, and to be particularly concerned about such matters.

It is on the basis of such an approach that John Paul can say:

> . . . the Church considers this concern for human beings, for their humanity, for the future of the human race on earth and therefore also for the direction of the totality of development and progress – to be inextricably linked to the Church's own mission and an essential element of it.[47]

This statement is a vindication of the position adopted by the bishops at the Synod of 1971. By using the word 'essential', the pope is really accepting what the bishops intended when they used the controversial phrase 'constitutive dimension'. As we saw in the previous chapter, Paul VI in *Evangelii Nuntiandi* provided a certain theological basis for the Synod statement. In *Redemptor Hominis* John Paul carries this a step further. In fact he deepens it considerably because he grounds all action for justice and human progress in a rich integral humanism. It is a humanism that is Christological; and this not in a superficial sense in which Christ is seen as adding something on to humanity or merely rescuing the human race from sin. It is more profound than that: for the pope, it is in Christ that we learn what it really means to be human.

The humanism of John Paul II is very comprehensive. He includes the economic and political dimensions; but, like Vatican II and Paul VI, he lays special stress on the cultural dimension. What is significant about his statements on culture is that there is no hint of dualism or escapism in them. One does not have any sense that he is stressing culture because it is easier and safer for a Church leader to talk about culture than about the more delicate and dangerous issues of economics and politics. If he speaks out strongly about culture — as indeed he does in Mexico,[48] and elsewhere[49] — this is because he sees people being injured and exploited in this area of culture as much as in the economic and political spheres. The cultural rights of people can be trampled on just as tragically as can their other rights. It is all part of the same process of marginalisation and impoverishment against which the Church is bound to protest.

Against the background of his integral humanism one can understand better the very fundamental misgivings expressed by John Paul about the present state of society. People, he says, now live 'increasingly in fear', afraid of a radical self-destruction.[50] The ordinary person lives under the constant threat of atomic warfare; and people also live under the threat of a ruthless oppression and subjugation that can deprive them of their freedom without even having to resort to military means.[51] The fundamental reason for all this is that we have adopted a type of 'development' that has got out of control, that is no longer serving humanity as any

219

genuine development ought to. What has been termed 'progress' now has to be called in question. Does it really make us more human? Of course it does, says the pope, in *some* respects. But, he asks, 'is man, as man, developing and progressing or is he regressing and being degraded in his humanity?'[52] Clearly the pope's own answer to that question is that in many respects modern 'development' is destroying humanity rather than promoting real progress.

First of all, the world economy is not solving the problems of starvation and malnutrition; in fact we have in the present world international order the parable of the rich man and Lazarus writ large.[53] The institutions on which the world economic order rests — the systems that control production, trade, and finance — have proved incapable, says the pope, of 'remedying the unjust social situations inherited from the past or of dealing with the urgent challenges and ethical demands of the present'.[54]

Secondly, modern so-called development is doing harm not only to the poorer peoples but also to those who live in the better-off countries — the very people who might have been expected to benefit most from it. The 'fever of inflation and the plague of unemployment' affect them at the economic and social level; while at the cultural and psychological level there is in them a sense of alienation.[55] People can easily be manipulated by political and economic means and also by the communications media. In fact we are running the risk of being enslaved by the very products we have made.[56] Furthermore, the massive social injustice that now exists in the world is giving rise to remorse and guilt in those who live in wealth and plenty.[57]

There is another major failure of modern development, one that affects the whole world, rich and poor alike. The world economy today depends on activities and systems that are 'depleting the earth's resources of raw materials and energy at an ever-increasing rate and putting intolerable pressures on the geo-physical environment'.[58] Here the pope is adverting to environmental issues — the poisoning of air, water, and land — and to the risk that we will exhaust the resources of energy and raw materials on which the whole modern type of production is based.

The pope's view is that the cumulative effect of all these

major inadequacies of modern development is the continual expansion of zones of grinding poverty, accompanied by anguish, frustration, and bitterness. This is aggravated by the fact that the extravagance and wastefulness of the people of the privileged classes and nations take place before the eyes of the poor. To make matters worse, the poorer nations are being offered armaments to serve nationalistic, imperialistic, or neo-colonial purposes, rather than being given the food and cultural aid that could be of real benefit to them. The arms race squanders resources that could have been used to overcome poverty.[59]

These very strong criticisms of the modern process of 'development' are in marked contrast to the optimism displayed by John XXIII and Vatican II. It is clear that John Paul II wants a very radical restructuring of our world order. And he is well aware that this will be no easy task:

> There is need for brave and creative initiatives . . .
> The task is not impossible . . .
> The only way forward is transformation of the structures of economic life. But this road is so difficult that it requires a real conversion of mind, will, and heart. The task calls for the strong commitment of individuals and peoples who are both free and in solidarity with each other.[60]

The pope is here taking it for granted that moral conversion is no substitute for structural reform of society. But at the same time he is insisting that such structural changes cannot be expected to take place without the free cooperation of morally committed people.

By what means can a more genuinely human type of development be brought about? The pope is not very specific as regards details but his general proposal is clear. Economic progress must be *planned*. The plan or programme must be one that takes account of each person and of all people, one that is universal and is based on the solidarity of all. It must above all ensure that economic growth does not damage society through becoming the highest value; economic growth must rather be at the service of people.[61] This proposal for a planned global economy follows in the line of Paul VI's *Populorum Progressio*, but makes it somewhat more explicit.[62]

The pope goes on to write movingly about human rights.

He insists that peace comes down to a respect for the rights of people. The real test of whether or not justice is present in a given situation is whether human rights are respected there.[63] The pope refers here to the United Nations' Declaration of Human Rights. A few months later, in his address to the United Nations, he called this document 'a milestone on the long and difficult path of the human race . . . the path of the moral progress of humanity'.[64] In this same address he invoked what he called *'the humanistic criterion'* as the proper standard for evaluating various systems:

> . . . the fundamental criterion for comparing social, economic and political systems . . . must be . . . *the humanistic criterion*, namely the measure in which each system is really capable of reducing, restraining and eliminating as far as possible the various forms of exploitation of man and of ensuring for him, through work, not only the just distribution of the indispensible material goods, but also a participation, in keeping with his dignity, in the whole process of production and in the social life that grows up around that process.[65]

The humanistic vision that pervades *Redemptor Hominis* and underlies the pope's addresses is filled out and rounded off by some deeply moving passages in *Dives in Misericordia*. There he notes how easily and often it happens that human actions which are 'undertaken in the name of justice' can in practice 'deviate from justice itself' by becoming distorted through spite, hatred, and cruelty.[66] He strongly resists the idea that justice and mercy are opposed to each other. Mercy and forgiveness, he maintains, do not 'cancel out the obligations of justice'; rather, mercy, when understood properly, is seen to be 'the most profound source of justice'.[67] Furthermore, mercy is not to be seen as something that leaves a distance between the benefactor and the recipient and creates a relationship that is one-sided. On the contrary, mercy includes the reciprocity of justice. Indeed, it even deepens this mutuality because it brings about an encounter between people that is not confined to external goods but is focused directly on the value of the persons involved; it enables them to meet in reciprocal tenderness and sensitivity.[68]

This teaching of Pope John Paul about mercy and forgive-

ness can go a long way towards allaying the fears and reservations experienced by some religious people in relation to an
'option for the poor'. The misgivings of such people arise
when they see how this phrase is invoked by certain angry
or over-enthusiastic activists to justify a strident, combative
attitude towards all authorities, towards ordinary 'respectable' people, and even at times towards anybody that ven-
tures to disagree with them! The pope's insistence on the
importance of mercy as well as justice does not by any means
result in a 'watering down' of the commitment of the Church
to an 'option for the poor'. What it does is to invite us to
think about the kind of world we would like to bring about
through such an option; and also to reflect about what would
be the most effective and human strategy for bringing such a
world into existence. If gentleness and human sensitivity are
to characterise the world we are working for, then they must
also be present in the manner in which we seek to attain it.

*The Brazil Addresses*

Of the various 'pastoral visits' made by John Paul II to different parts of the world, by far the most significant, from
the point of view of an 'option for the poor', was his trip to
Brazil. It lasted twelve days — from 30 June to 11 July 1980.
During that time he gave a very large number of addresses,
several of which made valuable contributions to the Church's
social teaching.[69] But perhaps more important than the content of his talks was the overall impression the pope gave,
which was that of being broadly in solidarity with the main
body of Brazilian bishops in their commitment to putting
the Church on the side of the poor and oppressed.

John Paul was well aware that the government would have
liked to use his visit to convey the impression that the
Brazilian bishops were being admonished for their outspoken
criticism of the regime. So he made his position clear from
the start. On the first day of his visit he addressed the president of Brazil. Having outlined his humanistic vision,[70] he
went on at once to state that the Church advocates 'reforms
that aim at a more just society';[71] and he insisted on the
importance of respect for human rights. That same day, in an
address to the diplomatic corps, he took up this theme again.
He made an obvious reference to the 'doctrine of National

Security' when he said that, while each country has the duty of preserving its internal peace and security, it must 'earn' this peace by ensuring the common good of everybody and by respecting human rights. He went on to insist that the Church 'will constantly endeavour to recall concern for "the poor", for those who are underprivileged in some way.'[72] In a very subtle way the pope took issue with another aspect of the National Security ideology when he spoke to Brazilian cultural leaders the following day at Rio de Janeiro. Stressing the importance of culture in the process of humanisation, he went on to insist that culture must not be imposed on people; there must be respect for their freedom.[73] This challenges the view of those right-wing Latin American ideologues who see culture, and indeed religion, as an integral and vital part of the system that is to be imposed on all, in the interests of the security of the State.

Two of the major addresses given by the pope in Brazil were the talk he gave to one hundred and fifty members of CELAM (the Latin American Conference of Bishops)[74] at Rio, and his speech at Fortaleza to the bishops of Brazil.[75] There are a number of similarities between the two talks. In each case there is generous approval for the general direction taken by the bishops, combined with some expressions of the need to avoid certain dangers. The tone of his CELAM speech is distinctly warmer than that of his opening address at Puebla eighteen months previously. He makes it quite clear that he had given a wholehearted approval to the Puebla document, after some modifications had been made to parts of the text in the interests of 'accuracy'.[76] Referring to Puebla he says, 'you rightly called for a preferential option for the poor, not an exclusive nor excluding one'.[77] In speaking to the Brazilian bishops he complimented them very warmly on their commitment in matters of poverty; he says it gives him joy to see their witness to poverty and simplicity and their insertion in the midst of their people.[78] A little later he clarified his understanding of the meaning of the term 'option for the poor':

> You know that the preferential option for the poor, forcefully proclaimed at Puebla, is not an invitation to exclusivism, and would not justify a bishop's refusal to proclaim the Word of conversion and salvation to this or that group

224

of persons on the pretext that they are not poor . . . because it is his duty to proclaim the *whole* Gospel to *all* men, that *everyone* should be 'poor in spirit'. But it is a call to a special solidarity with the humble and the weak, with those who are suffering and weeping, who are humiliated and left on the fringes of life and society, in order to help them to realise ever more fully their own dignity as human persons and sons of God.[79]

In various addresses — to CELAM, to the Brazilian bishops, to the shanty-dwellers of Vidigal, and to the workers of São Paulo — the pope insisted that the Church is completely opposed to class struggle. The aim of the Church is not to exacerbate divisions in society but to heal them; so it refuses to condone violence or to identify itself with the interests and ideology of any one group or class.[80] In his CELAM address he ruled out not merely the Marxist concept of class warfare but also the use of a Marxist analysis; but in doing so he carefully made use of the Puebla text on this question, without adding to it.[81] While stressing the need for effective structural reforms, he also maintains in several addresses that these must be introduced prudently and peacefully, and therefore in a gradual and progressive way.[82]

In an address to workers in the industrial city of Sao Paulo, Pope John Paul spoke very strongly and movingly about the plight of the urban poor, and the need to transform the city into a more human place. He referred to overcrowding and the frustration to which it gives rise. He also spoke about the pollution of the environment — a topic that was particularly relevant and urgent in view of the scandalous conditions in that city.[83] Just before he delivered this address, the pope had listened to a trade union activist speak in public of the economic and political repression of workers in Brazil.[84] Part of the pope's response to this cry was a firm insistence on the right of workers to form trade unions.[85] This is a right which had been affirmed by the Church as far back as the time of Leo XIII. But for John Paul to reaffirm it publicly in an address to workers in São Paulo, where in the previous months workers had been harrassed, arrested, and even shot for trying to exercise that right, was a clear challenge to the government. It also represented firm support for Cardinal Arns who had helped the workers during the strikes in which they sought to claim their rights.

In Recife, the city of Helder Camara, the pope spoke in an equally challenging way on the question of the ownership and use of land:

> ... the land is a gift of God, a gift that he gives to all human beings, men and women ... It is not lawful, there-fore, ... to use that gift in such a way that its benefits accrue to only a few, leaving the others, the vast majority, excluded ...[86]

Once again, the *content* of the pope's statement was by no means startlingly new; it was the *context* that made all the difference. He was speaking to exploited rural workers, people who were being impoverished through the loss of their title to the land they had considered their own, or people who were being deprived of work or of a living wage. In this situation the pope's address was a forceful protest against current abuses. It was also a strong vindication of the stand taken by Archbishop Camara, whom the pope pointedly called 'brother of the poor and my brother'.[87]

## The Poor and the 'Poor in Spirit'

The most striking witness by the pope to his concern for the poor and marginalised in Brazilian society was his visit to the *favela* or shanty-town of Vidigal, outside Rio de Janeiro. He told the people that what he had to say to them was also addressed to all those in Brazil who live in similar conditions.[88] And what he offers them is a reflection on the text, 'Blessed are the poor in spirit'. What the pope has to say on this ques-tion is of particular importance for this study of 'option for the poor'. So I propose to look closely at this address and to relate it to two other talks given by the pope in similar situ-ations and on the same theme; the other two talks are one given five days later in the *favela* of Alagados, near Salvador da Bahia in Brazil, and one given several months later to the shanty-dwellers of the Tondo area outside Manila in the Philippines.

In the first of these addresses the pope notes that the Church in Brazil wishes to be the Church of the poor; so he proposes to clarify what is meant by 'the poor in spirit' and to see who are these people. He says they are those who are open to God, ready to receive God's gifts, aware that they have received everything from God.[89] The 'poor in spirit' are merciful and generous. For to be 'poor in spirit' means to be open to others – to God and one's neighbours. Those who are not poor in spirit are closed to God and to other people; they are merciless.[90] Wealthy people are 'poor in spirit', says the pope, when they constantly give themselves and serve others in proportion to their riches.[91]

This last statement, taken on its own, could be used to justify a highly spiritualised notion of poverty of spirit that would have no connection with the presence or absence of wealth or with its use or abuse. The rich could then patronise the poor, for instance by giving them alms while leaving intact the structures in society that leave the poor trapped in poverty. But the pope makes his statement here in a context where he is trying very hard to show the inadequacy of such an approach; he wants to make clear that being open to God ('poor in spirit') is intimately linked to working for structural change in society. He does this by pointing out that the first beatitude, while addressed by the Church today to everybody, has in fact something different to say to each of three different categories of people:

— To those who live in want, it says that they are very close to God and that they must maintain their human dignity and their openness to others.
— To those who are somehat better off it says: ' . . . do not close yourself off in yourselves. Think of those who are more poor . . . share with them . . . in a systematic way . . . '
— To those who are very wealthy, the Church of the poor says: 'Do you not feel remorse of conscience because of your riches and abundance? . . . If you have a lot . . . you must give a lot. And you must think about how to give – how to organise socio-economic life . . . in such a way that it will tend to bring about equality between people, rather than putting a yawning gap between them.'[92]

There are two very important points to note in the pope's teaching here. First, being 'poor in spirit', though it is understood by him in a religious sense, is nevertheless firmly linked

227

to social justice because it means being open not only to God but also to other people. Secondly, if one belongs to the very wealthy group in society, then being open to others is not simply a matter of giving alms, however generously; it means transforming the unjust structures of society.

In the next section of his address the pope develops this point more explicitly when he makes a direct appeal on behalf of the Church of the poor to those who make the decisions that affect society and the world:

> Do all you can, especially you who have decision-making powers, you on whom the situation of the world depends, do everything to make the life of every person in your country more human, more worthy of the human person.
>
> Do all you can to ensure the disappearance, at least gradually, of that yawning gap which divides the few 'excessively rich' from the great masses of the poor, the people who live in grinding poverty.[93]

This eloquent appeal is addressed to the powerful, the decision-makers. It is up to them to change the structures of society. Though the task is urgent, the pope recognises that it may take time to bring about the necessary radical changes; so he asks that these decision-makers ensure that the wide gap between rich and poor disappears 'at least gradually'.[94]

What then does the pope have to say about economic poverty? On this point the main thrust of the Vidigal address may be summed up as follows: (i) Poverty is largely the result of injustice, structural injustice; therefore there is urgent need for a transformation of the structures that sustain it. (ii) The main responsibility for bringing about these radical changes falls on the rich and powerful, since it is they who are in a position to make the decisions that really matter, they on whom the future depends.

Without playing down the importance of the first of these two points (namely, the need for structural change) I want here to look particularly at the second point. According to this address the crucial agents of change are to be those who hold wealth and power in society. What are the implications of this for the poor, and for a Church that seeks to be the Church of the poor? If change is to be brought about mainly by the rich, what then does the pope, in the name of the Church, have to say to the poor? At Vidigal he tells them,

— that they are close to God;
— that they must 'do everything that is lawful to ensure for themselves and their families all that is required for life and upkeep';
— that they must maintain their human dignity and continue to have that magnanimity, openness of heart, and availability to others that characterise the 'poor in spirit'.[95]

The first and third points here offer some spiritual consolation to the poor; but from a practical point of view the crucial point is the second one. What does it mean to tell the poor to do everything that is lawful to support themselves? Does it, in effect, mean telling them *not* to do anything *unlawful*? Certainly, there is no indication here that the pope is encouraging the poor to organise themselves politically in order to bring about change. It must be admitted that anybody relying on this Vidigal address for guidelines about how to inspire the poor would find a notable gap at this point.

Pope John Paul may have sensed this, or even been advised about it by some of the Brazilian bishops. But, whatever the reason, he added some very important points to what he had to say to the poor, when he spoke a few days later to the shanty-dwellers at Favela dos Alagados, near Salvador da Bahia. In this address he notes that the poor are actively involved in shaping their own destiny and lives. Then he says:

> God grant that there may be many of us to offer you unselfish cooperation in order that you may free yourselves from everything that in a certain way enslaves you, but with full respect for what you are and for your right to be the prime authors of your human advancement.[96]

The important thing here is the pope's stress on the fact that the poor themselves are to be the main agents in bringing about their human development. Others are to see themselves not as making the changes in society needed by the poor, but simply as *cooperating* with the poor — with full respect for the right of the poor to take primary responsibility for their own lives. And in a humble and touching way the pope indicates that he himself would like to be one of those who cooperate with the poor.

229

John Paul goes even further. He encourages the poor to struggle to overcome their poverty:

> You must struggle for life, do everything to improve the conditions in which you live; to do so is a sacred duty because it is also the will of God. Do not say that it is God's will that you remain in a condition of poverty, disease, unhealthy housing, that is contrary in many ways to your dignity as human persons. Do not say, 'It is God who wills it.'[97]

In this passage the pope is addressing himself to the sense of apathy which helps to keep the poor in a state of poverty. He is aware that this apathy is given a religious legitimation — poverty is accepted as being the will of God. John Paul challenges this assumption, insisting that what God wants is not that the poor stay poor but that they struggle to escape it. He goes on to note that strong action is required not only by the poor themselves but also by others; but he insists that the prime movers have to be the victims of poverty themselves.[98]

It is quite significant that the pope, when speaking to the poor should encourage them to *struggle*. He does not, of course, say they should engage in a class struggle; his phrase is 'struggle for life'. And he clarifies what he has in mind by giving some examples:

> To wish to overcome the poor conditions, to help one another to find — together — better times, not to wait for everything from outside, but to begin to do all that is possible, to try to educate oneself in order to have greater possibilities of improvement: these are some important steps along your way.[99]

There is a very notable difference in emphasis between what the pope had to say to the poor in this address and what he had said at Vidigal. It is as though he had become convinced (perhaps during the Brazilian trip itself) that it is not enough to encourage the rich, the powerful decision-makers, to initiate and bring about social change. The Church must also encourage the poor to see themselves as the primary agents of change. This new approach was reiterated and carried a little further by Pope John Paul in his address to the shanty-dwellers of Tondo in the Philippines early the next year. The topic chosen by the pope for his address there was the same as that at Vidigal — the beatitude, 'Blessed are the poor in spirit'. Much of what he had to say was an echo of the earlier talk. But when he speaks to the poor on this occasion about what the beatitude says to them he includes the fact that 'their inviolable human rights must be preserved and protected'.[100] This is not, of course, the first time the pope had spoken of the rights of the poor. But here he is speaking directly *to* the poor, assuring them that the beatitudes tell them of their rights.

A little later the pope said:

> I encourage you, the people of Tondo, and all the People of God in the Philippines, to exercise your individual and corporate responsibility for increasing catechetical instruction as you endeavour to implement fully the social teachings of the Church.[101]

This is a very subtle passage. Three points may be noted. First, the pope is encouraging the poor themselves to work for social justice — and this is carefully expressed as the implementing of the social teaching of the Church (so a professedly Catholic regime cannot easily object to this!). Secondly, though addressed specifically to the poor people of Tondo, it is also directed to all the Christians in the Philippines; so there is nothing exclusive in this encouragement to the poor. Thirdly, the pope seems to be encouraging a continuance of the process of consciousness-raising; but this is expressed in the term 'catechetical instruction' which is both wider in scope and less radical in tone than the word 'conscientisation'; and as a traditional Church phrase it is not open to objection by the Filipino government.

In what it has to say to the poor, the Tondo speech is closer to the second of the Brazilian shanty-town addresses than to the one at Vidigal. John Paul tells them that, 'they themselves can achieve much if they pool their skills and talents, and especially their determination to be the artisans of their own progress and development.'[102] Like the address at Alagados, this goes notably further than the vague words of consolation offered at Vidigal. It is an encouragement to the poor to organise themselves, to take charge of their own desinty; they do not have to wait for the rich, 'the decision-makers', to initiate social change, for they themselves can become decision-makers. The pope tells the poor of Tondo and Alagados that they find 'strength in human solidarity'.[103] One may speculate that some of what the pope said later in his encyclical *Laborem Exercens* came out of what he experienced, and reflected on, in the shanty-towns of Brazil and the Philippines. Certainly, the new and more active encouragement to the poor, and the reference to their 'solidarity' with each other, are an anticipation of an important theme of the new social encyclical.

# 11

# A New Encyclical:
# Poverty and Solidarity

To commemorate the ninetieth anniversary of Leo XIII's *Rerum Novarum*, Pope John Paul prepared the encyclical *Laborem Exercens*, called in English, 'On Human Work'.[1] It was to have been issued on 15 May 1981 but its publication was delayed by four months as a result of the attempt on the pope's life. It is a document of major importance, a worthy successor to the encyclical it commemorates, and to the other great social encyclicals. It is not my intention here to make a study of all the points dealt with in this document — or even all the important ones; only those aspects which are relevant to the issue of 'option for the poor' will be considered. These can be treated under two main headings, namely, the concept of the indirect employer and the idea of solidarity. However, before dealing with these two points it may be well to make some more general remarks about the approach and contribution of this new encyclical.

## Social Teaching
*Laborem Exercens* represents a new *style* of social teaching. What it offers us is a painstaking and profound reflection on the nature of human work and the organisation of economic life. It is not teaching in the usual ecclesiastical sense of merely propounding truths. It is far more like teaching in the ordinary sense of the word, namely, explaining and helping people to understand why things are the way they are — and how they might be changed. In adopting this approach the pope goes a long way towards resolving the doubts that had arisen in relation to the very notion of a 'social teaching' of the Church. His approach is 'radical' in the literal sense: it goes to the root of the issues, rather than simply repeating or adapting traditional formulas.

John Paul believes that there are some general truths and values that underlie the particular teachings on social issues put forward by the Church over the years. Two of these underlying truths stand out in the encyclical. The first is that, 'the basis for determining the value of human work is not primarily the kind of work being done but the fact that the one who is doing it is a person.'[2] Therefore human labour may not be treated simply as a tool in the process of production and an item to be sold to those who control the means of production.[3] A second key point is that 'capital' is simply an instrument which is to be at the service of the human person, the worker. There is no opposition in principle between capital and labour, because what we call 'capital' is really the cumulative result of labour.[4] The present opposition between capital and labour is the result of a wrong direction taken by Western society in the last century.[5]

By using these key points the pope is able to bring out why the Church insisted on certain things in its social teaching in the past.[6] He can rightly claim that his reflections are 'in organic connection with the whole tradition' of the Church's social teaching and activity.[7] This organic unity can be seen despite the fact that the pope does not strive for a purely verbal coherence between what he is saying and what was said by his predecessors. In fact the continuity with the past is more clear because it is not forced; the pope resists the temptation to repeat *verbatim* the social teaching of earlier documents. It is remarkable that *Laborem Exercens*, which was issued to commemorate the ninetieth anniversary of *Rerum Novarum*, does not have a single footnote reference to that encyclical; and the references to the other social encyclicals are sparse.

Organic unity allows for notable differences in details and in priorities between the social teaching of earlier encyclicals and that of *Laborem Exercens*. It is clear that the attitude of John Paul towards socialism is significantly different from that of his predecessors. The earlier social encyclicals had critical things to say both about capitalism and about socialism; but they almost invariably showed a preference for the Western ideal of 'free enterprise'. Pope John Paul is more even-handed in his approach. There is great objectivity — indeed an almost ruthless honesty — in the way in which his philosophical and historical analysis shows up the weaknesses of the socio-economic models of society of East and West.[8]

It has been cogently argued that John Paul is advocating a modified version of socialism.[9] An assessment of that claim is not relevant to my present purpose, since I am directly concerned here with the specific issue of the pope's teaching about an option for the poor, rather than with his social teaching in general. Whether or not the pope is committing himself to some form of socialism, it is certainly clear that he is very trenchant in his criticism of capitalism. The encyclical contributes notably to a process which has been accurately described in these words by a left-wing writer: 'The Catholic Church is consciously, though slowly and deliberately, disassociating itself from capitalism and its institutions as presently structured.'[10]

Pope John Paul's distancing of himself from the capitalist order is perhaps less obvious than that of Pius XI in *Quadragesimo Anno*; but it is much more profound. The overall impression given by his approach is that he does not see it as part of his task to favour one of the existing systems over another, but rather to show where the different systems have gone wrong and the values they ought to promote.[11] And this is not done in a moralising way but by reference to the structural inadequacies of each system, understood in the light of their historical development. The presupposition of *Laborem Exercens* is that there may be a variety of quite different ways in which a structurally just society could take shape. The social teaching of the Church, according to this view, provides some basic principles by which any given society could be evaluated; but it does not opt for any particular socio-economic order as *the* correct one.[12]

## The Indirect Employer

Moving on from these rather general reflections on the contribution of *Laborem Exercens*, we can now look more closely at one of the more striking and effective elements in the teaching of the encyclical — the concept of 'the indirect employer'. The importance of this term lies in the fact that it can act as a bridge, leading the reader from an understanding of injustice in terms of a one-to-one relationship (which is easily grasped) to an understanding of structural injustice (a concept that many people find difficult to comprehend.)

If an employer refuses to pay a worker a living wage, that would seem at first sight to be an obvious case of one-to-one injustice. But what if the situation is such that it is economically impossible for the employer to pay a just wage? Many employers are trapped in an economic system that does not enable them to pay their workers properly; if they did so, their products would be priced out of the market. The encyclical notes how this kind of situation arises particularly in the Third World:

> The gap between most of the richest countries and the poorest ones ... is increasing more and more, to the detriment, obviously, of the poor countries. Evidently this must have an effect on local labour policy and on the worker's situation in the economically disadvantaged societies. Finding himself in a system thus conditioned, the direct employer fixes working conditions below the objective requirements of the workers ...[13]

The Third World is not the only place where conditions hinder or prevent the payment of an objectively just wage. There are sectors of the economy in practically all countries where this happens. It is most likely to arise in any situation where the workers are not in a position to become highly organised e.g. where there are migrant workers, or part-time women workers doing menial work, or in that rapidly growing sector called 'the black economy', where governmental and trade union controls are evaded.

The workers in these situations are undoubtedly the victims of injustice. But the person who is employing them may not be to blame for the evil, or may be only partly to blame. Who else may be held responsible for the injustice? To answer that question the pope introduces a distinction between what he calls the 'direct' employer (who is the employer in the usual sense of the word) and the 'indirect' employer. The latter term he explains as follows:

> ... we must understand as the indirect employer many different factors, other than the direct employer, that exercise a determining influence on the shaping both of the work contract and, consequently, of just or unjust relationships in the field of human labour.[14]

The encyclical goes on to mention some of these determining factors — but only in rather general terms. The State is mentioned, and later on there is reference to those ministries or public departments within the State which make decisions affecting workers or the rights of workers.[15] The pope also mentions 'various social institutions' set up for the purpose of safeguarding workers' rights.[16] These would presumably include such things as trade unions, farmers' organisations, and even employers' associations; voluntary agencies concerned with justice in the economic and social sphere could also be covered, as well as some political parties. However, the pope insists that his idea of the indirect employer is not adequately understood if it is limited to agencies *within* any particular State. Account must also be taken of the 'links between individual States' which, he says, 'create mutual dependence'; and this dependence 'can easily become an occasion for various forms of exploitation or injustice and as a result influence the labour policy of individual States; and finally it can influence the individual worker.[17] The pope goes on to spell out what this involves: the policy and practices of the highly industrialised countries and of the transnational companies cause the *national* income of poor countries to remain low; and this is directly related to the unjust wages paid by employers to *individual* workers in Third World countries — because there is simply not enough money in these countries to enable workers to get a just wage.[18]

To illustrate the kind of situation the pope is referring to, one might cite the international beef trade, or the sugar industry. Farming agencies in Western countries put pressure on their governments to protect their interests by restricting the entry of beef from Botswana or Argentina. Similarly, the entry of cane sugar from the Carribean is limited because of pressures from both industrial and farming agencies. What the pope is saying, in effect, is that the farmers, the industrialists, and other interested workers in the First World — as well as their trade unions or protective associations — are the 'indirect employers' of the cattle herders and sugar-cane cutters of the Third World. Through the restrictive policies they pursue they are partly responsible for the unjust wages paid to the Third World workers. By using the phrase 'the indirect employer' the pope succeeds in finding a vivid way of expressing the reality of that responsibility — and the fact that it may not be shirked on the plea that such matters are the concern of governments or international bodies.

If the concept of 'the indirect employer' is taken seriously it provides the basis for an answer to the objection that the pope is unrealistic in this encyclical. It is all too easy to accept that it is utopian of the pope to suggest that disabled people have a right to employment;[19] again, it is easy to assume that when he speaks about the right of workers to a vacation, or the right of the old and the sick to social welfare benefits, he could scarcely be taking account of the reality of the Third World.[20] But what he says about 'the indirect employer' is a clear challenge to all of us to create a world in which such apparently unrealistic ideas can in fact be realised universally. It is *not* unrealistic to envisage employment for most handicapped people, or a family wage and vacation for Third World workers, or adequate maternity leave for all mothers. All of these things are attainable if a sufficient number of people are prepared to pay the price. One part of the price is indicated — but tactfully understated — by the pope when he says, 'these changes . . . will very probably involve a reduction or a less rapid increase in material well-being for the more developed countries'.[21] There must, of course, be other things as well — notably a coordinated series of plans and education programmes aimed at bringing about a truly just international order.[22] But the crucial factor remains the willingness of people to submit to the sacrifices required by such programmes and their readiness to change their life-style accordingly.

To sum up this section we may say that the introduction of the term 'the indirect employer' helps one to have a better understanding of *what* an 'option for the poor' implies and of *why* such an option should be made. *What* it implies is a dedicated and consistent effort to disentangle oneself from the unjust structures, practices, and traditions that help to keep the poor in poverty; and a serious commitment to building alternatives that will be just and truly human. The reason *why* it should be done is that we cannot evade responsibility for the injustices that mark our world. Almost everybody has some degree of complicity in these injustices — the well-off who protect their own interests at the cost of the poor, and the poor themselves who often remain sunk in apathy.

238

*Poverty and Impoverishment*

The teaching of *Laborem Exercens* about 'the indirect employer' helps to bring home to people an important fact about poverty in today's world — the fact that it is generally not just an unfortunate reality, attributable to the lack of the bounty of nature, or even to laziness; it is more likely to be the result of injustice. This point has been stressed recently by Third World theologians, who distinguish between poverty and impoverishment.[23] Poverty is a state or condition which may be the result of misfortune — something that just *happens* to people. but the word 'impoverishment', as used by these theologians, connotes a deliberate action. To impoverish nations or people is to inflict poverty on them. Some recent studies have helped to bring out the fact that the misdevelopment and poverty of the Third World are due less to nature than to human intervention; they are largely the result of unjust actions in the past and present — mainly the actions of people in the wealthier countries (though now, increasingly, a small group of collaborators in the poorer countries must also be held responsible).[24] One must conclude that a crucial element in an 'option for the poor' should be a commitment to ensure that one is not guilty of complicity in the impoverishment of vulnerable individuals, or groups, or countries.

This distinction between poverty and impoverishment, together with the related notion of 'the indirect employer', can throw some light on a recent controversy between theologians on the subject of an 'option for the poor'. Ostensibly, the controversy is about the scriptural meaning of the word 'poor'. But this seems to be a case where the general attitude of the scholars affects the way in which they interpret the Scriptures. For instance, in an article about 'the Church of the poor', the Scripture scholar Martin Tripole claims that Moltmann and some Latin American theologians have understood the word 'poverty' too narrowly; he claims that the meaning of the term should be extended to cover those who, while being materially rich, are spiritually 'poor', in the sense of being open to the life of the Kingdom:

> While quantity of money and possessions is never totally to be ignored in this discussion, the more fundamental question is *how one makes use of them*. Thus, if one who has abundance of money and possessions is nevertheless

239

totally oriented to God for meaning and security in his life and uses his wealth in the service of God and mankind, he does not in effect fall under the category of 'the rich' as described in the Synoptic Gospels.[25]

Jesus was not really partisan to the poor in the way that society tends to use that term today.[26]

This author is quite explicit in drawing conclusions about what the Church should be doing today:

> The ecclesiological significance of this broader perception of 'poverty' is of enormous importance, for it allows us to overcome an overly confined perception of where the efforts of the Church need to be directed today. I am not saying that Jesus was not on the side of the poor. I am saying he was also on the side of those among the materially rich who were nevertheless numbered among those who were 'poor in spirit'; and that the efforts of the Church must be directed toward those as well.[27]

Tripole believes that he has provided a basis which would justify the Church in establishing 'a political theology of influence at the higher levels of our society' rather than one that calls for working 'against those in the upper levels of society on behalf of those materially deprived'.[28]

There are obvious differences between Tripole's scriptural position and the very brief outline of biblical teaching which I gave in the introduction to this book. However, I shall refrain from commenting here on the strictly biblical questions, because I am concentrating on an exposition of, and reflection on, Vatican teaching. What has to be commented on is the conclusion drawn by Tripole about what the Church ought to be doing today. Whatever one may say about poverty in the time of Jesus, the crucial point in today's world is that poverty is largely the result of injustice, of impoverishment. The concept of 'the indirect employer' as propounded in *Laborem Exercens* can help one to locate that injustice and see what needs to be done to eliminate it. To be a Christian today is to be called to work for justice in society; and an elementary (though difficult) part of this is to stop being unjust, to disentangle oneself from unjust structures for which one is partly responsible. It is true, of course, that wealthy people may become open to God, today as in

240

the past. But, as the pope pointed out in his address in the shanty-town of Vidigal, such openness involves a call to dismantle unjust structures. The situation of many rich people and of practically all rich nations today may be compared to that of the wealthy tax-collector Zaccaeus (*Luke* 19:1-10). His turning to Jesus involved a call to make recompense for the injustice he had practised in the past. Today, too, the call to openness to God is at the same time a call to moral conversion, to renunciation of the fruits of injustice. No exegesis of Scripture should be allowed to obscure this basic reality. Nor should 'a political theology of influence at the higher levels of society' be allowed to replace a preferential option for the poor.

To introduce a sharp distinction between material poverty and poverty of spirit is to invite a good deal of confusion into the discussion about the appropriate stance for the Church and the Christian in the face of poverty in the world today. We have been looking at the views of a writer who maintains that a wealthy person may be spiritually poor, in the sense of being open to God. Other people use the same kind of language but with an exactly opposite meaning; they say that the rich are spiritually poor in the sense that they are lacking in spiritual riches i.e. they are selfish, lonely, alienated from God and from other people. Some Church people use this kind of language to justify the work they are doing. They see themselves as helping the spiritually poor when they educate the children of the rich or provide medical services for the wealthy. This, they argue, is just as important for the Church as service of those who are materially poor. The effect of this use of language is to deprive the notion of an 'option for the poor' of any effective meaning, since everybody can be seen as poor in some respect.

The main problem here is a rather misleading use of language, which may or may not be deliberate. It may be helpful at this point to try to describe the situation of rich and poor in our world in a way that avoids a dualist opposition between material and spiritual poverty. In doing so I shall rely largely on the kind of integral humanist vision that is expounded so well by Pope John Paul in his first two encyclicals, and on the concept of 'the indirect employer' found in *Laborem Exercens*, as well as on the list of the

241

qualities of poor people given by the pope in his addresses in the shanty-towns of Brazil and the Philippines. Such a description might take this form:

In general the people at the bottom of society are being impoverished by the way in which our world is structured. This impoverishment is both material and spiritual (if one must use these unduly polarised terms): the poor are deprived of adequate food and housing; they are not allowed to participate in decision-making that affects them; they are despised because of their language, or accent, or customs; they are deprived of education and of the leisure and opportunity to cultivate the things of the spirit. Nevertheless, their humanity resists this multiple oppression; and to a surprising degree many of the poorest people succeed in finding ways of being deeply human and Christian – in spite of all the handicaps imposed on them.

On the other hand, the interests of the rich and powerful are served by the way in which our world is structured. The system offers them advantages of many kinds, both material and in the area of 'higher' or 'spiritual' values (e.g. education, and leisure for reflection and prayer). But most of these rich and powerful people must be held responsible in some degree for failing to change the unjust order of society. Because they fail to do so they may become corrupted to a greater or lesser extent – perhaps mainly through their selective and semi-deliberate blindness to social injustices. Furthermore, the present system has now become so distorted and misdirected – and so much out of human control – that it has become a major cause of alienation; it creates a sense of isolation and of threat even in those who are benefiting from it in economic and political terms. This combination of blindness and alienation in the 'privileged' ones of our society entitles one to say that they may be spiritually corrupted or at risk.

On the basis of this kind of description of the present situation of rich and poor, one may come to a better understanding of what is involved in an 'option for the poor'. It implies a commitment to trying to change the unjust structures of society. This includes giving encouragement and hope to those who are being impoverished, while challenging the com-

242

placency of those who are responsible for this impoverishment, or are guilty of complicity in it. How can this best be done? The answer will vary according to the situation, but some general points may be noted. Clearly there is a need for many people to work directly with the poor — not just *for* the poor but in a way that involves sharing their experiences in some degree. But there is no reason to believe that the rich and powerful should be entirely neglected or ignored; however, the crucial question is, what should committed Church people be saying to the rich, by their words and actions? What needs to be said and done *may* at times be rather different from what is being said and done at present. There are people who believe they can move the rich towards greater social awareness by working closely with and for them, for instance, by providing high-class — and expensive — educational services for their children. But more recently an increasing number of committed Church people have come to the conclusion that this approach is not sufficiently effective; so they choose to challenge the rich by transferring their energies to working with the poor.

Does an 'option for the poor' mean an option *against* the rich and powerful? By no means — at least not in John Paul's view. As we shall see in the next section, the pope is firmly opposed to class struggle; so he does not advocate the rejection of rich *people*. However, an option for the poor does mean the rejection of an evil system and of bad *structures* in society. The Church has always insisted that people make an 'option against sin'. In recent years theologians and Church leaders have come to realise more clearly that this should include an option against what is called 'social sin'. One aspect of social sin is the embodiment of injustice in the unequal distribution of wealth and power in the world. Informed Church leaders are becoming more aware that in today's world (especially), great wealth and power are very often linked to injustice — either in the way they are acquired or in the refusal to share them with others. Christians are now being helped to see than an option against sin includes an option against embodied injustice — and therefore in favour of the victims of injustice. Correctly understood, an 'option for the poor' is simply one aspect of an 'option against sin'. If we opt to resist injustice we must be opposed to the process of impoverishment and the systems that promote poverty.

*Solidarity*

The foregoing reflections flowed from an examination of the concept of the 'indirect employer', which was the first of the two main points in *Laborem Exercens* that are especially important from the point of view of an 'option for the poor'. The second of these points is the concept of solidarity. The issue here is one that we were concerned with at the end of the previous chapter — namely, what does the Church have to say to the poor? We saw that, in two of his addresses to shanty-dwellers in Brazil and the Philippines, the pope stressed the importance of the poor taking responsibility for their own destiny; and he also mentioned the solidarity of the poor in helping each other as one of their virtues. In *Laborem Exercens* these points are elaborated more fully. They are also situated against a historical background, namely the struggle of workers in the last century to break out of the degradation that was imposed on them through the industrial revolution.[29]

*Laborem Exercens* offers a trenchant criticism of the two major economic systems of today's world — that of the West and that of the East.[30] It is insistent in calling for a transformation of the present structures, with the aim of ensuring that the person is respected. But what kind of action does the pope envisage to bring about such radical changes? Not a class struggle. In this encyclical, as elsewhere, the pope rejects the idea that the way to achieve social justice is to struggle 'against' others.[31] He favours a struggle *for* justice, rather than *against* other people or classes.

However, Pope John Paul is quite prepared to approve of resistance to exploitation. He accepts that in the last century industrial workers had to oppose a 'system of injustice and harm that cried to heaven for vengeance', in order to protect their human rights and dignity.[32] There is a certain solemnity — almost a judicial quality — in the way in which the pope states that this reaction of the workers 'was justified from the point of view of social morality'.[33] In the remainder of the same paragraph he goes on to examine the need for similar action to secure social justice in *today's* world. He notes

244

that there are various sectors where the old injustices persist, or other forms of injustice are present — injustices that are 'much more extensive' than those of the last century.

The key word used by Pope John Paul in this connection — the word that for him seems to play a role analogous to the phrase 'class struggle' in Marxist writings — is 'solidarity'. He uses the word ten times — nine of them in the space of one paragraph.[34] Needless to say he does not spell the word with a capital letter. But his repeated use of this term, when he refers to the reaction of workers against an unjust and exploitative system, suggests that the 'Solidarity' union of Lech Walesa and his ten million fellow workers was very much in the mind of this Polish pope.

The fact that a pope from Poland spoke so strongly about solidarity at the very time when the Polish trade union 'Solidarity' was so much in the news could give a wrong impression. It might appear that his ideas about worker solidarity were inspired mainly by what was happening in Poland at the time. This would be quite incorrect. In fact, if anything, the position might be the other way round: John Paul's views about solidarity, propounded several years earlier, undoubtedly played some part in creating a climate in Poland favourable to the emergence of the 'Solidarity' trade union — and may well have helped to inspire this choice of name for the movement.

In 1969, when John Paul was still Karol Cardinal Wojtyla, archbishop of Cracow, he published a study entitled *Osoba i Czyn* (The Self and the Act).[35] In it he put forward a philosophical analysis of the concept of solidarity. This provides a very important background for an understanding of what he wrote twelve years later in *Laborem Exercens*. So it is worthwhile quoting some important passages from this study.

A first passage indicates what the author means by 'solidarity'; and it shows how it relates to participation by people in the building of community:

The attitude of solidarity is a 'natural' consequence of the fact that a human being exists and acts together with others. Solidarity is also the foundation of a community in which the common good conditions and liberates participation, and participation serves the common good,

245

supports it, and implements it. Solidarity means the continuous readiness to accept and perform that part of a task which is imposed due to the participation as member of a specific community . . .[36]

The attitude of solidarity respects the limits imposed by the structures and accepts the duties that are assigned to each member of the community.[37]

The next point is particularly important in our present context. It is that solidarity does not always exclude opposition and confrontation. The following passages throw light on what *Laborem Exercens* has to say about oppressed people asserting their rights — and being entitled to do so:

The attitude of solidarity, however, does not exclude the attitude of opposition. *Opposition is not a fundamental contradiction of solidarity*. One who expresses opposition does not remove himself from participation in the community, does not withdraw his readiness to act for the common good.[38]

There are instances . . . when solidarity demands . . . contrariness. In such instances, restricting oneself to the assigned duty only could be tantamount to a lack of solidarity.[39]

Opposition is also an expression of the vital need for participation in the community of existence, but especially in the community of action. Such opposition has to be viewed as constructive . . .'[40]

The author goes on to make it clear that it is not sufficient to have an opposition which emerges spontaneously, more or less in spite of the existing structure. The structure itself must facilitate the expression of opposition:

We are concerned with such a structure of community that permits the emergence of opposition based on solidarity. Moreover, the structure must not only *allow the emergence of the opposition, give it the opportunity to express itself, but also must make it possible for the opposition to function for the good of the community* . . .[41]

The final point to note in this important study by Cardinal Wojtyla before he became pope is his notion of dialogue. For him, dialogue serves the function of ensuring that opposition is not cut off; it ensures that the structures which seek to promote the common good do not become too restrictive. It is especially important in a situation characterised by militancy, since it can help the participants to eliminate purely personal attitudes and preferences, and enable them to agree on what is objectively required. In this way opposition, though it can make it difficult to live and act together, can at the same time contribute to a deepening of human solidarity.[42]

In the light of this account of the meaning of solidarity, one can now see how ideal a word it is for the pope's purposes in the encyclical *Laborem Exercens*. The word 'solidarity' is action-oriented. But it does not have the negative connotations of the word 'struggle'. Instead of evoking an image of divisiveness, it suggests that the primary thrust of the workers' activity is towards unity and community. Of course this unity comes largely in and through confronting those who try to maintain unjust structures. But that is an unfortunate fact, not a necessary part of the order of reality. In fact it is due to a perversion of the way things ought to be. And it certainly cannot be attributed to the workers but only to those who are exploiting them.

In the paragraph in which the pope examines the concept of 'solidarity' in some depth he never once speaks of the 'struggle' of the workers for justice. Instead he speaks of a 'reaction' — a justified reaction — of the workers to an unjust and exploitative system.[43] This nuanced use of language suggests that what he sees taking place is not the struggle of two morally equal groups, the employers and the workers. Rather there is 'a wide-ranging anomaly', a perversion of right order, which calls forth a justified 'reaction'. It is only in a much later paragraph, dealing with the role of trade unions, that the pope speaks of the *struggle* of workers; and then it is only with the qualification noted above, namely, that it is always a struggle for justice, rather than against other people or classes.[44]

A further advantage of the choice of the word 'solidarity' is that the confrontational aspect of working for justice does not have to be spelled out. Anybody reading the newspapers in the months prior to the publication of the encyclical would be very well aware that action for justice through workers' solidarity is not all sweetness and gentleness; the story of the

Polish 'Solidarity' shows that quite clearly. This means that the pope does not have to explore hypothetical issues about the morality of different kinds and levels of confrontation in a variety of different situations. Had he done this, it could have given the wrong impression: it might have seemed as though the attention he devoted to the issue implied that he was in some way inciting workers and others to *seek* confrontation. But there is no indication either in his encyclical or in other writings or addresses that John Paul wanted to provoke confrontation. What he has to say about opposition is only a small part of his teaching on solidarity; and this in turn is just one part of a balanced and comprehensive social teaching. Indeed, there is a sense in which I may appear to have given an inordinate amount of space to this one issue. But it was necessary to go into the question in some detail because what the pope has to say about opposition is a small but crucial part of the whole edifice of his social teaching. Its significance lies above all in the fact that it plugs a gap that had existed in previous papal teaching.

A final advantage in the choice of the word 'solidarity' (and one that was probably quite important for the pope personally) is that the repeated use of this word in a papal encyclical undoubtedly had the effect of giving a certain discreet aura of Vatican approval to the Polish workers' movement – at least in its overall direction. And why not? If the pope could pronounce a judgment that the reaction of nineteenth-century workers to an oppressive system was justified, why should he not imply that the same is true of the activity of Polish workers today?

Pope John Paul does not claim to have made an exhaustive listing of the kinds of injustice in the present world that call for 'new movements of solidarity of the workers and with the workers'.[45] But he goes quite some distance in that direction. He mentions 'various ideological or power systems, and new relationships which have arisen at various levels of society'; these have, he says, 'allowed flagrant injustices to persist or have created new ones.'[46] This general statement can be taken to refer, among other things, to power bureaucracies in East and West and to the ability of rich nations to exercise economic power for their own advantage through such agencies as the International Monetary Fund, as well as to the economic abuses of transnational corporations. But the pope's words may apply equally well to structures that give undue or unchallenged power at the local level to politicians or administrators — or even to clergy.

The pope also notes that he has in mind not only industrialised countries but also those countries where most workers are engaged in agricultural labour. It can be taken that he is alluding here to the gross injustices associated with land ownership in many Third World countries — and to other abuses in the less industrialised parts of the world. The pope also makes specific mention of the need for a movement of solidarity among groups of people who may have had a privileged position in the past but now find themselves in a 'proletariat' situation; these would include some categories of the working intelligentsia.[47] The point here is an important one: the proletariat is no longer confined to those who work with their hands; old-style Marxist descriptions are no longer adequate to describe the present reality.

The introduction of the concept of solidarity provides a perfect solution to a problem that had arisen for Paul VI and even for John Paul himself in earlier teaching. They could point out and condemn injustices in society at the international or national level. They could appeal to those in authority to put things right. But if that was not enough, as clearly it was not, what then? Should a pope invite the poor and oppressed to take matters into their own hands and put things right? Would this not amount to an incitement to open confrontation? Is it not likely that any such statement would be hailed by revolutionary groups as approval for their cause and their activity? All this would seriously weaken the stance of the Church in favour of non-violence. It could also lessen the effectiveness of the Church from a purely strategic point of view: the explicit identification of the Church with the struggle of the oppressed could provoke further repression and persecution by those in power.

The word 'solidarity' offers a way out of this dilemma. As has been noted already, it is not to be identified with an all-out revolutionary struggle. But on the other hand it does not exclude whatever degree of confrontation is necessary and prudent. No *a priori* theory can enable one to predict the risks that are involved or how far the workers would be entitled to go in pressing for justice. Traditional Catholic principles about violence, war and rebellion, could help one in exploring each individual unique situation; but they would not excuse one from the need to make prudent judgments in each case.

By coming out strongly in favour of 'solidarity', Pope John Paul is accepting the need for confrontation. This means he has evaded the false dilemma of having to choose between direct approval for violent action or on the other hand simply issuing warnings against resistance in a way that almost amounts to acquiescence in the *status quo*. The effect is that the stance of the Church in the struggle for justice is strengthened considerably. It seems, then, that the pope's Polish experience has provided the basis for an important new step in the social teaching of the Church. It may be noted in passing that the later sad story of the Polish trade union 'Solidarity' is not an argument against the rightness or relevance of the pope's teaching. The value of such teaching is not to be assessed in terms of immediate 'success'.

## The Role of the Church

One of the most surprising features of the whole encyclical is how little it has to say about the role of the Church in working for justice. Of course, in John Paul's view, the great contribution of the Church lies precisely in the teaching he is now proposing — and the long tradition of experience and reflection out of which this teaching comes. But the pope says little in this encyclical about the role of the Christian Church in actually implementing the principles and proposals. This is scarcely an accident. Presumably one reason for it is because in this encyclical, as in his first one, John Paul wishes to emphasise his 'humanistic' perspective.[48] Christians can stand alongside sincere non-Christians in working for the kind of just society which he envisages.

What Pope John Paul has to say about the action of the Church in the effort to overcome injustice is brief but powerful. Significantly, it comes towards the end of the paragraph dealing with the need for new movements of solidarity of and with those who are degraded and exploited. He says: 'The Church is firmly committed to this cause, for she considers it her mission, her service, a proof of her fidelity to Christ, so that she can truly be the "Church of the poor".'[49] What more needs to be said? These lines offer a firm commitment to the cause of the poor and the oppressed, together with the fundamental reasons for this engagement. On other occasions the pope has elaborated on these points. One has the impression that here he prefers to be short and pungent because that makes it clear that what is now called for is action — action by committed Christians in solidarity with the poor of the world.

If this study of Vatican teaching on 'option for the poor' had been written a few years ago, the ending would have had to include a major question-mark about the adequacy of this teaching. The failure to face up to the question of confrontation was a serious weakness. With the publication of *Laborem Exercens* this weakness has been eliminated. The result is a very rounded body of teaching which offers both inspiration and guidance to Christians concerned about issues of social justice.

It is interesting to reflect that the major advance made by Pope John Paul on the issue of organised opposition by 'the poor' to oppressive authorities, is closely related to the pope's own experience in Poland. Church leaders in other parts of the world who become fully committed to the promotion of social justice can, like the pope, develop a theology that is rooted in practical experience. Obviously, the theology that emerges in each region will have its own specific flavour. But there will also be common themes — among them the major themes the pope has taken up in *Laborem Exercens* and in his other writings and addresses. For the Polish experience is now echoed in different ways in many parts of the world: great masses of people are left voiceless or marginalised, the victims of an insensitive ruling group; and their only realistic hope lies in learning how to assert their dignity and in organising themselves to claim their basic human rights. The pope himself spelled this out quite explicitly during his visit to Central America in March 1983. He spoke there to a group of people who are among the most oppressed in the whole world — the American Indians of Guatamala. To them he said: 'Your brotherly love should express itself in increasing solidarity. Help one another. Organise associations for the defence of your rights and the realisation of your own goals.'[50]

251

# 12

# An Organic Tradition?

In this concluding chapter I shall try to draw together the threads from the preceding chapters by summarising some of the main points that have emerged in regard to the teaching of various popes and conferences of bishops. This will lead me on to reflect on the question of whether, or in what sense, there is a coherent and organic tradition of social teaching in the Catholic Church, stretching over the period of a hundred years. I shall also have something to say on the closely related question of whether there has been any significant change of direction in the social teaching of the Church. Finally, I shall reflect rather briefly on two key issues that seem to me to require further thought and dialogue in the Church today.

## From Leo XIII to Pius XII

There is a sense in which the first four chapters of this book, dealing with the period prior to John XXIII, have to be seen as a preliminary to the remainder of the book. A full historical study of the early social encyclicals would have required a much more extensive treatment of the background of the period and a detailed account of the policies of the popes of that time. However, in view of the broad sweep of this present study I decided to limit myself, in the main, to the actual text of the various documents under review. This approach is justified, I believe, in a study of social teaching by the fact that the documents themselves remain as part of the body of social teaching inherited by the Catholic Church today. They are by no means mere historical relics. Quite frequently one or other of these documents is quoted in contemporary controversies. It is important then to examine what they have to say. But in presenting their teaching I have tried, within the available space, to indicate *why* the popes emphasised certain points and overlooked or played down others.

Leo XIII's *Rerum Novarum* was the first major step by the Vatican towards putting the Church on the side of the poor and the working class. It can be seen as the beginning of a process which has eventually led Church leaders, including Pope John Paul II, to approve of the notion of an 'option for the poor'. *Rerum Novarum* cannot itself be said to represent an 'option for the poor' in the sense I have outlined in the introduction to this book. Leo's encyclical expresses deep *concern* for the plight of the poor, makes a strong protest on their behalf, and calls for changes in society. But Leo failed to make a clear *option* in favour of the poor. He wished for changes in the economic order; but he was not prepared to approve of the kind of political activity that would be likely to bring such changes about. He was so convinced of the importance of order in society — and so concerned about the evil effects of revolution — that his political theology was built around *stability* as the key value.

Pope Leo called for major changes in the socio-economic order. But such changes would have to come 'from the top down'. They would have to be introduced by the very people or classes who were benefiting from the existing liberal-capitalist order. If no action were taken by them to introduce a more equitable society, Leo was not prepared to encourage confrontation. He defended the right of workers to form trade unions. But he did not want Catholics to join with other workers in the kind of strong united trade union movement that could bring about major social changes. In certain circumstances — notably where the rights of the Church were interfered with — Catholics were encouraged to seek political change; but only by legal means. In the last analysis, where changes could not be brought about without a threat to social order, Christians were expected to put up with injustice. Leo's spirituality was in line with his theology. It was of a kind that actively discouraged the poor from confronting the wealthy to claim their rights; it promised reward in Heaven to those who were the victims of injustice on earth.

The next pope, Pius X, was much more conservative than

253

Leo himself on social issues; the result was that the Church moved backward from Leo's fairly advanced position. Benedict XV, who followed Pius, was more flexible in his *policy*; but his *statements* on social issues were quite like those of Pius X. So there was little advance in social teaching during his papacy.

In 1931, forty years after the first social encyclical, Pius XI issued *Quadragesimo Anno*. It challenged the capitalist model of society much more strongly and more specifically than Leo's encyclical had done. This challenge was all the more powerful because it was accompanied by the proposal, in general terms, of an alternative model of society — a corporatist-vocational one. Perhaps the most significant effect of this, the second of the social encyclicals, was that it convinced many Catholics that the Church was called to be an agent of major socio-political change in society. It could no longer be assumed that the Church was, in the final analysis, a conservative force in society. The later encyclical *Firmissimum*, issued by Pius XI in 1938, represented a break with the political theology of Leo XIII on the vital question of loyalty to an unjust regime; it suggested that, in an extreme situation, resistance and rebellion could be justified.

These two encyclicals of Pius XI were issued at a time when the Vatican was very unsympathetic to left-wing economics and politics. For this reason their significance has not been fully appreciated by those who favour radical change in society. If one prescinds from the particular issues of the period, what is left is rather less time-conditioned: it is the conception of the Church as having a strongly 'prophetic' or challenging role in socio-political and economic affairs. The Church's call to promote justice in the world provides the ultimate reason why the Church should play such a prophetic role.

The position of Pius XII was much less radical than that of his predecessor. In his concern about the dangers of Communism, Pius XII took a strong stand on the side of Western democracy. During his pontificate the Catholic Church gave strong religious and ideological support to those who opposed Communism and socialism at the international, national, and local levels.

Pius XII gave tacit support to the capitalist economic

model that went hand in hand with the Western political system. He held that the worst excesses of capitalism had already been curbed in the Western world; and he believed that further gradual reforms were possible. While expressing misgivings about certain aspects of the 'free enterprise' approach, he apparently felt that it was the best available option in his time; he saw it as more effective in overcoming poverty and safeguarding human freedom and dignity than the likely alternatives. His chief concern about the new developments in society related not so much to economic poverty as to the *powerlessness* that arises when people are subjected to bureaucratic structures of any kind. From a 'doctrinal' point of view the main contribution of Pius XII to social teaching was his insistence that the right of private property is subordinate to the general right of all people to the goods of the earth; this principle was given much greater prominence in the teaching of later popes.

During the seventy-year period between 1891 and 1961, 'Catholic Social Doctrine' developed into a fairly coherent body of teaching. While theoretically offering 'a third way' that was neither capitalist nor socialist, in practice it gave solid religious legitimation to the 'free enterprise' model of society. Its protests against the excesses of capitalism — protests that had reached a peak in the early 1930s — had become muted during the later years of the papacy of Pius XII. The Church still challenged the ideology of liberal capitalism; but its opposition to socialism was far more explicit, systematic, and effective.

At this stage, Catholic social teaching had come to represent in practice almost the exact opposite of what is now meant by an 'option for the poor'. Changes began to take place from 1961 onward — but without any formal admission that the Church's social teaching was beginning to move in a different direction. It is not surprising, then, that people accustomed to the older version have found it hard to believe that major Church leaders are now calling for an 'option for the poor'. In many cases the reaction of 'respectable' Catholics is not even one of formal opposition to this call; it is one of real incomprehension, and a feeling that there must be a mistake somewhere. Sometimes this gives way to a sense of betrayal and even a suspicion that left-wing theorists have managed to delude the bishops or even the pope.

*A New Direction*

It was with John XXIII's *Mater et Magistra* in 1961 that the change in direction began. I have suggested that his teaching can best be understood not precisely as 'an opening to the left' but more as a decisive move away from the right. Pope John himself does not seem to have doubted that the Western 'free enterprise' system, linked to Western democracy, was the best hope for overcoming poverty in the world. But he shifted the focus of Catholic social teaching: he came out in favour of what amounts to a 'Welfare State' model of society. The result was that 'the social doctrine of the Church' could no longer be invoked to give unilateral legitimacy to the values of a 'free enterprise' approach; and the right to private property no longer held a uniquely privileged place in Catholic social teaching. None of this amounts to an 'option for the poor'; but it was undoubtedly a major step in dissociating the Church from the forces in society that were most opposed to structural change.

The Second Vatican Council showed considerable concern about the problem of poverty on a global scale. However, the leaders in the Council were from the Western world; and they seemed to assume that the main solution to the problem of poverty lay in following the Western model of economic development. Despite the resulting inadequacy in the vision of the Council, Vatican II nevertheless contributed to Catholic social teaching in a number of important ways. It presented *justice* as central both to the issue of poverty and to that of peace. It stressed the right of the poor of the earth to their share of its goods — and insisted that this imposed on the rich more than the obligation of giving alms from their superfluous goods. It envisaged a new international economic order in which the poorer countries would have a more equal share not merely of goods but also of power. It accepted that some huge land-holdings might have to be expropriated and given to the poor. However, the most significant contribution of Vatican II to social teaching was perhaps the fact that it committed the Church to a relinquishment of its privileges where that is required to make its witness sincere and effective. I believe that it is at this point that 'the liberal agenda' leads on to the 'radical agenda'. For it is only when the Church is prepared to

256

renounce the patronage and privileges which the State can offer, that it is in a position to take a prophetic stand against those who hold power.

Less than two years after the end of Vatican II Paul VI issued the encyclical *Populorum Progressio*. In it he called for an integral human development of each person and of all peoples. Recognising the massive problem of poverty at the global level, the pope sought a solution in 'bold transformations' of the way the international economic order is structured. What he was proposing amounted, in effect, to the replacement of the present structures of international capitalism.

How did Paul VI envisage such changes coming about? Through negotiation and consensus rather than violent revolution. The encyclical came out strongly against violence, though it did seem to imply that in certain extreme circumstances rebellion might be justified. Pope Paul was opposed not merely to violence but to a confrontational approach. He did not see the poor as the ones called to play a key role in bringing about change.

At Medellín in 1968 the Latin American bishops took the single most decisive step towards an 'option for the poor'. While pointing out the massive structural injustice in society in their part of the world, they committed themselves and the Latin American Church to giving 'effective preference to the poorest and most needy sectors of society'. They accepted the obligation to be in solidarity with the poor and marginalised. Most important of all, they came out in favour of a process of 'conscientisation' of the poor, the masses of ordinary people; this process involves educating the poor to an awareness of the basic causes of the marginalisation they experience, and helping them to organise themselves to overcome injustice and achieve liberation.

Three years later, in *Octogesima Adveniens*, Pope Paul offered what may be taken as his response to Medellín. It is a remarkable document which integrated a good deal of what the Latin American bishops had said. Above all, it recognised that economic problems call for political solutions. The pope stressed the importance of people being allowed to participate in the decision-making that shapes society. But he still retained his hope that change could come about through consensus. Another important point in this document was the acceptance by the pope of the need for an inductive approach to social problems – and his admission that this would result in a certain pluralism; in different parts of the world different approaches might be adopted.

The document 'Justice in the World', issued by the 1971 Synod of Bishops, made a major contribution to the development of the social teaching of the Church. It held that the promotion of justice is 'a constitutive dimension' of the preaching of the Gospel. It questioned the myths of 'development' – and especially the assumption that the Western type of economic development could be applied all over the world. It also accepted that a Church that presumes to speak to the world about justice must itself practise justice in its own life and structures.

In 1975 Pope Paul issued the document *Evangelii Nuntiandi*. From our present point of view an important feature of it was the way in which the pope accepted the word 'liberation' and clarified its theological meaning. He did this especially by relating it to the liberating work and word of Christ. The pope made a particularly valuable contribution by his emphasis on the cultural aspects of liberation – the need for a change in the structures of thought as well as in economic and political structures. In some respects, however, this document reflects the caution of an ageing pope living with people who, like himself, were fearful of liberation movements and liberation theology.

John Paul II became pope in 1978, and within a few months he had to face his first big challenge in the area of social justice. In January 1979 he went to Puebla and played a major role in the Conference of Latin American Bishops there. The big issue was whether or not the conference would reaffirm the basic thrust of Medellín. In spite of a lot of opposition, it eventually did so. The more radical bishops at Puebla had to make some compromises on 'doctrinal' topics; but there was no drawing back from the options taken at Medellín. The final document of Puebla has one section entitled, 'A Preferential Option for the Poor'. The Puebla document as a whole is a consensus statement in which Paul VI's *Evangelii Nuntiandi* and the Mexican addresses of John Paul II provided the basis for agreement on some of the more divisive issues.

The addresses given by the pope in Mexico encouraged the Latin American Church to continue to take a strong prophetic stance on questions of injustice; but John Paul also spoke out quite sharply against the danger of seeing Christ as a political revolutionary. The pope's strong statements about poverty and oppression indicated that in his view the Church is called to have a special concern for the poor. But it was only in the following year, during his visit to Brazil, that he openly approved and made use of the controversial phrase, 'a preferential but not exclusive option for the poor'.

In his first two encyclicals and his address to the United Nations, John Paul put forward his own vision of what it means to be human, of the place of Christ in this, and of the mission of the Church. It is a vision of integral humanism in which the spiritual is not opposed to the material, in which social justice is of major importance, and in which mercy is essential — but is not to be seen as a substitute for justice. For him, respect for human rights is the test for whether a society is truly just. The pope challenged and criticised in a very radical way the current model of 'development' — seeing it as a cause of injustice, poverty, alienation, destruction of traditional cultures, and ecological disaster.

In Brazil and Mexico the pope addressed himself to the issue of the role of the poor in bringing about change in society. He indicated that they are to be the main agents of their own advancement, struggling together to improve their conditions. In the encyclical *Laborem Exercens* of 1981 this point was taken further: great stress was laid on the *solidarity* of the poor and oppressed, and they were encouraged to struggle to overcome the disadvantages imposed on them. John Paul stressed especially the importance of trade unions in the struggle for the protection of workers' rights. But he insisted that what is in question is a struggle *for* justice rather than *against* other people or classes. The Church, he maintained, is firmly committed to the cause of the solidarity of those who are poor and oppressed in various ways. The pope's understanding of solidarity includes an element of opposition: confrontation of this kind may be a real service to the common good. This recognition is a very important contribution to the tradition of social teaching, which had previously been slow to acknowledge the need for opposition or confrontation.

## Continuity or Discontinuity?

Pope John Paul II does not hesitate to use the phrase 'social teaching' — or even, occasionally, 'social doctrine'. He sees his own teaching on socio-political and economic issues as part of an organic tradition. By this he does not mean a rigid system made up of a body of immutable truths, but rather a pattern of teaching which has been consistent over the years, while allowing for development and even, perhaps, changes of emphasis. In this view the coherence or consistent character of the teaching is based on an enduring commitment of the Church to certain basic values such as human dignity, the right of everybody to the conditions required to be free and responsible, the importance of human community, and the notion of the common good as meaning the welfare of all — in a way that gives priority to the person rather than the State. These values, in turn, are based on certain fundamental truths about the human person, the nature of society, and the role of the Church. These truths would include the fact that every person is called by God to share in the divine creative work, in the redemption of the world, and in the promotion of the Kingdom. A further truth, following from this, is the fact that the human co-operation in creation, redemption, and the building of the Kingdom is brought about through an integral development of social, economic, political, cultural, and religious aspects — a type of development that is misunderstood if the spiritual and the temporal are sharply opposed to each other and if the mission of the Church is limited to purely religious matters.

To what extent is it true that there is an organic and consistent tradition of 'Catholic social teaching'? If the term 'organic tradition' is understood in the sense just described, then it can hardly be denied that such a tradition has existed at least since the time of *Rerum Novarum*. There has been a fairly consistent insistence by popes and other Church leaders on the kind of basic values and truths

260

I have listed (though with varying degrees of explicitness). In regard to the practical *application* of these truths and values there has also been general continuity, despite some changes in emphasis. For instance, John Paul II, when defending the right of Brazilian workers to form trade unions, could present his teaching as part of a tradition stretching back to Leo XIII. Again, there is a real continuity in the misgivings about capitalist society expressed by Leo XIII, Pius XI, Paul VI, and John Paul II.

A good case can be made for saying that there are two central themes that lie at the heart of Catholic social teaching. The first is a particular concern for the poor and powerless, together with a criticism of the systems that leave them vulnerable. The other central theme is a defence of certain personal rights against collectivist tendencies. Many *radicals* could find common cause with Catholic social teaching in its concern for the poor and its criticism of the systems that create poverty and marginalisation. On the other hand, many *liberals* share the Church's concern for personal rights and its resistance to encroachment on personal responsibility by the State. But there are differences also — elements that give a distinctive character to Catholic social teaching. Despite its criticism of unjust structures and systems, Catholic social teaching has not, on the whole, been radical: it has not acted as a powerful force for social change, at least until quite recently. On the contrary, it has tended to set a high value on stability and order — and it continues to do so even today. Again, despite its concern for personal rights, which it shares with the liberals, the social teaching of the Catholic Church, taken as a whole, could scarcely be called liberal in tone. There is in it an emphasis on the organic nature of society which contrasts with the more individualistic character of the liberal tradition. Furthermore, the Catholic social tradition — at least until recently — has been much more selective than the liberal tradition in its choice of the personal rights which it stressed; in fact its main emphasis was on just one right — the right to own private property.

A notable feature of Catholic social teaching over the past hundred years is that it has tended on the whole to react more strongly and more quickly against left-wing

261

excesses than against those of the right-wing. During one period early in the 1930s, the pope, along with many other Church people, seems to have flirted with fascist-corporatist systems and their leaders; but this did not last very long, except in the cases of Spain and Portugal. However, even apart from this, there has been a tradition of hostility to almost all forms of socialism – a hostility that has generally been much more explicit and obvious than the Church's criticism of right-wing regimes. In very recent times, however, John Paul has largely succeeded in distancing the Church from authoritarian and oppressive governments of left and right, in more or less equal degree.

I have been looking at some elements of continuity in Catholic social teaching. But one can also find some discontinuity. Already I have mentioned one instance: there was a period, mainly in the first half of the 1930s, when Vatican teaching seemed to favour a corporatist model of society as an alternative to the capitalist order. What was untypical in this was that it seemed rather more specific than has been customary. Perhaps this impression came not mainly from the content of *Quadragesimo Anno* but from the context: the Italian State was at that very time implementing an elaborately worked out corporatist plan. As time went on, the context changed – and there was a readjustment of emphasis in the interpretation of the papal teaching, with little formal recognition that this was taking place; the teaching of Pius XI simply came to be understood in a less specific way, more typical of the general tradition of 'social doctrine'. In the chapter on Pius XII, I mentioned how he presented his predecessor's view as an ideal that was not realisable until some indefinite future time; this is one of the few occasions when there was an implicit acknowledgment that there was some incompatibility between the teaching of the two popes.

A much more significant element of discontinuity came with the teaching of John XXIII. I have already suggested that the sense of confusion and betrayal that some people now feel in regard to the Church's social teaching must be attributed to a process which began when Pope John issued the encyclical *Mater et Magistra*. One way of understanding what was happening is to see it as a move by the Church to dissociate itself from right-wing forces in society. Further light may be thrown on the process by seeing it as a shift of emphasis from the second to the first of the two main themes in Catholic social teaching — from concern about the right of private ownership to concern about poverty.

From the point of view of 'doctrine', that is, the *content* of the teaching, this shift does not involve major discontinuity; the same truths and values are insisted upon — although Church leaders since the time of Pope John have seen more clearly and insisted more forcefully that the main purpose of the Church's concern about private property was to ensure that people would not be left defenceless. However, when it comes to practical *consequences* of the change of emphasis, the repercussions are considerable — amounting to a major discontinuity in the tradition. The full implications were not apparent at first. Over the past twenty years, however, Church social teaching has been taking a notably different direction, not in its basic truths and values but in the practical implications for the life of the Church.

At the end of Chapter Five, I suggested that John XXIII's encyclical *Mater et Magistra* stands as a turning-point in Catholic social teaching — the beginning of a process in which the Church came to have new allies and new opponents. This is a process that could eventually lead to a change as profound as that which took place when the Emperor Constantine made Christianity the religion of the Roman Empire.

Since the time of Constantine, the Christian Church has generally been part of 'the establishment' in most of the Western world (allowing for occasional harassment of the Church by governments). On the frontiers of the Western world — in such places as North and South America and Africa — the Christian religion was seen as going hand in hand with Western 'civilisation', offering little effective challenge to Western imperialism (again allowing for some few exceptions). But, quite recently, the stance of the Church has begun to change — most obviously in the frontier situations, especially Latin America and South Africa. The Church is coming to be seen — both by defenders of the *status quo* and by those seeking liberation — as one of the most effective opponents of oppressive governments. Far from offering religious legitimation to unjust regimes, it is becoming a powerful 'voice for the voiceless', as John Paul said to the Mexican Indians.

Though it is mainly on the frontiers of the Western world that the strong prophetic voice of the Church is emerging, the repercussions are gradually beginning to be felt nearer the centre. All the Churches — and the Catholic Church especially — are international movements of solidarity. When Christians are persecuted in one area the sense of outrage tends to spread to fellow-Christians elsewhere. This process is speeded up enormously on those occasions when the martyrs of the Third World happen to be citizens of North America or Europe. For instance, the murder of four women missionaries from the U.S.A. in El Salvador helped Christians in North America to realise what had been going on in Central America.

It is also becoming clearer that Western governments — and Western-based multi-national companies — cannot disclaim all responsibility for the poverty and exploitation that characterise the Third World. Some Christians in the West are beginning to challenge their own governments to take action. Meanwhile, rising unemployment and other economic difficulties have hit the poorest section of the population of the Western countries; and some Church leaders, among them the pope himself, are protesting more strongly against a system which creates so much suffering, alienation, and powerlessness. As the 'national security' mentality and ideology seeps back to the West from the Third World, there is a corresponding growth in the willingness of some Church members and leaders to adopt a prophetic stance.

Nobody can foretell the outcome of this process. It is possible that most Church leaders will suffer a failure of nerve and will continue to remain establishment figures who occasionally make ineffectual sounds of disquiet. If this happens, then the more prophetic-minded Christians will probably become more and more alienated from the Church leadership. On the other hand, it is possible that many Church leaders will take a prophetic stance and will be willing to suffer the consequences; the treatment of people like Helder Camara and Oscar Romero shows what they can expect. Even if most bishops and other Church leaders take up a challenging position, it is unlikely that they will carry the whole Church membership with them. Some divisions and polarisation are almost inevitable; but their extent will depend on the degree of moral authority the leaders can exert. The position of the pope will be of crucial importance.

Both directly through his own moral authority and charisma, and indirectly through his influence on local bishops and hierarchies, the pope has played — and will continue to play — a major role in determining the direction and effectiveness of Catholic social teaching. The tradition of social teaching in the Catholic Church might be compared to a very large earth-moving machine. For years it was moving forward in one direction, with some relatively minor diversions due to the surrounding terrain. When Pope John got into the driver's seat he began to turn it in a different direction. At first there was much grinding of gears and lurching in the mud — and many observers thought the machine was falling to pieces. But eventually the new direction has become established — due to skilful and determined handling by Paul VI and John Paul II.

This image brings out the important role played by recent popes in setting the direction of Catholic social teaching. Needless to say, some local bishops or hierarchies may be still quite far to the left or right of the pope. But what the pope says is usually taken very seriously; Puebla is perhaps the best instance of that. The moral authority of John Paul II has made it more likely that the line he has taken on social issues will have great influence on local Churches throughout the world. That is why I consider it worthwhile to spend time spelling out the nuances of his position to date, and placing his statements within the context of what he himself sees as the organic tradition of Catholic social teaching.

There are some who recognise the importance of John Paul's position, but who seek to interpret his teaching quite differently. It has been argued, for instance, that Paul VI's *Populorum Progressio* and the documents of the Synods of 1971 and 1974 represent a drift away from the mainstream of Catholic social teaching — a drift that has been sharply corrected by John Paul II.[1] To sustain such an argument requires a very selective reading of recent Church documents and statements. I hope that the previous chapters have brought out the real continuity that exists between the teaching of John Paul and that of his predecessor and the Synod. One of the few significant differences between John Paul and Paul VI lies in the greater willingness of John Paul to use the *terms* 'Catholic social teaching' or even 'Catholic social doctrine'. But as regards the *content* of that teaching there can be no serious doubt that his position is far closer to that of Paul VI and the Synod of 1971 than to earlier social teaching. Indeed, on the key issues of justice, liberation, 'option for the poor', and solidarity of and with the poor, John Paul has moved further forward in the line of Paul VI and the Synod rather than backward to an older line.

It is in the interest of the defenders of the *status quo* to present John Paul II as the one who has corrected the deviations of Paul VI and has returned to an older, more 'authentic' line of teaching. This interpretation is furthered by giving special weight to a few selected passages from his statements, while playing down the rest. Some sections of the mass media cooperate in this process of distortion, either because the journalists have been misled or because they have been given the task of showing that the pope is opposed to 'liberation', and to 'interference in politics'. I feel it is better for me not to bother trying to correct a whole series of such misrepresentations; but perhaps the material of the last two chapters will help interested readers to do this for themselves. But before I conclude this book it may be well to look rather briefly at two issues which can give rise to genuine confusion, quite apart from any unbalanced reporting of the pope's position. The first has to do with the opposition of John Paul to class struggle; the second is concerned with the role of the institutional Church in facing political issues.

## Class Struggle or Solidarity?

As I said in the previous chapter, the word 'solidarity' seems to play, in the thinking of John Paul, a role analogous to 'class struggle' in Marxist writings. 'Solidarity' is a master-image which does not have the overtly aggressive overtones of the phrase 'class struggle'. But how different really is the pope's position from Marxism? Is it mainly a matter of words and a different emphasis, or is there a fundamental incompatibility between the two approaches? I shall not attempt here to answer this question fully; but the following remarks may at least help to open up the topic for further discussion. I must, however, preface my remarks by noting that what is in question here is the relationship between two political philosophies — that of Marxism and that of John Paul — and not the attitude of the pope towards governments and leaders in Communist or Marxist countries.

In presenting the human person as fundamentally a *worker*, the pope in *Laborem Exercens* is in line with the Marxist tradition. Marxism does not, however, have a monopoly on such a conception, so the pope does not become a Marxist merely by adopting this approach. Nevertheless, it is evident that his understanding of human life and of society have been profoundly affected by some aspects of Marxist philosophy. Catholic thinkers in the past were more inclined to begin from a Greek notion of the human person as a thinker rather than a worker.

However, it must be added at once that the pope takes a much broader view of what is meant by 'work' than is common in the Marxist tradition. In a good deal of Marxist writing there is a tendency to use the word 'work' mainly to refer to industrial labour[2] — or at most to manual labour. For John Paul, on the other hand, the meaning of the word 'work' is so comprehensive that *everybody* can be called a worker in some sense.[3] Work, for him, includes such intellectual occupations as study; and it also takes in organisational work such as management, as well as the work of caring for a family. What about the unemployed, the disabled, those who are retired, and children? It would appear that the pope intends his teaching on human work to refer to them also, since they can all in a certain sense be thought of as potential workers. This may sound rather contrived — but only if one is thinking of work in the limited sense of doing a task for which one can be paid. The pope's conception, however, is one of *homo faber* — the human person as a 'maker', one who shares in the making of the world.

One of the most important effects of this broadening of the conception of work and the worker is that the notion of 'the working class' ceases to have the meaning it had in traditional Marxism. Central to Marxist thinking was the view that the interests of the working class were different to those of owners and managers. What happens when the definition of the worker is extended to cover everybody? The idea of a fundamental clash of interest between 'the workers' and others is eliminated. This is the conception that lies behind John Paul's insistence that cooperation is fundamental, and that solidarity is more basic than opposition.[4]

So much for the fundamental nature of society as it ideally exists. But John Paul is also prepared to look at the actual situation. He is not so foolish as to think that the problem of class struggle is eliminated by re-defining the word 'worker'. He recognises that there have been major clashes of interest between employers and their employees. In his view, however, this did not occur because of any necessary law. It was not predetermined that things should happen in this way. Rather it was due to free decisions made by human beings. Initially, the people mainly responsible were the early capitalists; they were determined to maximise their profits — and they did so by exploiting their workers.[5] This provoked what the pope calls a justified 'reaction' on the part of the workers.[6]

Having begun in this way, the struggle between the classes has, according to the pope, gone on to develop into an ideological and political struggle between capitalism and Marxism.[7] John Paul's purpose in *Laborem Exercens* is to unmask the myths and over-simplifications that are part of this struggle. He points out the inadequacy of economic liberalism, the ideology of capitalism. He also rejects the Marxist notion that class struggle is a matter of historical necessity. For him, as we have just seen, it is the result of human decisions[8] — and it is something that can be avoided. More fundamentally, the pope rejects the view of those Marxists who maintain that history is totally determined by economic processes and that human freedom is an illusion. He is opposed to Marxism understood as an ideology: he does not accept that it provides a system that has universal applicability, giving one a 'scientific' understanding of reality;[9] such a notion of Marxism as an exact science is bound up with the belief that history is determined by economic factors which follow rigid 'laws'.[10]

It should be noted, however, that there are thinkers within the Marxist tradition whose views on these issues are quite close to those of John Paul. Their conception of history is not a determinist one; rather it finds a place for human responsibility.[11] These Marxists agree with the pope in rejecting the kind of doctrinaire approach that would claim to be able to understand the world 'scientifically' by means of a ready-made theory.[12]

Even on the question of class struggle, there is by no means as much difference as might appear at first sight between the views of the pope and those of some of the more 'critical' Marxists. He would agree with them that class struggle has actually taken place. They could perhaps agree with him that this was not due to some necessity of nature but was a matter of history in which humans played a determining part — a history that might well have developed differently in other circumstances and if different key decisions had been made. These Marxists could even agree that, in the long run, human solidarity is more basic than class struggle. After all, they would say, do we not envisage a classless society in which the divisions between the classes are finally resolved? Is not this, fundamentally, the same goal as the one to which the pope aspires, when he seeks the elimination of class struggle and the effective solidarity of all? As for the crude accusation that Marxism calls for the elimination of the enemies of the working class: their response would be that what is sought is the ultimate elimination of *classes*, but not of the *people* who belong to the upper classes.

Another point on which there is room for clarification is the motivation of the poor in struggling to overcome injustice. One of the major objections of Church leaders to the Marxist conception of class struggle seems to be the belief that it stirs up the instincts of hatred and revenge.[13] But does it necessarily do so? Or has it even done so invariably in practice? These are questions requiring careful answers. Certainly, it is not part of Marxist belief to hold that the poorer classes can be moved to action only by the crudest of motives; and if the ultimate aim is the achievement of a classless society then there is room for higher ideals than those of 'class interest'.[14]

I am not suggesting that there are no real differences between the views of John Paul and those of 'critical' Marxists. But there is certainly room for dialogue; and such a dialogue may show that some of the differences are due to a somewhat different use of language. The dialogue might also lead

269

to a discovery, by people on either side, of points which they had not taken sufficiently seriously. By way of example I mention here a question to which I believe those who propound Catholic social teaching have not given enough attention. The question is: to what extent do the poor and oppressed need to *win* the struggle against oppressive forces? Or what is meant by 'winning'? From a practical point of view what is at stake is the vital issue of when to stop the struggle. There are cases where liberation movements, having more or less won a political and military victory over their oppressors, stopped short of dismantling those State structures in which the oppression was embodied — and the result was a change of rulers rather than the elimination of injustice. The Marxists — particularly those who follow the Leninist line — envisage an intermediate stage, called 'the dictatorship of the proletariat', prior to the emergence of a classless society. Church leaders would be understandably uneasy about such a term — as indeed some Marxists are. But there is need for serious consideration of the need to replace existing unjust structures with ones that are not merely just in theory but that provide a remedy for the imbalances that have developed over a long period of oppression.

I have said enough to indicate that there is room and need for a good deal of study, reflection, and dialogue on the relationship between the new current in Vatican social teaching and the more liberal and critical strands in the Marxist tradition. I must add at once that there is need for a similar dialogue with the more moderate strands in the tradition of liberal political philosophy.[15] If I have not said much about this, it is simply because this dialogue has been going on over many years and is not seriously questioned. Largely as a result of this dialogue, Church leaders now find a wide measure of agreement with moderate Western politicians and economists about the kind of values they would like to see embodied in society. The difficulties that committed Church leaders (and others) need to raise have to do not so much with the ideals, but with the capacity of the present system to attain them. The failure to find answers to certain urgent questions is raising widespread doubt about the validity of the whole Western system of economics and politics:

— Can international agencies such as UNCTAD be used more

effectively to overcome the imbalances and injustices of the international economic order; and will there be a willingness to make the necessary changes in those agencies, such as the International Monetary Fund, which need to be reformed?

— Is it possible to slow down 'the growth imperative' in capitalist society to a level that is environmentally acceptable, without creating even greater unemployment than we have at present?

— Can the problem of 'structural unemployment' be overcome?

— Is it possible that there can be sufficient cooperation between all the nations to put adequate controls on the operation of transnational corporations?

— Can the drift towards 'the national security state' be halted — and the corresponding drift towards ever greater international competition, with the risk of nuclear war?

Those who propound Catholic social teaching cannot afford to neglect dialogue with *either* of the major systems which dominate the world today. For there is a pluralist principle built into the Catholic teaching. It was put forward explicitly by Pope Paul in *Octogesima Adveniens*; and it is a presupposition of John Paul's approach in *Laborem Exercens*. What it implies is that we must not expect some ideal system which will perfectly embody all the values of Catholic social teaching. Rather we must hope for a variety of different systems, each embodying certain fundamental values in a very successful way but exemplifying other important values only imperfectly. A crucial factor in evaluating any concrete system will be the extent to which it remains open to the criticism that points out its weaknesses and leads on to improvement.

*The Church and Politics*

The final point on which I wish to comment is the role of the Church in politics. Newspaper readers sometimes find reports of the same speech of the pope under very different headlines. One paper may say, 'Pope Condemns Unjust Regimes', while another paper says, 'Pope Warns Church to Keep Out of Politics'. How can this apparent contradiction be explained?

There are some general guidelines which have developed as

271

part of the tradition of Catholic social teaching; and a speech by the pope which keeps within these guidelines lends itself to being reported in either of the ways just noted. Central to the accepted approach was a practical distinction between the area of 'politics' and that of 'religion' — though it was accepted that the two overlapped to some extent. Within the terms of this distinction, the Church's main concern was with 'religion' although it did not confine itself to a purely religious sphere which would exclude all involvement in the social and political spheres of life. However, it came to recognise that Church leaders are not entitled to claim any special competence in purely political matters. On the other hand, individual Christians, in their capacity as citizens, were encouraged to take part in politics, even party politics. But Church authorities discouraged priests and religious from becoming actively involved in overtly political activity, or party politics; the aim was to ensure that the Church as such would not become too closely identified with any particular party.

These guidelines have served the Church well and are not to be discarded lightly. But they still leave some awkward questions — particularly now that Church leaders are insisting so strongly on social justice and are committing the Church to the defence of the poor and oppressed. When Church leaders speak out on such issues they enter on an area which has traditionally been regarded as 'political'. Furthermore, it is an area which may be the subject of disagreement between political parties. Among the questions which then arise more acutely than before, are:

— What exactly does one mean by the term 'Church' — and who is entitled to speak on its behalf, committing it to a position on issues of justice?

— How can the Church as such remain aloof from party politics while taking a stance on matters that are in dispute between parties?

We can begin to consider these interlocking questions by noting the different shades of meaning that are given to the word 'Church'. It can refer to the institutional Church — and this in turn is frequently taken to mean the clergy and religious, since it is they who most commonly articulate Church policy. So, when newspapers report that the pope is warning 'the

Church' to keep out of politics, it usually turns out that his message is directed to priests and religious. In Latin America, especially, John Paul insisted that politics should be left to lay people. Unfortunately, these speeches are sometimes cited as a proof that the pope is reversing the trend established by Paul VI and the Synod; his words are taken to show that John Paul does not want 'the Church' to take a strong and specific stance on issues of justice in society.[16] In fact, however, John Paul is merely continuing the insistence of his predecessors that politics should normally be left to lay people.[17]

Even if political action is to be mainly the preserve of lay people, a question remains. It arises from the fact that the Church is not primarily an institution or the clergy but a community of people. The Church as a community is called to promote justice in society as an essential element in its work of evangelisation. It is as citizens that particular Christians take specific action in the area of politics; but the community as such has some responsibility to educate its members (and others) to an understanding of how injustice is caused and how it can be overcome. Church leaders have a duty to promote such education. One of the ways in which they do so is by establishing and supporting 'Commissions for Justice and Peace' and agencies dedicated to the promotion of truly human development on a global level. The activities of these agencies and commissions touch on very sensitive political issues.

It is the sensitivity of these questions that leads one to consider more closely the issue of the distinction between politics in a broad sense and 'party politics'. Does it provide a basis for deciding the limits to the involvement of Church agencies in politics? The distinction is very helpful where a number of different democratic parties, sharing the same fundamental moral values, differ in regard to priorities and programmes; the Church can then maintain its neutrality in relation to each of them. But what happens when some parties follow a line that overtly maintains an unjust social order? Such parties are bound to feel threatened by Church action in support of social justice; and they have good grounds for saying that the Church is 'interfering' in party politics.

The question is made more complex by the fact that the

273

staff and committee members of many of the Church agencies concerned with issues of justice are laity. Would the pope wish to extend to these lay men and women the kind of reservations he has expressed about priests and religious becoming involved in political affairs? If so, then his remarks about priests leaving politics to the laity would need to be modified. But if his reservations about involvement in politics are not extended to cover such lay people, then it would seem that the latter, acting in the name of the Church, are entitled to commit the Catholic Church as such on issues that are political. At this point it is no longer valid to invoke the distinction between the Church as such and the individual Christian acting as a citizen. The important issue here is on what grounds the pope is opposed to involvement by priests and religious in politics. Is it because of his theology of the priesthood and the religious life? Or is it because of his understanding of the role of the Church? The general tone of his addresses suggests that it is the former; but I am not sure that he or other Church leaders or theologians have worked out a fully coherent theology of Church activity performed by lay people.

Perhaps more urgent than this theological question is the practical issue of consistency in the teaching and witness of the Church. Cynics sometimes suggest that the Vatican is reluctant to allow Church leaders in Latin America to apply in their region the principles the pope applies in relation to Poland. To assess the validity of this claim would take me into the area of Vatican *policy* as distinct from Vatican *teaching*. I have tried to concentrate on the latter and to refer to the former only in a peripheral way.[18] I must say, however, that if social teaching is to be credible and effective, then it must be applied consistently. Furthermore, the most crucial test of all is whether Church leaders are prepared to take seriously the commitment made in the Synod of 1971 — to witness more effectively to justice within the life of the institutional Church itself.

I have been suggesting that a socially committed Church stands in need of further dialogue with the dominant political philosophies of our time; and also that there is need for further reflection about the manner in which the Church is to work for justice — and the limits of its action. The more clarity

274

there is about the goals and the appropriate means, the more effectively the Church can carry out its task of evangelisation. A major part of that task is to promote social justice in this world where oppression and exploitation are rampant. The task of helping to build a just and truly human world is formidable. But it is a source of hope that the Church, through its highest authorities, is teaching more and more clearly the need for an 'option for the poor' — and is committing itself to such an option. The poor are being recognised as the most important agents of social change. In view of the inspiring vision that now permeates Catholic social teaching, they can no longer be seen as passive recipients of alms; they are, under God, the makers and subjects of their own history, the ones who play a major role in shaping the destiny of the world.

# Notes

Chapter 1
(pp. 11-28)

1. *Rerum Novarum*, 15 May 1891, *Acta Sanctae Sedis* 23(1890—1) 641-70; also available in Latin (together with a French translation) in *Actes de Léon XIII, Encycliques, Moto Proprio, Brefs, Allocutions, Actes de Dicastrères etc.*, Paris (Bonne Presse: n.d.), III, 18-70. In neither of these texts are the paragraphs numbered. But the numbering of the paragraphs was added by the Vatican in a revised edition, issued in 1931. The official Vatican translation into English is available in Anne Freemantle (ed.), *The Social Teachings of the Church*, New York (Mentor-Omega: 1963) 20-56. I have used the revised translation published in *The Workers' Charter, On the Condition of the Working Classes*, London (CTS:1960). In these two texts the paragraphs are numbered in accordance with the Vatican edition of 1931. References will be given by citing the paragraph number, preceded by the initials RN.
2. E.g. RN 16-17, 33-4.
3. RN 13.
4. RN 2.
5. Ibid.
6. Alec R. Vidler, *A Century of Social Catholicism*, London (SPCK: 1964) 127.
7. Marie-Dominique Chenu, *La 'doctrine sociale' de l'Église comme idéologie*, Paris (Cerf: 1979) 15, 18; cf. John Courtney Murray, 'Leo XIII: Two Concepts of Government', in *Theological Studies* 14 (1953) 551; cf. Arthur F. McGovern, *Marxism: An American Christian Perspective*, Maryknoll (Orbis: 1981) 99; cf. Pius XI, *Quadragesimo Anno*, para. 14.
8. RN 34.
9. Ibid.
10. RN 16.
11. RN 3-12. Leo's account does scant justice to the Catholic socialists of his time.
12. RN 6, 9, 10, 11; for a helpful account of Leo XIII's position on the limits of the State's competence and duty of intervention in economic affairs see, Murray, art. cit. (note 7 above) 552-60.

13. RN 27.
14. RN 29.
15. RN 32-4.
16. In RN 29 Leo contrasts the 'richer class' with 'the mass of the poor' and adds that wage-earners 'mostly belong to that class' (i.e. the poor).
17. E.g. RN 35: '. . . the gulf between vast wealth and sheer poverty will be bridged over, and the respective classes will be brought nearer to one another'; RN 15: in a State it is 'ordained by nature that these two classes should dwell in harmony and agreement'.
18. RN 12.
19. RN 29.
20. RN 26-7.
21. RN 15.
22. Ibid.
23. RN 35.
24. Ibid.
25. RN 26-34.
26. RN 16.
27. RN 36.
28. RN 16-17.
29. RN 16.
30. RN 31.
31. RN 29.
32. In the very first sentence of the encyclical (RN 1) the pope distinguishes between 'the sphere of politics' and 'the cognate sphere of practical economics'. The Latin text reads: '. . . ut commutationum studia a rationibus politicis in oeconomicarum cognatum genus aliquando defluerent.' — Acta Sanctae Sedis 23(1890—1) 641. The Italian draft text on which the Latin was based reads: 'Le gravi agitazioni . . . che travagliano da tempo la presente società non potevano rimanere nei soli confini dell' ordine politico, ma, come era naturale, dovevano farsi sentire anche nell' ordine economico e sociale, per la connessione che esiste tra i diversi ordini dell' umano consorzio.' — see Giovanni Antonazzi (ed.), L'enciclica Rerum Novarum: testo autentico e redazioni preparatorie dai documenti originali, Roma (Edizioni de Storia e Letteratura: 1957) 78. Cf. Leo XIII, Encyclical, Praeclara Gratulationis Publicae, 20 June 1894, Bonne Presse edition (note 1 above) IV, 102 — English translation in Leo XIII, The Great Encyclical Letters of Pope Leo XIII, New York (Benziger Brothers: 1903) 316-17: 'There are two questions . . . the one called the social, and the other the political question. . .' He says he has treated the former in an earlier encyclical (i.e. Rerum Novarum) and then he goes on to speak of the political question. Cf. also Leo XIII, Encyclical, Graves de Communi, 18 January 1901, translated as 'On Christian Democracy' in ibid., 482-3.
33. RN 35.
34. RN 16.

35. RN 29.
36. This question of working for change by democratic means comes up elsewhere in Leo's teaching; see the following chapter.
37. RN 2.
38. Cf. Vidler, op. cit. (note 6 above) 144; also Jean-Yves Calvez and Jacques Perrin, *The Church and Social Justice: The Social Teaching of the Popes from Leo XIII to Pius XII (1878–1958)*, Chicago (Regnery: 1961) 353: 'It would be foolish to conclude ... that Leo XIII entertained any romantic attachment to the past. The men of the last years of the eighteenth century were blameworthy, not because they had destroyed the "ancient working-man's guilds", but because they had put no other organization in their place.'
39. RN 2.
40. Chenu, in op. cit (note 7 above) 25, maintains that Leo's evangelical concern about the misery of workers did not lead to a structural analysis of its causes.
41. RN 29.
42. RN 15.
43. RN 2.
44. RN 36.
45. RN 36-44.
46. For the various words used in the original Italian drafts and in successive Latin texts, see Antonazzi, op. cit. (note 32 above) especially 157-75.
47. RN 36.
48. RN 42.
49. RN 40. In an address which he gave six years before *Rerum Novarum*, Leo had followed a similar line. He called for unity — but what he had in mind was that Catholics should unite with each other rather than with others; see Leo XIII, *C'est avec une particulière satisfaction*, 24 February 1885, translated as 'Working-Men's Clubs and Associations' in *The Pope and the People: Select Letters and Addresses on Social Questions by Pope Leo XIII* (revised edition), London (CTS: 1913) 68-9.
50. RN 40.
51. Ibid.


Chapter 2.
(pp. 29-56)
1. Alec R. Vidler, *A Century of Social Catholicism*, London (SPCK: 1964), 91.
2. Encyclical *Quod Apostolici Muneris*, 28 December 1878, *Actes de Léon XIII, Encycliques, Motu Proprio, Brefs, Allocutions, Actes de Dicastrères, etc.*, Paris (Bonne Presse: n.d.) I, 40. (This Bonne Presse seven-volume Latin-French collection will be used as the main source for references to the writings of Leo XIII, since it offers a more complete and accessible compilation of his works than the *Acta Sanctae Sedis*; in subsequent notes the references to

this collection will be given in abbreviated form by citing the volume and page number, preceded by the initials BP — for Bonne Presse.) The English translation quoted in the text is taken from the version given in Leo XIII, *The Great Encyclical Letters of Pope Leo XIII* (with a preface by John J. Wynn), New York (Benziger Brothers: 1903), 33. (In subsequent references this collection will be cited as *Great Encyc.*).

3. Encyclical *Inscrutabili*, 2 April 1878, BP I, 16-18; cf. *Quod Apostolici Muneris*, BP I, 38, *Great Encyc.* 32: '. . . the relations of the State and Religion are so bound together . . . that whatever is withdrawn from religion impairs by so much the dutiful submission of the subject and the dignity of authority.' In a valuable study of Pope Leo's teaching, John Courtney Murray notes that his polemical bias led him closer to absolutist conceptions than to Christian and medieval ones; so he put the stress 'on the duty of the people to consent to the king's legislation, rather than on the duty of the king to obtain the consent of the people . . .' — see J.C. Murray, 'Leo XIII on Church and State: The General Structure of the Controversy', in *Theological Studies* 14 (1953) 23; cf. idem, 'The Church and Totalitarian Democracy, in ibid. 13 (1952) 546, note 50.

4. *Quod Apostolici Muneris*, BP I, 28, *Great Encyc.* 23.

5. Ibid.

6. BP I, 32, *Great Encyc.* 27.

7. *Diuturnum*, 29 June 1881, BP I, 144; not in *Great Encyc.*; an English translation is given in Etienne Gilson (ed.), *The Church Speaks to the Modern World: The Social Teachings of Leo XIII*, Garden City (Doubleday Image: 1954) 144-5.

8. BP I, 146.

9. BP I, 154: 'Quod autem inquiunt ex arbitrio illam pendere multitudinis. . . nimium levi ac flexibili fundamento statuunt principatum.'

10. BP I, 150-2.

11. BP I, 154: 'Postea vero quam respublicae principes christianos habuerunt, multo magis Ecclesia testificari ac praedicare instituit, quantum in auctoritate imperantium inesset sanctitatis: ex quo futurum erat, ut populis, cum de principatu cogitarent, sacrae cujusdam majestatis species occurreret, quae ad majorem principum cum verecundiam tum amorem impelleret.'

12. BP I, 156.

13. BP I, 158.

14. Encyclical *Auspicato Concessum*, 17 September 1882, BP I, 176: 'Praeterea qui religione christiana penitus imbuti sunt, sentiunt judicio certo, legitime imperantibus conscientia officii obtemperari, nullaque in re violari quemquam oportere: qua animi affectione nihil est efficacius ad extinguendam radicitus omnem in hoc genere vitiositatem, vim, injurias, novarum rerum libidinem, invidiam inter varios civitatis ordines . . .' Six years later the pope followed the same line in his encyclical *Libertas Praestantissimum*, 20 June 1888, BP II, 194-6, where he said that since religion 'derives the prime origin of all power directly from God Himself . . . it ad-

279

monishes subjects to be obedient to lawful authority as to the ministers of God ... forbidding all seditious and venturesome enterprises calculated to disturb public order and tranquillity ...' (English translation taken from *Great Encyc.* 151). It is on this basis that Leo can claim that religion of its essence is wonderfully helpful to the State — ibid.

15. BP II, 18, *Great Encyc.* 109.
16. BP II, 20.
17. BP II, 30.
18. Encyclical *Quamquam Pluries*, 15 August 1889, BP II, 256-8: 'Harum cogitatione rerum debent erigire animos et aequa sentire egeni et quotquot manuum mercede vitam tolerant: quibus si emergere ex egestate et meliorum statum anquirere concessum est non repugnante justitia, ordinem tamen providentia Dei constitutum subvertere, non ratio, nec justitia permittit.'
19. *Quod Multum*, 22 August 1886, BP II, 88. It should perhaps be noted that when Leo speaks of seditious activity ('religio ... vetat ... seditiose facere') he is using a term which has a moral judgment built into it; in Catholic tradition (and elsewhere) sedition means not just resistance to authority but *unjustified* resistance; on this question see A. Bride, articles 'Tyranni' and 'Tyrannicide' in *Dictionnaire de théologie catholique* XV, especially cols. 1969-71 and 1987.
20. *Quod Apostolici Muneris*, BP I, 34, *Great Encyc.* 28.
21. BP I, 36-8.
22. *Diuturnum*, BP I, 148: 'Una illa hominibus causa est non parendi, si quid ab iis postuletur quod cum naturali aut divino jure aperte repugnet: omnia enim, in quibus naturae lex vel Dei voluntas violatur, aeque nefas est imperare et facere.'; cf. *Quod Apostolici Muneris*, BP 34, *Great Encyc.* 28: 'But should it please legislators and rulers to enjoin or sanction anything repugnant to the divine and natural law, the dignity and duty of the name of Christian and the Apostolic injunction proclaim that one "ought to obey God rather than men" (*Acts* 5:29).'; cf. *Libertas Praestantissumum*, BP II, 202, *Great Encyc.* 156: 'But when anything is commanded which is plainly at variance with the will of God ... it is right not to obey.'
23. *Libertas Praestantissimum*, BP II, 202, *Great Encyc.* 156.
24. *Diuturnum*, BP I, 148: '... si principum voluntas cum Dei pugnat voluntate et legibus, ipsi potestatis suae modum excedunt justitiamque pervertunt: neque eorum tunc valere potest auctoritas, quae, ubi justitia non est, nulla est.'
25. Encyclical *Au milieu des sollicitudes*, 16 February 1892, BP III, 119, *Great Encyc.* 258.
26. BP III, 119-20.
27. Because of the importance of this text I quote it here in the original French: 'Et voilà précisément le terrain sur lequel, tout dissentiment politique mis à part, les gens de bien doivent s'unir comme un seul homme, pour combattre, par tous les moyens légaux et

honnêtes, ces abus progressifs de la législation.' — BP III, 119. In other circumstances the phrase 'legal means' might be understood to include ways of acting that, though declared illegal by the government, were lawful in the eyes of God; but the context here, and the other statements of Leo which I have quoted, make it clear that the word 'legal' here has a more limited meaning.

28. *Diuturnum*, BP I, 142-4; cf. encyclical *Graves de Communi*, 18 January 1901, BP VI, 210.
29. BP II, 18.
30. *Libertas Praestantissimum*, BP II, 210.
31. Ibid.: '... fas est aliam quaerere temperationem reipublicae ...' The common English translation says simply, 'it is lawful to seek ... a change of government'. The French translation in the Bonne Presse edition is, 'il est permis de chercher une autre organisation politique' — see BP II, 211.
32. *Au milieu des sollicitudes*, BP III, 112-22; *Great Encyc.* 249-62.
33. BP III, 117 (my translation, since that given in *Great Encyc.* 256 could be misleading).
34. BP III, 117, *Great Encyc.* 256.
35. BP III, 118.
36. BP III, 118, *Great Encyc.* 257.
37. BP III, 118, *Great Encyc.* 258.
38. BP III, 118: 'Thence it follows that, in these kinds of situations, all the newness pertains to the political form of civil power, or to its mode of transmission; it in no way affects the power considered in itself. .... in all hypotheses, civil power, considered as such, is from God, always from God.' (Translation based on that in *Great Encyc.* 257-8, but slightly emended.)
39. It should be noted that this teaching of the pope was given in the same encyclical in which he ruled out any attempt to overthrow existing governments.
40. As an indication that Leo continued to hold this view to the end, one may note the following passage from his encyclical on Christian Democracy, *Graves de Communi* (1901): '... the mind and the action of Catholics who are devoted to the amelioration of the working classes, can never be actuated with the purpose of favouring and introducing one government in place of another.' — BP VI, 210, *Great Encyc.* 483.
41. *Summa Philosophica* III, Lyon (4th ed: 1882) 266-7 — quoted in A. Bride's *DTC* article (referred to above in note 19), col. 1970. According to Zigliara 'defensive resistance' in this case would not be a rejection of the authority of God since the ruler, through the abuse of power, would no longer be acting as the agent of God. For background on the traditional teaching and an account of how this teaching came to be modified in the nineteenth century see, J. Leclercq, *Leçons de droit naturel, II: L'État ou la politique* (2nd ed.), Namur (Wesmael-Charlier: 1934) 163-207; cf. René Coste, 'Le Problème de la légitimité de principe de la guerre révolutionnaire', in Pierre Marie Theas et al, *Guerre révolutionnaire et conscience chrétienne*, Paris (Pax Christi: 1963) 191-208.

42. *Au milieu des sollicitudes*, BP III, 119-20; *Libertas Praestantissimum*, BP II, 210.

43. Cf. Encyclical *Sapientiae Christianae*, 10 January 1890, BP II, 282, *Great Encyc.* 196: 'The Church . . . since she not only is a perfect society in herself, but superior to every other society of human growth, . . . resolutely refuses, prompted alike by right and by duty, to link herself to any mere party and to subject herself to the fleeting exigencies of politics.'

44. Letter to Cardinal Rampolla, Secretary of State, 15 June 1887, BP VIII, 73.

45. Cf. *Rerum Novarum* paras 13-16.

46. *Diuturnum*, BP I, 154.

47. This is treated in Vidler, op. cit. (note 1 above) especially 126, 144-5.

48. *Rerum Novarum* para. 2.

49. For general background to the political teaching of Leo XIII, and particularly for an explanation of its polemical context, as well as a careful identification of the forces identified by the pope as 'the Enemy' see the articles by John Courtney Murray referred to in note 3 above; also the same author's other articles — 'Leo XIII: Separation of Church and State', 'Leo XIII: Two Concepts of Government', and 'Government and the Order of Culture', in (respectively) *Theological Studies* 14 (1953) 145-214, 551-67; 15 (1954) 1-33. For more general background on the period see Roger Aubert, *Le pontificat de Pie IX* (vol. 21 of *Historie de l'Église*, ed. A. Fliche et V. Martin), Paris (2nd ed: 1963); also the early chapters of R. Aubert (with others), *The Church in a Secularized Society* (vol. 5 of *The Christian Centuries*) London (Darton, Longman and Todd: 1978) and New York (Paulist: 1978).

50. On the change of approach by Leo XIII see the articles by J.C. Murray referred to in the previous note, and especially 'Leo XIII: Separation of Church and State'. See also Joe Holland and Peter Henriot, *Social Analysis: Linking Faith and Justice*, Washington D.C. (Center of Concern: 1980) 31: '. . . Leo XIII . . . while still a traditionalist, had switched from hostile rejection to diplomatic outreach toward the modern world.'

51. *Auspicato Concessum*, BP I, 176.

52. *Quod Apostolici Muneris*, BP I, 30; cf. encyclical *Exeunte Jam Anno*, 25 December 1888, BP II, 232, *Great Encyc.* 168: '. . . rationalism, materialism, and atheism have begotten socialism, communism, and nihilism — fatal and pestilential evils, which naturally, and almost necessarily, flow forth from such principles.' In the encyclical *Laetitiae Sanctae*, 8 September 1893, BP III, 244-6, Pope Leo bemoans the growth of discontent and envy between the classes of society; he finds in the workman 'a tendency . . . to shrink from toil, . . . to have expectations of things above him, and to look forward with mindless hope to a future equalisation of property.' (My translation.)

53. *Immortale Dei*, BP II, 34.

54. *Quod Apostolici Muneris*, BP I, 26, *Great Encyc.* 22: '... We are alluding to that sect of men who, under the motley and all but barbarous terms and titles of Socialists, Communists, and Nihilists, ... bound intimately together in baneful alliance, ... strive to carry out the purpose long resolved upon, of uprooting the foundations of civil society at large.'; cf. *Diuturnum*, BP I, 156, translation in Gilson, op. cit. (note 7 above) 151: 'From this heresy there arose in the last century a false philosophy — a new right, as it is called, and a popular authority, together with an unbridled licence which many regard as the only true liberty. Hence we have reached the limit of horrors, to wit, communism, socialism, nihilism, hideous deformities of the civil society of men and almost its ruin.'

55. Encyclical *Humanum Genus*, 20 April 1884, BP I, 264-6, *Great Encyc.* 99: '... the fear of God ... being taken away, the authority of rulers despised ... a change and overthrow of all things will necessarily follow. Yea, this change and overthrow is deliberately planned and put forward by many associations of *Communists* and *Socialists*; and to their undertakings the sect of Freemasons is not hostile, but greatly favours their designs, and holds in common with them their chief opinions.'

56. *Graves de Communi*, BP VI, 220, *Great Encyc.* 490.

57. *Quod Apostolici Muneris*, BP I, 36-8, *Great Encyc.* 31; cf. *Quod Multum*, BP II, 88.

58. Marie-Dominique Chenu, *La 'doctrine sociale' de l'Église comme idéologie*, Paris (Cerf: 1979) 22. René Laurentin, in *Liberation, Development and Salvation*, Maryknoll (Orbis: 1972) 96-7, refers to a growing misunderstanding of the teaching of St Thomas, a misunderstanding which affected the drafting of *Rerum Novarum*; cf. also Richard L. Camp, *The Papal Ideology of Social Reform: A Study in Historical Development 1879-1967*, Leiden (Brill: 1969) 55.

59. *Rerum Novarum* para. 7.

60. *Rerum Novarum* para. 35.

61. See *Rerum Novarum* paras. 19, 25-40; cf. *Graves de Communi*, BP VI, 218-20.

62. E.g. Encyclical *Il fermo proposito*, 11 June 1905, *ASS* 37(1904–5) 741-67.

63. Cf. Camp, op. cit. (note 58 above) 14.

64. Vidler, op. cit. (note 1 above) 139-40.

65. Cf. Camp, op. cit. (note 58 above) 117 (on the question of 'integrism'); also Chenu, op. cit. (note 58 above) 29-30.

66. Camp, op. cit. 14.

67. *Motu proprio*, *Fin dalla prima*, 18 December 1903, *ASS* 36 (1903-4) 341. In a comment on this statement Calvez and Perrin say: 'If one did not take account of the polemical context, one could well be astonished at such a list, where natural and institutional inequalities are jumbled up together.' — see Jean-Yves Calvez and Jacques Perrin, *The Church and Social Justice: The Social Teaching of the Popes from Leo XIII to Pius XII (1878–1958)*, Chicago (Regnery: 1961) 356.

68. *Rerum Novarum* para. 35.
69. Letter on *Le Sillon*, 25 August 1910, *AAS* 2(1910) 613-33.
70. *Fin dalla prima*, *ASS* 36(1903–4) 341-2, 344. The English translation quoted is a slightly emended version of that given in *The Pope and the People: Select Letters and Addresses on Social Questions by Pope Leo XIII, Pope Pius X, Pope Benedict XV and Pope Pius XI* (1929 ed.), London (CTS: 1937 reprint) 184, 187.
71. A footnote in the English translation says tactfully that Leo's documents do not 'explicitly' state what Pius says – see ibid, 184.
72. Encyclical *Ad Beatissimi*, 1 November 1914, *AAS* 6(1914) 570-1, English translation in *The Pope and the People* (note 70 above).
73. Ibid. 571.
74. Letter to the Bishop of Bergamo, 11 March 1920, *AAS* 12(1920) 111.
75. Ibid.: 'Quapropter, si sapient, nec ad altiora quam queant attingere, frustra enitentur, et quae mala defugere non possint, ea quiete et constanter perferent in spem bonorum immortalium.'
76. *Ad Beatissimi*, *AAS* 6(1914) 571-2.
77. Ibid.; English translation taken from *The Pope and the People* (note 70 above) 208.


Chapter 3
(pp. 57-75)
1. Dated 15 May 1931, *AAS* 23(1931) 177-228; English translation: *The Social Order* London (Catholic Truth Society) and Oxford (Catholic Social Guild). A second English translation is incorporated in Raymond J. Miller, *Forty Years After: Pius XI and the Social Order: A Commentary*, St Paul, Minn. (Radio Replies Press: 1947). A third English translation is to be found in Oswald Von Nell-Breuning, *Reorganization of Social Economy: The Social Encyclical Developed and Explained* (English edition prepared by Bernard W. Dempsey), Milwaukee (Bruce: 1936) 401-42. The paragraphs are not numbered in the original Latin text but they are numbered in each of the above three translations. References to the encyclical will be given in abbreviated form by citing the number of the paragraph preceded by the initials QA. Unless otherwise stated all quotations will be from the first of the three translations mentioned above. For some background, and a contemporary commentary, see, Action Populaire, *L'Encyclique sur la Restauration le l'Ordre Social: Texte française complet, table analytique, étude doctrinale*, Paris (Éditions Spes: 1931) 81-108.
2. QA 59, 112.
3. QA 10, 88.
4. QA 112, 117-20.
5. QA 40, 117.
6. QA 105. Cf. encyclical *Divini Redemptoris*, dated 19 March 1937, *AAS* 29(1937) 65-106 (Latin text) and 107-38 (Italian text); English translation in *Twelve Encyclicals of Pius XI* (with a fore-

word by Mgr P.E. Hallett), London (C.T.S.: 1943). The original Latin text does not have the paragraphs numbered, but the paragraphs are numbered in the Italian and English texts. References will be given by citing the number of the paragraph preceded by the initials DR. The reference in this case is to DR 8. Cf. also encyclical *Caritate Christi Compulsi*, dated 3 May 1932, *AAS* 24(1932) 179: '. . . that unjust distribution of goods, the effect of which is to concentrate the wealth of the nations in the hands of a small group of private citizens who . . . regulate the markets of the world according to their choice, to the great detriment of the mass of humankind' (my translation).

7. QA 105-8.
8. QA 59.
9. QA 74. Cf. encyclical *Nova Impendat*, dated 2 October 1931, *AAS* 23(1931) 393-7.
10. Marie-Dominique Chenu, *La 'doctrine sociale' de l'Église comme idéologie*, Paris (Cerf: 1979) 35. It should be noted that the paragraph numbering system used by Chenu to refer to this encyclical is quite different to the one used in the English translations.
11. QA 77; cf. QA 97, 98, 127.
12. QA 132-5.
13. QA 125.
14. QA 137.
15. Ibid.
16. DR 61, 63, 70; also encyclical *Firmissimum* dated 29 March 1937, *AAS* 29(1937) 193; English translation in *Twelve Encyclicals of Pius XI* (note 6 above); paragraph numbers are added in this translation. The reference in this case is to para. 22.
17. QA 142.
18. Ibid.
19. DR 50.
20. DR 53.
21. Cf. Jean-Yves Calvez and Jacques Perrin, *The Church and Social Justice: The Social Teaching of the Popes from Leo XIII to Pius XII (1878–1958)*, Chicago (Regnery: 1961) 350.
22. QA 108.
23. QA 109; cf. QA 4: the open violation of justice is sometimes not merely tolerated but even ratified by legislators.
24. QA 109.
25. QA 107.
26. Cf. Miller, op. cit. (note 1 above) 233.
27. QA 88.
28. QA 110. In reference to this development of capitalism into a system where domination replaces competition, Christine E. Gudorf claims that, 'Pius XI placed the blame . . . not on any natural direction of the system of capitalism, but on the lack of moral restraint of the individuals concerned.' — See her book *Catholic Social Teaching on Liberation Themes*, Lanham (University Press of America: 1980) 10. Her remark seems to miss the point. It is true

of course that the pope blamed capitalists for lack of restraint. But his main point here is the need for some limits to be imposed on free competition; and these limits are to be not merely moral but *structural*, since they are to be imposed by public authorities. It is an uncalled-for polarisation of the issue to see it simply in terms of choosing between lack of moral restraint of individuals on the one hand and the 'natural direction of the system of capitalism' on the other.

29. QA 92-4. For the historical background see Miller, op. cit. (note 1 above) 190-7.
30. The phrase 'attentive benevolence' was used by Pius XI two weeks after he had issued *Quadragesimo Anno*, to describe its attitude to the Italian system. See address of 31 May 1931, *AAS* 23(1931) 231: '... nella Enciclica *Quadragesimo Anno* tutti hanno facilmente riconosciuto un cenno di benevola attenzione agli ordinamenti sindicali e corporativi italiani.' It may be noted here that a very different interpretation of these paragraphs is given by Oswald Von Nell-Breuning in op. cit. (note 1 above) 254-7. He sees delicate irony and under-stated criticism in the pope's references to the Italian system. Since Nell-Breuning was a principal drafter of the encyclical, his interpretation must be taken seriously; but in this case it would seem that his own antipathy to corporatism has led him to read more of his own views into the text than is apparent to others.
31. QA 82.
32. QA 86.
33. QA 74.
34. QA 79.
35. QA 30, 34, 35, 87. For background information on the development of trade unions see Henry Somerville, *Studies in the Catholic Social Movement*, London (Burns Oates and Washbourne: 1933).
36. QA 30-1; DR 50.
37. QA 30, 34.
38. QA 31 — he says socialist unions are not the *sole* defenders ...
39. QA 33 — through the unions, workers 'learned to defend their temporal rights and interests energetically and efficiently, retaining at the same time a due respect for justice ...'
40. QA 82-5.
41. QA 85.
42. QA 81-3; *Rerum Novarum* 15, 35, 41.
43. QA 83-4; *Rerum Novarum* 15.
44. QA 82.
45. QA 83.
46. QA 85.
47. QA 86.
48. QA 88.
49. I cannot then agree with the view of Villain who maintains that the Church 'does not condemn the principles of capitalism but condemns the liberalism which in fact has vitiated the working and evolution

of capitalism, and consequently condemns "actual" capitalism.' (my translation) — Jean Villain, *L'enseignement social de l'Église, I: Introduction, capitalisme et socialisme*, Paris (Spes: 1953) 233. The distinction between the principles of capitalism on the one hand and economic liberalism on the other is so strained that it has little meaning. It can only be sustained by taking capitalism in the attenuated and incorrect sense which I shall outline in the following paragraph.

50. A rather similar distinction between two meanings of capitalism, and a similar conclusion about the attitude of Pius XI may be found in John A. Ryan, *A Better Economic Order*, New York (Harper: 1935) 181.

51. QA 100-1.

52. QA 88 — Miller translation, op. cit. (note 1 above) 179.

53. Cf. Richard L. Camp, *The Papal Ideology of Social Reform: A Study in Historical Development 1878–1967*, Leiden (E.J. Brill: 1969) 65, 97.

54. See especially QA 61-90.

55. QA 95.

56. Camp, op. cit. (note 53 above) 40.

57. QA 41.

58. QA 42. The C.T.S. translation of the Latin phrases '*oeconomica res*' and '*moralis disciplina*' gives 'economic life' and 'moral conduct' respectively; for the translation used in the text I have taken the Von Nell-Breuning rendering of the first term and the Miller version of the second term — see Von Nell-Breuning, op. cit. (note 1 above) 77 and Miller, op. cit. (note 1 above) 42.

59. Camp, op. cit. (note 53 above) 40.

60. QA 42.

61. QA 41 — Latin text, '*quae artis sunt*'; C.T.S. translation, 'in matters of technique'.

62. Cf. QA 7, 8, 41, 117, 122.

63. See, for instance, Von Nell-Breuning, op. cit. (note 1 above) 219-32, 256.

64. Even the nicely balanced and non-controversial treatment given by John A. Ryan seems to presuppose that the pope had 'the answer'; see op. cit. (note 50 above) 178-84.

65. QA 105-9.

66. QA 78, 97; *Rerum Novarum* 2.

67. QA 112.

68. *Mit brennender Sorge*, dated 14 March 1937, *AAS* 29(1937) 143-67; English translation in *Twelve Encyclicals of Pius XI* (note 6 above); the English text has the paragraphs numbered; the reference here is to para. 33.

69. Ibid. paras. 41, 42, 47.

70. DR (note 6 above).

71. DR 30.

72. DR 33.

73. See note 16 above. This encyclical is also known as *No es muy*.

74. *Firmissimum* para. 35. It may be noted that in this passage the pope is recounting the teaching of the Mexican bishops; but he leaves no room for doubt about his own acceptance and approval of this teaching. It should also be noted that when Pius XI makes use here of the phrase 'by lawful and appropriate means' ('licita atque idonea auxilia adhibentes' — *AAS* 29(1937) 193) the context makes it quite clear that he is not leaving it to the oppressive regime itself to define what is 'lawful' or 'unlawful'; otherwise his remarks would be pointless. It is precisely at this point that Pius XI goes further than the position of Leo XIII outlined in the previous chapter.

75. Ibid. para. 36.

76. Ibid. paras. 34, 36.

77. For a brief account of some of the earlier skirmishes (political and military) between the socialist government and Catholic resisters see, Anthony Rhodes, *The Vatican in the Age of the Dictators 1922—45*, London (Hodder and Stoughton: 1973) 94-102.

78. DR 19.

79. E.g. DR 21.

80. Cf. René Coste, 'Le problème de la légitimité de principe de la guerre révolutionnaire', in Pierre Marie Theas et al., *Guerre révolutionnaire et conscience chrétienne*, Paris (Pax Christi: 1963) 200-1.


Chapter 4
(pp. 76-86)

1. Cf. Christmas Message, 23 December 1950, *AAS* 43(1951) 55-9. Part Three is concerned with internal peace while Part Four deals with peace between peoples. The former treats of some economic issues while the latter refers mostly to political rather than economic matters.

2. Christmas Address, 24 December 1939, *AAS* 32(1940) 6-13; Christmas Radio Message, 24 December 1941, *AAS* 34(1942) 10-21; Christmas Radio Message, 24 December 1942, *AAS* 35(1943) 9-24; Christmas Radio Message, 24 December 1943, *AAS* 36(1944) 11-24; Christmas Radio Message, 24 December 1944, *AAS* 37(1945) 10-23.

3. *AAS* 37(1945) 10-23. An English translation is available in Pius XII, *Selected Letters and Addresses of Pius XII*, London (CTS: 1949) 299-318.

4. Ibid. para. 9.

5. Ibid. para. 41: 'If the future is destined to belong to democracy . . .'

6. Ibid. para. 6.

7. Ibid. para. 12.

8. Ibid. para. 8. Cf. Joseph N. Moody, *Church and Society: Catholic Social and Political Thought and Movements 1789—1950*, New York (Arts Inc.: 1953) 71: 'While the attitude of neutrality to the various forms of government still stands, there is evident a pronounced papal benevolence toward the active participation of all

citizens in government and a strong rejection of absolutism in all its forms.' It is clear that democracy as such was by no means an absolute for the pope; what he was concerned about was the needs of a healthy community. These, he said, can also be met under other legitimate forms of government — see Address of 2 October 1945, *AAS* 37(1945) 258.

9. See the addresses given in January of the years 1942, 1945, 1946, 1947, 1949, and 1952 which are given in French translation in Alain Savignat (ed.), *Relations humaines et société contemporaine: synthèse. chrétienne directives de S.S. Pie XII*, Fribourg (St Paul: 1956), II 1575-1607 (paras. 3308-74). (Savignat's compilation is an expanded version of the one done by Utz and Groner.)

10. Ibid. II, 1603 (January 1947).

11. Ibid. II, 1605 (January 1952).

12. Ibid. II, 1586 (January 1945).

13. Ibid. II, 1595-6 (January 1946).

14. For instance, Pius XII in his Christmas Radio Message 1954, *AAS* 47(1955) 25, when speaking of the possibility of coexistence, finds no solid basis for it in the communist system, since he sees this as a system completely detached from the base provided by natural law. The implications of such a judgment are far-reaching: it could be concluded that a communist regime lacks the moral authority to command its citizens and is incapable of entering into morally binding international agreements. It is not a mere flight of fancy to suggest that such conclusions could be drawn. See, for instance, the following statement made by the well-known moralist Jacques Leclercq in *Leçons de droit naturel: II, L'État ou la politique* (2nd ed.), Namur (Wesmael-Charlier: 1934) 182: '. . . le gouvernement bolchevique fonde toute sa politique sur une philosophie qui va a l'encontre des exigences de la nature humaine. Il ne peut être légitime . . .'

15. Cf. Richard L. Camp, *The Papal Ideology of Social Reform: A Study in Historical Development 1878–1967*, Leiden (E.J. Brill: 1969) 40.

16. Radio Message of 14 September 1952, *AAS* 44(1952) 791-2: '. . . die Not des Prolitariats unt die Aufgabe, diese den Zufälligheiten der wirtschaftlichen Konjuktur schutzlos preisgegebene Menschenklasse emporzuheben zu einem den anderen gleichgeachteten Stand mit klar umschribenen Rechten. Diese Aufgabe ist, jedenfalls im Wesentlichen, gelöst . . .'; cf. Christmas Message of 1954, *AAS* 47 (1955) 20.

17. Camp, op. cit. (note 15 above), 104.

18. Radio Message *La sollenità della Pentecoste* 1 June 1941, *AAS* 33(1941) 198.

19. E.g. Radio Message 1 September 1944, *AAS* 36(1944) 252-3; Address 15 November 1946, *AAS* 38(1946) 435-6; Christmas Radio Message, 1942, *AAS* 35(1943) 16-7.

20. *La sollenità della Pentecoste* 1 June 1941, *AAS* 33(1941) 195-205 (Italian text), 216-27 (English text).

21. Cf. Christmas Message 1942, *AAS* 35(1943) 11; and Address of 1 November 1947 quoted in Savignat, op. cit. (note 9 above) II, 1774 (para. 3715).

22. Radio Message of 14 September 1952, *AAS* 44(1952) 792: 'Die Überwindung des Klassenkampfes durch ein organisches Zueinanderordnen des Arbeitgebers und Arbeitnehmers.'

23. Letter to Charles Flory 14 July 1954, in Savignat, op. cit. (note 9 above), II, 1748 (para. 3674).

24. Ibid.

25. Address of 7 May 1949, *AAS* 41(1949) 284.

26. Ibid. 285.

27. E.g. Christmas Message of 1942, *AAS* 35(1943) 5-24.

28. Ibid. 17: 'Che questa servitù derivi dal prepotere del capitale privato o dal potere dello Stato, l'effetto non muta . . .'; cf. Radio Message of 1 July 1944, *AAS* 36(1944) 252-3.

29. E.g. Address of 3 June 1950, *AAS* 42(1950) 487.

30. Christmas Radio Message, 1952, *AAS* 45(1953) 42.

31. *La sollenità della Pentecoste* (note 20 above).

32. Ibid. 200. This need for stability is only adverted to briefly on this occasion but the pope developed it more fully later. See Christmas Message 1942, *AAS* 35(1943) 13; also Address of 17 February 1956, *L'Osservatore Romano* 18 February 1956.

33. *La sollenità della Pentecoste* 200-1.

34. Ibid. 198-9. Pius XII had already made a more brief and vague statement on this question in the final section of his encyclical *Sertum Laetitiae* of 1 November 1939, *AAS* 31(1939) 642, where he said that the goods of the earth have been created by God for all people and the basic point of the social question was that they should be equitably shared out with justice as the guide and charity as the support. In his radio message, however, his teaching is much more specific. See, for instance, *AAS* 33(1941) 199 (English text 221): 'Undoubtedly the natural order, deriving from God, demands also private property. . . But all this remains subordinated to the natural scope of material goods and cannot emancipate itself from the first and fundamental right which concedes their use to all men; but it should rather serve to make possible the actuation of this right in conformity with its scope.'

35. *Rerum Novarum* para. 19; *Quadragesimo Anno* paras. 45-6.

36. Address of 7 May 1949, *AAS* 41(1949) 284.

37. Address of 31 January 1952, in Savignat, op. cit. (note 9 above), II, 1670 (para. 3507); cf. Address of 3 June 1950, *AAS* 42(1950) 487.

38. Address of 13 June 1943, *AAS* 35(1943) 175.

Chapter 5.
(pp. 87-116)

1. *Mater et Magistra*, dated 15 March 1961 but actually issued just two months later. *AAS* 53(1961) 401-64. There are at least five

English versions, of which the most widely used at present seems to be that of W.J. Gibbons for the Paulist Press. This text is available in Joseph Gremillion (ed.), *The Gospel of Peace and Justice: Catholic Social Teaching Since Pope John*, Maryknoll (Orbis: 1976) 141-200; also in David J. O'Brien and Tnomas A. Shannon (ed.), *Renewing the Earth: Catholic Documents on Peace, Justice and Liberation*, Garden City (Doubleday Image: 1977) 50-123. J.R. Kirwan made an interesting translation which often succeeds in expressing the underlying meaning of the text much better than the other versions, but is occasionally unacceptable. It can be found together with some helpful comments by Kirwan, in the the *The Social Thought of John XXIII*, Oxford (Catholic Social Guild: 1964). A very careful French translation is to be found in Paul-Emile Bolté, *Mater et Magistra: texte latin, nouvelle traduction, index and analytique*, Montréal (Univ. de Montréal: 1968). As a companion to his translation, Bolté has produced a four-volume commentary on the text: Paul-Emile Bolté, *Mater et Magistra, commentaire*, Vol. I 1964, Vol. II 1966, Vol. III 1967, Vol. IV 1968, Montréal (Univ. de Montréal). References to the text of *Mater et Magistra* will be given by citing the paragraph number preceded by the initials MM.

2. *Pacem in Terris*, dated 11 April 1963, *AAS* 55(1963) 257-304. There are a number of English versions, some of which differ from each other only in minor respects. The easiest to read is that of Henry O. Waterhouse, available in *The Social Thought of John XXIII*, Oxford (Catholic Social Guild: 1964); but it seems rather less accurate in some important places than the version of Donald R. Campion available in Joseph Gremillion (ed.), *The Gospel of Peace and Justice . . .*, (see note 1 above) 201-41. References to the text of *Pacem in Terris* will be given by citing the paragraph number preceded by the initials PT.

3. See Raymond Williams, *Keywords: A Vocabulary of Culture and Society*, Glasgow (Collins Fontana: 1976) 209-11; cf. Joe Holland and Peter Henriot, *Social Analysis: Linking Faith and Justice*, Washington D.C. (Center of Concern: 1980) 13-9.

4. PT 161-2 (Waterhouse version, adapted).

5. Cf. John F. Cronin, 'A Commentary on *Mater et Magistra*' in John XXIII, *The Encyclicals and Other Messages of John XXIII*, Washington D.C. (T.P.S. Press: 1964) 242.

6. MM 107.

7. MM 149.

8. PT 150 (Campion version).

9. PT 152 (Campion version).

10. PT 46.

11. PT 47.

12. PT 49.

13. PT 51, 61.

14. PT 84.

15. PT 104 (Campion version).

16. PT 52.

17. MM 155-65, 170-7; PT 80-145.
18. PT 156 (Campion version).
19. MM 62. Bolté makes the interesting suggestion that the 'negandum' of the Latin text should be translated not as 'it will not happen' but as 'it must be resisted' i.e. not allowed to happen. This translation would certainly fit in better with what the pope says in the following two paragraphs; but neither the Italian text nor the letter of the Holy See to the French Social Week (the text of which seems to have been the original source for the passage in the encyclical) is open to this interpretation; see Bolté's commentary referred to in note 1 above, I, 289.
20. MM 67.
21. MM 68. See Bolté, op. cit. II, 376-7 for the nuances of the translation.
22. MM 163; cf. MM 154 which speaks of primitive and obsolete methods of agriculture.
23. MM 124-5.
24. MM 154.
25. MM 104, 118.
26. MM 198, 69, 204; PT 109.
27. MM 69.
28. On 'development' in relation to capitalism and socialism see Jean-Yves Calvez, *The Social Thought of John XXIII: Mater et Magistra*, London (Burns and Oates: 1964) 64-6.
29. PT 159. The translation of the passage is itself a matter of controversy. I have taken the phrase 'false philosophical theories' from the Waterhouse version since it is clearer than the Campion version which uses the word 'teachings' instead of 'theories'. But I have used the phrase 'historical movements' from the Campion version in preference to Waterhouse's vague phrase 'practical measures'. The translations into other European languages speak of 'movements' (see Bolté, op. cit. II, 613); and the latter part of the paragraph clearly refers to developments within such movements.
30. Cf. Arthur Fridolin Utz, *Die Friedensenzyklika Papst Johannes XXIII: Pacem in Terris*, Freiburg (Herder: 1963) 136, note 47; Jeremiah Newman, *Principles of Peace*, Oxford (Catholic Social Guild: 1964) 199-201. The following remark by Cronin sums up the position: 'It is widely held that they apply to contacts with the Communist world. . . But the principles as given in the encyclical are general in nature, and we cannot quarrel with those who also see in them reference to anti-clerical movements in Europe and Latin America, or the "opening to the left" in Italian politics, Spanish fascism or any similar accommodation with historic antagonists.' — John F. Cronin, 'A Commentary on *Pacem in Terris*' in John XXIII, *The Encyclicals and Other Messages of John XXIII* Washington D.C. (T.P.S. Press: 1964) 325.
31. *Ad Petri Cathedram*, 29 June 1959, *AAS* 51(1959) 497-531. English text in John XXIII, *The Encyclicals* . . . (note 30 above) 33; cf. MM 48.
32. Ibid.

33. MM 115.
34. Cf. Harold Brookfield, *Interdependent Development*, London (Metheun: 1975) 38.
35. MM 113-14.
36. MM 115.
37. MM 73-4.
38. MM 74 (my translation, with emphasis added). The sentence quoted is not a direct quotation from Pius XII but a summary of an important part of a radio message he gave — see Pius XII, *La solennità della Pentecoste*, 1 June 1941, *AAS* 33(1941) 200-1.
39. MM 115 (Gibbons version).
40. See Chapter Ten below — especially the treatment of *Redemptor Hominis*.
41. Richard L. Camp, *The Papal Ideology of Social Reform: A Study in Historical Development 1878–1967*, Leiden (E.J. Brill: 1969) 159.
42. Ibid. 160.
43. *Quadragesimo Anno*, paras. 91-7.
44. Bolté, op. cit. II, 321-5. (Note that Bolté's numbering of the paragraphs of *Quadragesimo Anno* differs from that of the English text.)
45. John F. Cronin, 'Significance of John XXIII' in Benjamin L. Masse (ed.), *The Church and Social Progress: Background Readings for Pope John's Mater et Magristra*, Milwaukee (Bruce: 1966) 44.
46. MM 124, 150, 154, 157-74, 185; PT 88, 95, 96, 101, 103-7, 121-5.
47. MM 59-60 (my translation). For the nuances of meaning see Bolté, op. cit. I, 231-57; cf. the note by J.R. Kirwan to his translation in *The Social Thought of John XXIII* (note 1 above) 90-3; and publisher's note, ibid., (v); cf. also Jean-Yves Calvez, op. cit (note 28 above), publisher's note, (v)-(vi), and 102, footnote 13 to Chapter I. In the English version given above I have translated *ius privatum* as 'contractual law' in order to give some approximation to what the pope has in mind — see Bolté, op. cit. I, 247-8.
48. '*Socialium rationum incrementa*'; equivalent Latin phrases are used in each of the paragraphs from 59-67 inclusive; in each of these nine cases the Italian text uses '*socializzazzione*'. Many translations in other European languages used words equivalent to the Italian word; but one authoritative German version and Bolté's later, careful, French text gave a more literal translation of the Latin.
49. The Gibbons version speaks of 'the multiplication of social relationships'; that of Kirwan gives 'the development of the network of social relationships'.
50. Kirwan sees it as quite significant that the official Latin text 'rejected the term' (op. cit. 92); Bolté (op. cit. I, 241) inclines to the opposite view — that the reason the word was omitted was simply to avoid a Latin neologism.
51. See Address of 11 March 1945, *AAS* 37(1945) 68-72; and radio message to Austrian *Katholikentag* 14 Sept 1952, *AAS* 44(1952) 792.

52. Cf. John F. Cronin, 'Significance of John XXIII' (note 45 above) 44.
53. MM 62.
54. MM 60.
55. MM 62.
56. Calvez, op. cit. (note 28 above) 8-9.
57. MM 63; cf. Calvez, op. cit. (note 28 above) 14: 'Socialisation has no meaning in reality save as . . . a "should" of personal freedom.'
58. MM 53, 117, 152.
59. MM 65. J.R. Kirwan, op. cit. (note 1 above) 93-4, points out that the terms used echo those of *Quadragesimo Anno*. For a careful study of the relationship between the words used in the two encyclicals see Bolté, op. cit. I, 317-25.
60. MM 117, 152.
61. *Quadragesimo Anno*, para. 65.
62. Pius XII, Address of 3 June 1950, *AAS* 42(1950) 487.
63. MM 75.
64. MM 92-3, 97.
65. MM 97.
66. MM 104.
67. MM 116-7.
68. MM 120.
69. MM 128-41.
70. MM 133.
71. MM 134.
72. MM 135.
73. MM 136.
74. MM 137.
75. MM 140.
76. MM 141.
77. Bolté's very comprehensive study at times gives the impression that his discovery of such parallels has led him to play down the difference in approach between Pius XII and John XXIII; for instance, on the question of 'socialisation', op. cit. I, 246.
78. MM 51, 55.
79. MM 109.
80. MM 65.
81. PT 62 (Campion version).
82. PT 65. The Campion text quoted here is preferable to the Waterhouse version which does not bring out the contrast in the first sentence (Latin: *'tum . . . tum'*).
83. MM 119 (my translation). The phrase *'munus . . . sociale'* is very difficult to translate accurately. Kirwan gives 'social function' and the Italian and French texts use a corresponding phrase. But in English this is too vague. The Gibbons text gives 'social responsibility'; this is excellent except that it only conveys one of the two aspects of the meaning of *'munus'*. I have added 'role' to express the second aspect.
84. *Rerum Novarum*, para. 19.
85. *Quadragesimo Anno*, para. 45.

86. *La solennità della Pentecoste, AAS* 33(1941) 198-9.
87. See notes 29 and 30 above. It has been noted that Pope John's 'opening to the left' was actually a belated response of the Vatican to the overtures of the Italian Communist Party, led by Gramsci and Togliatti — see Carl Marzani, 'The Vatican as a Left Ally?', in *Monthly Review*, July/August 1982, 14-6.
88. MM 135. See also the details referred to in notes 70-6 above.
89. MM title.
90. Bolté, op. cit. I, 245-6.
91. E.g. M.-D. Chenu, *La 'doctrine sociale' de l'Église comme idéologie*, Paris (Cerf: 1979). This issue will be discussed below, in Chapter Ten.


Chapter 6
(pp. 117-138)
1. In his study of papal teaching Camp does not include any serious study of the teachings of Vatican II; see Richard L. Camp, *The Papal Ideology of Social Reform: A Study in Historical Development 1879–1967*, Leiden (Brill: 1969).
2. *Nuntius ad Universos Homines Summo Pontifice Assentiente a Patribus Missus Ineunte Concilio Oecumenico Vaticano II, AAS* 54(1962) 823-4; English translation in Joseph Gremillion (ed.), *The Gospel of Peace and Justice: Catholic Social Teaching since Pope John*, Maryknoll (Orbis: 1976), 353. For background information on this document see Marie-Dominique Chenu, 'Le Message au monde des Pères conciliaires (octobre 1962)', in Yves M-J Congar et M. Peuchmaurd (ed.), *L'Église dans le monde de ce temps: Constitution pastoral 'Gaudium et Spes': Tome III, Réflexions et perspectives* (Unam Sanctam, 65c), Paris (Cerf: 1967), 191-3.
3. See Willem J. Schuijt's history of the text in Herbert Vorgrimmler (ed.), *Commentary on the Documents of Vatican II*, Vol. 5, London (Burns and Oates: 1969) and New York (Herder and Herder: 1969), 339.
4. Bishops from dioceses in Asia, Africa, and Latin America constituted about 40 per cent of the bishops at the Council — see Roger Aubert et al, *The Christian Centuries, Vol. 5: The Church in a Secularized Society*, London (Darton, Longman and Todd: 1978) and New York (Paulist: 1978), 627-8.
5. E.g. *Gaudium et Spes* 69.2, 70. In footnote references in the remainder of the chapter the initials GS will be used to designate *Gaudium et Spes*. The numbers indicate the paragraph and, where relevant, the sub-paragraph, as given in the Latin text. For the Latin text see *AAS* 58(1966), 1025-1115. There are three English translations in common circulation. They are to be found in the following three collections: Walter M. Abbott (ed.), *The Documents of Vatican II*, New York (America Press: 1966) and London/Dublin (Chapman: 1966) 199-308; J.L. Gonzalez and the Daughters of St Paul, *The Sixteen Documents of Vatican II*, Boston (St Paul

Editions: n.d.) 513-624; Austin Flannery (ed.), *Vatican Council II: The Conciliar and Post Conciliar Documents*, Northport, New York (Costello: 1975, 1977) 903-1001. The second of these almost always follows the sub-paragraphing of the Latin text; the third does so in most cases; the first does not do so. In quoting in English from GS, I shall make use of whichever of the available translations seems most accurate for the particular passage; on some occasions, in the interests of accuracy, I shall adapt the translation or give my own translation of the text.

6. For the names on the various committees see Charles Moeller's history of the text in Vorgrimmler, op. cit. (note 3 above), 21, 39, 40, 49, 63.

7. GS 53-62, 64-5; there seems to be a patronising tone in GS 69.2 — customs may be useful if brought up to date. Even during the Council, drafts of GS were criticised as being too Western in outlook — e.g. intervention by Bishop James Corboy from Zambia in *Acta Synodalia Sacrosancti Concilii Oecumenici Vaticani II*, Vol. III, Pars V, Roma (Vatican Press: 1975) 625-6.

8. E.g. GS 69.2, 71, 86.

9. Cf. René Coste's commentary in Vorgrimmler op. cit. (note 3 above) 368.

10. For instance GS follows *Mater et Magistra* in what it says about the process of socialisation (GS 6, 23.1, 25.2, 75.3) — and in 75.3 the official Latin text includes the word *socializatio*, in contrast to the Latin text of Pope John's encyclical. *Pacem in Terris* was issued while GS was being drafted, so on the more practical aspects of the question of peace and war the authors of GS could add little to it; they did however offer a richer theology of peace as we shall note later.

11. E.g. GS 63.3: economic progress can lead to contempt for the poor.

12. *Dignitatis Humanae*, *AAS* 58(1966), 929-41.

13. Especially GS 78.

14. GS 33-9, 67.

15. GS 74.

16. GS 40-4.

17. GS 25-32, 63-72, 85-90.

18. GS 53-62.

19. E.g. GS 78 on peace; GS 34, 37, 39, 57 on work.

20. GS 57, 72.

21. GS 78.1.

22. Ibid.: '. . . the fruit of that right ordering of things with which the divine founder has invested human society . . .' (Flannery translation).

23. Ibid.: '. . . the achievement of peace requires . . . unceasing vigilance . . .' (Flannery translation).

24. Ibid.: '. . . the common good of mankind . . . depends . . . upon circumstances which change as time goes on; consequently, peace will never be achieved once and for all, but must be built up continually.' (Flannery translation).

25. GS 83-7.
26. Pius XII, *La solennità della Pentecoste*, 1 June 1941, *AAS* 33(1941) 200-1; John XXIII, *Mater et Magistra*, para. 74, 161; for references to two addresses in which Pope John mentions the point see Paul-Emile Bolté, *Mater et Magistra, commentaire*, III, Montréal (Univ. de Montréal: 1967) 899-90.
27. GS 69.1 (Abbot translation, slightly emended).
28. Cf. Jean-Yves Calvez's remarks in Vol. II of the Cerf commentary on GS (referred to in note 2 above) 502.
29. GS 85.2.
30. GS 85.3 (my translation).
31. GS 86.6. The following statement by Gamani Corea, Secretary-General of the United Nations Conference on Trade and Development (UNCTAD), will indicate the close correspondence between what GS asked for and the NIEO concept: 'The theme of structural change is one of the crucial concepts of the New International Economic Order. It signifies the conviction of the developing countries that the development process ... requires ... changes in some of the prevailing mechanisms and systems that govern international economic relations.' — *Restructuring the international economic framework: Report by the Secretary-General of the United Nations Conference on Trade and Development to the fifth session of the Conference*, New York (United Nations: 1980), 2.
32. GS 26.1.
33. GS 63.5: '... reformationes multae in vita oeconomica-sociali atque mentis et habitudinis conversio ab omnibus requiruntur.' The Italian translation brings out the fact that what is in question is structural reform: 'si richiedono molte riforme nelle strutture della vita economico-sociale ...' Enrico Chiavacci understands the Council to be calling for a fundamental reform of the economic system; see his *La costituzione pastorale sulla Chiesa nel mondo contemporaneo: Gaudium et Spes*, Roma (Studium: 1967), 314.
34. In his commentary on this part of GS, L.J. Lebret is rather more specific; he maintains that reform of international trade requires reform of the structures of production, of the monetary systems, and of the economic regimes which actually are in force at present — see H. de Riedmatten et al, *La Chiesa nel mondo contemporaneo: commento alla costituzione pastorale: 'Gaudium et Spes'*, Brescia (Queriniana: 1966), 224.
35. GS 86.7 (my translation).
36. The Abbott version speaks of the need for a 'reform' of the structures while the St Paul version uses the verb 'revamp'; the Flannery version is more accurate here since it uses the word 'reassess' to translate the Latin *'recognoscendi'*. The Italian text has *'una revisione'*. The French text speaks of a 'recasting' (*'une refonte'*); this was probably the working text of the drafting group; but the toning down of the phrase in the Latin text (which is of course the official one) is hardly accidental.
37. GS 86.7 (my translation).

297

38. GS 69.1.
39. GS 29.3 (my translation).
40. GS 71.6: '. . . *ut distribuantur fundi non satis exculti* . . .'.
41. It may be noted that this vagueness is to be found not merely in the text but also in some of the commentaries on it. For instance the lengthy commentary by Augustino Ferrari Toniolo on this section of GS does little more than repeat the words of the document itself, when treating of this delicate issue — see his commentary in E. Guano et al, *La costituzione pastorale sulla Chiesa nel mondo contemporaneo: introduzione storico-dottrinale; testo latino e traduzione italiano; esposizione e commento*, Torino-Leamann (Elle di Ci: 1966), 984-5.
42. Lebret, art. cit. (note 34 above), 228-9.
43. GS 69.1 (Abbott translation).
44. Cf. Jean-Yves Calvez's comments in Vol. II of the Cerf commentary (note 2 above), 503; also Ermenegildo Lio, 'Povertà (Theol morale)', in Salvatore Garofalo (ed.), *Dizionario del Concilio Ecumenico Vaticano Secondo*, Roma (Vatican Press: 1969), col. 1646.
45. *Rerum Novarum*, para. 19.
46. *Quadragesimo Anno*, paras. 50-1.
47. E.g. Raymond J. Miller, *Forty Years After: Pius XI and the Social Order: A Commentary*, St Paul, Minn. (Radio Replies Press: 1947), 91.
48. GS 69.1.
49. In *Quadragesimo Anno*, para. 51, the only proviso made by Pius XI is that the work should be devoted to the production of really useful goods.
50. GS 65.3 insists that the common good is seriously threatened by those who hoard their wealth unproductively. Other statements in favour of investment can be found in GS 70 and 85.2.
51. Pius XII, *La solennità della Pentecoste, AAS* 33(1941), 199.
52. GS 69.1, 85.1.
53. GS 83.
54. GS 69.1.
55. GS 80.4.
56. GS 79.4. Originally it was proposed to insert in the text of GS the passage in Pope John's *Pacem in Terris* (para. 127) which states that it is unreasonable to hold that war can any longer be seen as a means to obtain justice for violated rights. But difficulties and objections led to the passage being relegated to a footnote (at GS 80.3). On this point see the remarks of D. Dubarle in Vol. II of the Cerf commentary (referred to in note 2 above), 581, footnote 11. This change was obviously significant. So too was the fact that the footnote is appended to a passage in which the Council is condemning *total* war. In this way the authors of GS imply that Pope John was outlawing only total war, not all kinds of war; and there is some basis for this interpretation since the relevant passage in *Pacem in Terris* includes a reference to atomic weapons.

57. Alfred de Soras, *International Morality (Faith and Fact Books, No. 58)*, London (Burns and Oates: 1963) 87, 95. (This is a translation from a French original published a little earlier.)

58. Cf. comment by D. Dubarle in de Riedmatten, op. cit. (note 34 above), 276-9; comment again by D. Dubarle in Vol. II of the Cerf commentary (note 2 above), 582; comment by Raimondo Sigmond in E. Guano et al, op. cit. (note 41 above), 1087-8.

59. Cf. D. Dubarle in Vol. II of the Cerf commentary (note 2 above), 581-2.

60. GS 78.5. A proviso is added: 'so long as there is no injury to the rights and duties of others or of the community' (my translation).

61. GS 79.3: 'It seems proper (*aequum videtur*) that the law should make humane provision for those who for reasons of conscience refuse to bear arms . . .' (my translation). This way of expressing the point allowed the Council to by-pass the question of the correctness of such a conscientious judgment.

62. GS 78.5.

63. GS 74.

64. GS 74.5.

65. GS 32.2 (my translation).

66. *AAS* 54(1962), 823; English translation in Gremillion, op. cit. (note 2 above), 353. Note that in GS 1 there is a certain sense of solidarity with the poor: 'The joy and hope, the grief and anguish of the people of our time, *especially of those who are poor or afflicted in any way*, are the joy and hope, the grief and anguish of the followers of Christ as well.' (Flannery translation, emended slightly and emphasis added). But this sense of solidarity is not very evident later in the document.

67. *Perfectae Caritatis, AAS* 58(1966), 708 (para. 13).

68. Apostolic Exhortation *Evangelica Testificatio*, 29 June 1971, *AAS* 63(1971) 506-7 (paras. 17-18) — English text in Flannery, op. cit. (note 5 above) 688-9.

69. GS 65-71, 85-8.

70. GS 72.1 (my translation). This passage may have been influenced by Paul VI's first encyclical, *Ecclesiam Suam* (6 August 1964), which had emphasised the spirit of poverty — see *AAS* 56(1964), 634-5. Various documents of Vatican II refer to the need for Christians to follow Christ who became poor for our sake and came to bring good news to the poor, e.g. *Lumen Gentium*, *AAS* 57(1965), 12, 45-7 (paras. 8, 41); *Apostolicam Actuositatem*, *AAS* 58(1966), 841 (para. 4); *Perfectae Caritatis*, ibid. 702, 708 (paras. 1, 13); *Ad Gentes*, ibid. 949, 952 (paras. 3, 5); *Presbyterorum Ordinis*, 1018 (para. 17). But none of these documents offers a developed spirituality of poverty which integrates the christological and evangelical aspects with the economic and social reality.

71. GS 21. The clear recognition by the Council of the pluralist character of modern society was recognised as a significant change. See, for instance, the following statement by a Church represen-

299

tative at the International Labour Office (ILO): 'The impact of the Council from the point of view of society springs from the fact that in it the Church sketched the guiding lines along which it reckons to be able to play its part in a pluralistic society and that it called on its members to accept the rules laid down. The Church's message and mission remain unaltered, but the framework within which it has to deliver the one and accomplish the other has changed.' – J. Joblin, '"The Church in the World": a Contribution to Pluralism', reprinted from the *International Labour Review*, Vol. 93, No. 5, May 1966, Geneva (ILO: 1966), 20.

72. GS 92. In this paragraph there are obvious echoes of the passage about dialogue at a variety of levels, in Pope Paul's encyclical *Ecclesiam Suam*, *AAS* 56(1964), 654-9.

73. GS 40-5.

74. GS 40.3.

75. GS 41.3.

76. GS 42.2.

77. GS 76.

78. GS 76.5 (my translation). In his commentary on this part of GS, Giuseppe Mattai calls this a truly fundamental proposition; but unfortunately he does little to explain its importance – see his commentary in E. Guano et al, op. cit. (note 41 above), 1049. Oswald von Nell-Breuning sees this relinquishment of privilege as the culmination of this chapter of GS and as a major challenge to the Church – a cheque that must be honoured – see his commentary in Vorgrimmler, op. cit. (note 3 above), 326-7.


Chapter 7
(pp. 139-56)

1. Cf. Marie-Dominique Chenu, La *'doctrine sociale' de l'Église comme idéologie* Paris (Cerf: 1979) 75.

2. *Populorum Progressio*, 26 March 1967, *AAS* 59(1967) 257-99, para. 3; English translation of Vatican Polyglot Press in Joseph Gremillion (ed.), *The Gospel of Justice and Peace: Catholic Social Teaching since Pope John*, Maryknoll (Orbis: 1976) 387-415; also David J. O'Brien and Thomas A. Shannon (ed.), *Renewing the Earth: Catholic Documents on Peace, Justice and Liberation*, Garden City (Image Doubleday: 1977) 313-51. A slightly different (and better) version of this translation is in *Encyclical Letter of his Holiness Pope Paul VI: On the Development of Peoples* (with commentary by Barbara Ward), New York (Paulist: 1967) – and quotations from the encyclical in English will be taken from this last text except in cases where I consider it necessary to give my own translation from the Latin. References to *Populorum Progressio* in the remainder of this chapter will be given by using the abbreviation PP followed by the number of the paragraph.

3. PP 7-9, 52, 56-8.

4. PP 7.

5. Cf. Vincent Cosmao, *Dossier: nouvel ordre mondial; les chrétiens provoqués par le développement*, (Chalet: 1978) 51: '... ce que nous appelons le sous-développement s'explique en effet, bien plus fondamentalement, par un *processus de déstructuration des sociétés polarisées par la société dominante en expansion*' (emphasis in the original); cf. Vincent Cosmao, *Changer le monde: une tâche pour l'Église*, Paris (Cerf: 1979) 44-8. For a historical account of how this process took place over several centuries see Leften Stavros Stavrianos, *Global Rift: The Third World Comes of Age*, New York (Morrow: 1981).

6. See for instance, Charles Elliot, *Patterns of Poverty in the Third World: A Study of Social and Economic Stratification*, New York (Praeger: 1975), 228-76; also Michael P. Todaro, *Economic Development in the Third World: An introduction to problems and policies in a global perspective*, London (Longman: 1977), 235-65. Both of these authors show how Western schooling is used to reinforce the gap between the rich and the poor and has other damaging effects on the economic and social structures of poor countries.

7. PP 7; cf. PP 57.

8. PP 52.

9. PP 9.

10. PP 57-60.

11. PP 57.

12. In PP 48, however, there is reference to 'the gifts that providence has bestowed' on a country; this phrase, coupled with the general tone of the paragraph, could give the impression that the pope sanctions the view that the so-called 'underdeveloped' countries have been given less of such resource gifts; although this may be true about some individual countries it cannot be said of the poorer countries as a whole; in fact it is a myth which people in the First World often cling to — perhaps to avoid the implications about the past exploitation and present injustice that have to be drawn once the myth is challenged.

13. PP 29.

14. PP 32. The standard English translation, 'innovations that go deep', does not do justice to the Latin phrase *'rerum forma penitus renovetur'*.

15. PP 58.

16. PP 59.

17. PP 61.

18. PP 60-1.

19. Barbara Ward, 'Looking back on *Populorum Progressio*', in *Doctrine and Life* 29(1978), 202.

20. Chenu, op. cit. (note 1 above) 72.

21. One finds, for instance, a strong moralistic note in PP 66: 'The world is sick. The cause lies less in the lack of resources, or their monopolisation by a small number of men, that in the lack of brotherhood among individuals and peoples.'

22. PP 26.

301

23. PP 56-9.
24. PP 26.
25. PP 48-9, 76-7.
26. PP 54, 73.
27. PP 50-2, 60-1, 64, 78.
28. PP 61.
29. PP 33 (translation emended).
30. PP 78; cf. address of Pope Paul to the United Nations where he spoke of the need to move progressively towards the establishment of a world authority — *AAS* 57(1965), 880.
31. PP 50-5.
32. PP 9, 58-60.
33. PP 59. Pope Paul here recalls the teaching of Leo XIII's *Rerum Novarum* and adds: 'What was true of the just wage for the individual is also true of international contracts . . .'
34. Cf. PP 9.
35. PP 65 (my translation).
36. PP 77; cf. PP 35, 70.
37. PP 84.
38. PP 85.
39. PP 83.
40. PP 82.
41. PP 81.
42. PP 55; cf. PP 76, 86.
43. PP 49.
44. PP 30.
45. PP 31.
46. PP 32.
47. PP 31 (my translation).
48. PP 31. In this final sentence of the paragraph the pope moves on to speak of what ought to be done, as distinct from what happens in fact.
49. In an article on the encyclical written shortly after its publication Joblin remarked about these words that 'those who are struggling bravely against injustices will undoubtedly interpret them as approval of their activities'; see Joseph Joblin, 'Towards Complete Development', reprint from the *International Labour Review* (Geneva) 96 (September 1967) 5.
50. Encyclical *Quod Apostolici Muneris*, 28 December 1878, *Actes de Léon XIII, Encycliques, Motu Proprio, Brefs, Allocutions, Actes de Dicastrères, etc*, Paris (Bonne Presse; n.d.) I, 34.
51. PP 51.
52. PP 48-9.
53. PP 61.
54. PP 50.
55. PP 78.
56. PP 64.
57. PP 54.
58. PP 79.

59. PP 49.
60. PP 30.
61. PP 55.
62. PP 64.
63. PP 65.
64. E.g. PP 15, 20, 65, 70.
65. PP 15, 25, 27.
66. PP 35 (my translation).
67. PP 44, 48, 49, 84.
68. PP 46, 78, 83.
69. PP 83, 84, 85.
70. PP 68.
71. PP 71-4.
72, PP 12.
73. PP 13.
74. PP 13 (my translation).
75. PP 14-21.
76. PP 81.
77. Ibid.
78. PP 35. The words within double quotation marks are from an earlier message of Pope Paul, which he quotes here.
79. Freire became famous for his literacy work in a national programme in Brazil in 1963-4. He was put in prison by the new military regime in 1964 and there he began to write the essay 'Education as the Practice of Freedom'; this appeared in English only in 1973, in *Education for Critical Consciousness*, New York (Seabury) and London (Sheed and Ward). So his thought would have been well known at the time of writing of *Populorum Progressio* even though his better-known works were not written until later. For background on Freire see Denis Collins, *Paulo Freire: His Life, Works and Thought*, New York (Paulist: 1977).
80. PP 35.
81. PP 30, 49.


Chapter 8
(pp. 157-76)
1. Second General Conference of Latin American Bishops, *The Church in the Present-Day Transformation of Latin America in the Light of the Council, II: Conclusions*, Washington D.C. (Secretariat for Latin America, National Conference of Bishops: 3rd ed. 1979). There are sixteen main documents, numbered 1 to 16. Each of these is divided into numbered 'paragraphs'. References to the documents will be given by giving the number of the document, followed by the number of the paragraph within the document, followed by a page reference, within brackets, to the above edition.
2. E.g. ibid. 1.2 (p. 33); 2.16 (p. 53); 10.2 (p. 126); 15.1 (p. 182).
3. Ibid. 2.16 (p. 53).

303

4. Ibid. 2.2-9 (pp. 46-9).
5. Ibid. 14.2 (p. 172).
6. Ibid. 14.4 (pp. 173-4).
7. Ibid. 14.5 (p. 174).
8. Ibid. 14.9 (p. 175).
9. Ibid. 14.10 (p. 176).
10. Ibid. 2.18 (p. 54); for other references to this 'awakening' see, 2.7 (p. 48); 7.19 (p. 103); 10.2 (p. 126); 16.2 (p. 194).
11. Ibid. 4.16 (p. 76).
12. Ibid.
13. Ibid. 2.7 (pp. 47-8).
14. Ibid. 1.3-4 (pp. 33-4); 4.2, 9 (pp. 70, 73); 5.15 (p. 87); 8.6 (p. 110); 10.2, 9, 13 (pp. 126, 128, 130); 14.2, 7 (pp. 172, 174).
15. Ibid. 10.2, 9, 13 (pp. 126, 128, 130).
16. Ibid. 2.19 (pp. 54-5): 'If it is true that revolutionary insurrection can be legitimate in the case of evident and prolonged "tyranny that seriously works against the fundamental rights of man, and which damages the common good of the country", whether it proceeds from one person or from clearly unjust structures, it is also certain that violence or "armed revolution" generally "generates new injustices, introduces new imbalances and causes new disasters; one cannot combat a real evil at the price of a greater evil".' The passages within double quotation marks are taken from *Populorum Progressio* para. 31 (in a different translation from the one I used in the previous chapter).
17. Ibid. 2.19 (p. 55). The option for non-violence expressed in this passage fits in with the reference in an earlier paragraph to 'the pacifist position of the Church' — ibid. 2.17 (p. 54).
18. Apostolic Letter, *Octogesima Adveniens*, 14 May 1971, *AAS* 63(1971) 401-41. English translation from the Vatican Press in Joseph Gremillion (ed.), *The Gospel of Justice and Peace: Catholic Social Teaching since Pope John*, Maryknoll (Orbis: 1976) 485-512; also in David J. O'Brien and Thomas A. Shannon (ed.), *Renewing the Earth: Catholic Documents on Peace, Justice and Liberation*, Garden City (Image Doubleday: 1977) 352-83. A slightly emended version of this text is given in the booklet, *Social Problems: Apostolic Letter of Pope Paul VI: 'Octogesima Adveniens'* (No. S 288), London (Catholic Truth Society: n.d.). Quotations in English will be taken from this booklet, unless otherwise stated. References will be given by using the initials OA, followed by the number of the paragraph.
19. OA 41. But there are indications that Paul VI was still influenced by this concept of development — see, for instance, his references to 'stages' in OA 2 and OA 10.
20. E.g. OA 28, 45.
21. Philip S. Land, 'The Social Theology of Pope Paul VI', in *America*, 12 May 1979, 394.
22. OA 45-7 (translation emended considerably).
23. OA 42.

24. OA 44.
25. OA 20.
26. OA 47.
27. Ibid.
28. OA 14.
29. OA 20.
30. OA 25.
31. This sentence and the rest of this paragraph are an attempt to para-phrase a particularly difficult and obscure passage in OA 25.
32. OA 27-8.
33. OA 30 and *Pacem in Terris*, para. 159.
34. OA 33.
35. OA 34.
36. OA 31: 'This insight will enable Christians to see the degree of commitment possible along these lines . . .'
37. Ibid.
38. OA 4; cf. OA 42: the Church 'does not intervene to authenticate a given structure or to propose a ready-made model . . .'
39. OA 49-50. The reference to *Gaudium et Spes*, para. 43, confirms this understanding of the text.
40. OA 3, 4.
41. OA 31.
42. *Quadragesimo Anno*, paras. 113-26.
43. Land, art. cit. (note 21 above) 394.
44. Marie-Dominique Chenu, *La 'doctrine sociale' de l'Église comme idéologie*, Paris (Cerf: 1979) 80.
45. OA 35.
46. OA 8-21.
47. OA 47.
48. OA 23.
49. Ibid.
50. Ibid.
51. Ibid.
52. OA 3.
53. Medellín documents (note 1 above) 2.18 (p. 54).
54. OA 14.
55. OA 46.
56. OA 14.
57. OA 47.
58. OA 4.
59. OA 43. The Latin and Italian versions of the text are equally vague.
60. OA 3-4.


Chapter 9
(pp. 117-206)
1. *De Justitia in Mundo*, *AAS* 63(1971) 923-42. English translation: *Justice in the World*, Roma (Vatican Press: 1971); this translation is also given in Joseph Gremillion (ed.), *The Gospel of Justice and*

305

*Peace: Catholic Social Teaching since Pope John*, Maryknoll (Orbis: 1976) 513-29; also in, David J. O'Brien and Thomas A. Shannon (ed.), *Renewing the Earth: Catholic Documents on Peace, Justice and Liberation*, Garden City (Image Doubleday: 1977) 390-408. The paragraphing in each of these three English texts is the same; but that of the Latin text is slightly different. Only the Gremillion text actually numbers the paragraphs. References to this document will be given by using the initials JW followed by the number of the paragraph, as in Gremillion; in cases where the paragraphing in the Latin text (as given in AAS) is different, a reference will be given also to the number of the paragraph in the Latin text — although the paragraphs are not given numbers in the Latin text, they can be counted. Quotations in English are from the Vatican text unless otherwise stated.

2. Apart from its full-time staff the Commission could draw on the expertise of several highly competent scholars who were members of the Commission or consultants to it. One such person was Barbara Ward-Jackson, whose study, *The Angry Seventies: The Second Development Decade: A Call to the Church*, was published by the Commission in 1970.

3. O'Brien and Shannon, op. cit. (note 1 above), introduction to the document.

4. For some background on the use of the phrase 'the signs of the times' see Peter Hebblethwaite, 'The Popes and Politics: Shifting Patterns in "Catholic Social Doctrine"' in *Daedalus: Journal of the American Academy of Arts and Sciences*, Winter 1982, 88-9.

5. JW 16.

6. Ibid.

7. *Populorum Progressio* paras. 7, 52, 57.

8. For the references see note 14 of Chapter Eight (above).

9. JW 16.

10. JW 10.

11. Ibid.

12. JW 11.

13. JW 9.

14. JW 9-10.

15. In his brief but valuable study of the Synod document Hollenbach says: 'Lack of adequate nourishment, housing, education and political self-determination are seen as a consequence of this lack of participation.'; and he maintains that for the Synod the fundamental right to participation 'integrates all other rights with each other and provides their operational foundation'; see David Hollenbach, *Claims in Conflict: Retrieving and Renewing the Catholic Human Rights Tradition*, New York (Paulist: 1979) 86-7. Hollenbach is undoubtedly correct in holding that participation is a central issue; but the texts to which he refers are not quite so clear as he is in seeing economic and social deprivations as the *consequence* of lack of participation; the document seems at times to locate lack of participation *alongside* other lacks.

16. JW 20. It is not clear whether the 'we' used in this paragraph is intended to mean 'we, the authors of this document, i.e. the Synod bishops', or whether it is a more generic 'we' meaning people who are reflecting on the world situation and committed to working for justice; but even the more generic 'we' would clearly include the bishops and other Church leaders.
17. JW 20 (translation slightly emended and emphasis added).
18. OA 46.
19. For references see notes 11 and 13 of Chapter Eight (above).
20. JW 20-6 (Latin text paras. 20-7).
21. Ibid.
22. JW 18.
23. JW 17.
24. JW 27-8 (Latin text paras. 28-9).
25. JW 39 (Latin text para. 40); cf. JW 71 (Latin text para. 72) which lays great stress on cooperation.
26. JW 51-2 (Latin text paras. 52-3).
27. JW 77 (Latin text para. 78) (Emphasis added).
28. JW 40 (Latin text para. 41).
29. JW 41-6 (Latin text paras. 42-7).
30. JW 47 (Latin text para. 48).
31. JW 47-8 (Latin text paras. 48-9).
32. JW 30-1 (Latin text paras. 31-2).
33. JW 34 (Latin text para. 35).
34. JW 35 (Latin text para. 36).
35. JW 36 — my translation (Latin text para. 37).
36. JW 6.
37. I am indebted to Mgr. Charles O'Connor for background information on this controversy.
38. Cf. O'Brien and Shannon, op. cit. (note 1 above) 385 — their introduction to the Synod document.
39. Cf. Philip S. Land, 'The Social Theology of Pope Paul VI' in *America*, 12 May 1979, 393.
40. Apostolic Exhortation, *Evangelii Nuntiandi, AAS* 68(1976) 5-76. There are two easily available English translations: one is published by the Vatican Press and distributed by CTS, London; the other is by Dom Matthew Dillon and is published in a special issue of *Doctrine and Life*, March—April 1977, 3-52. The latter is based on the Latin text whereas the former appears to follow the Italian text. Neither translation is wholly satisfactory so in many cases I shall give my own translation of the official Latin text. References to the document in this chapter will be given by using the initials EN followed by the number of the paragraph. For the pope's references to the request of the Synod see EN 2 and 5.
41. EN 8 (my translation).
42. EN 13 (Dillon translation). The document is at pains later to ensure that its teaching does not involve any playing down of the importance of the Church — e.g. EN 28; cf. Bede McGregor, 'Commentary on *Evangelii Nuntiandi*', in *Doctrine and Life*, March—April 1977, 70-1.

43. EN 21-2 (my translation); cf. EN 41-2.
44. For instance in paragraph 6 of the Vatican II Decree on the Church's Missionary Activity (*Ad Gentes*) the Council says that in situations where there is no possibility of preaching the Gospel directly, missionaries ought at least to bear witness to the love and kindness of Christ and thus prepare a way for the Lord and in some way make him present.
45. EN 10.
46. EN 6.
47. EN 9 (my translation).
48. Cf. Bernard J.F. Lonergan, *Insight: A Study of Human Understanding*, London (Longmans: revised ed. 1958) and *Method in Theology*, London (Darton, Longman and Todd: 1972).
49. EN 17; cf. McGregor, art. cit. (note 42 above) 63.
50. EN 27.
51. EN 28. In translating the Latin in this case I have allowed myself to be influenced by the Italian text because it seems more in harmony with the dynamic quality of the relationship between the present and the future as developed in the rest of the sentence. The Dillon translation which follows the Latin more literally speaks of 'another life' which is 'at once connected with and distinct from' the present state.
52. EN 27.
53. EN 27 (my translation).
54. EN 33 (my translation, partly based on the Dillon version).
55. EN 34.
56. Indeed it is interesting to note that in EN 32 the pope quotes from an address he gave at the opening of the 1974 Synod. He spoke then of the need to re-affirm the specifically religious purpose of evangelisation. There is a discernible shift of emphasis in the text of EN itself — an avoidance of the tendency to present the issue in terms of a sharp contrast between the 'religious' and the 'worldly'. The quotation from the earlier address may even have been included here precisely in order to ensure that it is interpreted in the light of the more comprehensive teaching of the later document — and in this way to suggest a continuity between the two.
57. EN 32.
58. EN 33, 31.
59. *Octogesima Adveniens*, para. 42.
60. EN 35 (my translation).
61. E.g. 'Final Document: International Ecumenical Congress of Theology, February 20—March 2, 1980, São Paulo, Brazil' (EATWOT Conference), para. 33, in *Occasional Bulletin of Missionary Research*, July 1980, p. 129.
62. EN 37.
63. There are two significantly different translations of the first sentence in EN 37. The Vatican translation reads: 'The Church cannot accept violence . . . and indiscriminate death as the path to liberation'. The Dillon translation has: 'The church cannot accept any

form of violence ... nor the death of any man as a method of liberation.' The Vatican English text may find some basis in the Italian, *'la morte di chicchessia'*, while the Dillon text is closer to the Latin *'cuiusvis mortem hominis'*. The French text is *'la mort de qui que ce soit'*, which still leaves one not quite clear about what is intended. Is the writer saying that the goal of liberation does not justify the death of even one person? Or is it simply that one must not seek liberation through a type of violence that is liable to cause the death of anybody (at random, or indiscriminately)? The former would be a strongly pacifist position, while the latter could be understood as simply a rejection of an arbitrary kind of violence. It is not unlikely that it was the intention of the writer to leave a degree of ambiguity in the text.

64. E.g. EN 30.
65. EN 36 (my translation).
66. EN 18 (my translation).
67. EN 19 (my translation).
68. EN 20 (my translation).
69. EN 18.
70. Ibid. (my translation).
71. EN 36 (my translation).
72. EN 30 (my translation).
73. EN 6.
74. EN 58.


Chapter 10
(pp. 207-32)
1. Cf. Penny Lernoux, 'The Long Path to Puebla'; Moises Sandoval, 'Report from the Conference'; Jon Sobrino, 'The Significance of Puebla for the Catholic Church in Latin America'; all in John Eagleson and Philip Scharper (ed.), *Puebla and Beyond: Documentation and Commentary*, Maryknoll (Orbis: 1979) 3-27; 28-43; 289-309.
2. 'Documento: As Reflexões da Assembléia Geral Extraordinária realizada em Itaici, de 18 a 25 de abril [1978]', published in, *O São Paulo*, 29 April–5 May 1978.
3. For instance the document accepts that there is need also for the Church to minister to elite groups, and that it must face difficult questions regarding evangelisation of the upper classes, military chaplaincies, etc.
4. 'Sugestões para elaboração do Documento de Puebla ... Tome o *'Evangelii Nuntiandi'* como documento de referência no estilo e na forma da elaboração.'
5. Sobrino, art. cit. (note 1 above), 300.
6. Third General Conference of Latin American Bishops, *Puebla: Evangelization at Present and in the Future of Latin America: Conclusions* (Official English Edition), Middlegreen and London (St Paul Publications and CIIR: 1980). The text is also given in

*Puebla and Beyond* (note 1 above). The paragraphs of the text are numbered. References will be given by citing the paragraph numbers. The section referred to here is *Puebla* 1134-65.

7. E.g. Paulo Evaristo Cardinal Arns, 'The Church of the Poor: A Persecuted Church', in, *Center Focus: News from the Center of Concern*, July 1981, p. 2: 'The option for the poor is not a class option in the Marxist sense . . .'; Gregory Baum, 'Liberation Theology and "The Supernatural"', in *The Ecumenist* 19(1981), 84: 'The Marxist position is . . . quite different from the Christian option for the poor.'

8. E.g. Elsa Tamez, *The Bible of the Oppressed*, Maryknoll (Orbis: 1982); Gustavo Gutierrez, *A Theology of Liberation: History, Politics and Salvation*, Maryknoll (Orbis: 1973) and London (SCM: 1974) 287-306; Benedito Ferraro, *A Significaçao Politica e Teologica da Morte de Jesus à luz do Novo Testamento*, Petropolis (Vozes: 1977) 92-5.

9. *Puebla* 1134, 1154, 1160. It should be noted that at Puebla the bishops also committed themselves to a preferential option for young people (*Puebla* 1166-1205). This had the effect of playing down to some degree the uniqueness of the phrase 'option for the poor' and in this way making it less threatening and more widely acceptable.

10. *Puebla* 1155.

11. *Puebla* 1156. For a helpful treatment of the concept of an 'option for the poor', based on *Puebla* and on Pope John Paul's addresses in Mexico, see, Ricardo Antoncich, *Los Cristianos ante la Injusticia: Hacia un lectura latinamericano de la doctrina social de la Iglesia*, Bogota (Ediciones Grupo Social: 1980) 108-15.

12. Cf. Julian Filochowski, 'Medellín to Puebla', in Pope John Paul II and others, *Reflections on Puebla*, London (CIIR: 1980) 18.

13. The official texts of the pope's addresses, in the original languages, are given in *AAS* 71(1979) 164-246. In the case of all of the addresses except one, the English text used here will be taken from, *John Paul II in Mexico: His Collected Speeches*, London and New York (Collins: 1979); this is the Vatican translation of *L'Osservatore Romano*. In the case of the opening address of the pope to the conference, a different, and better, translation will be used. It is to be found in the two English editions of the Puebla document referred to in note 6 above; since this address is divided into numbered sections and paragraphs, references can be given simply by referring to these numbers. In the case of the other addresses, page references will be given to the original text in *AAS* and to the English translation referred to in this note. The passage quoted in the text here is the pope's opening address I, 4.

14. Ibid.

15. Ibid. I, 8.

16. Ibid. III, 6.

17. Ibid. III, 2.

18. Ibid. III, 3. An earlier English text issued by the Vatican and used

in *John Paul II in Mexico: His Collected Speeches* (p. 79) omits the word 'primarily'; so too does the Italian text in, *Giovanni Paolo II alla Chiesa che é in Messico: Discorsi del primo viaggio apostolico*, Alba (Figlie di San Paolo: 1979) 37; however, the Spanish text as published in *AAS* 71(1979) 79, has *'sobre todo'*.

19. Sermon at Guadalupe, para. 3, *AAS* 174, *John Paul II in Mexico* . . . 44; cf. address of John Paul II to the Pontifical Commission 'Justice and Peace', in, *L'Osservatore Romano* (English edition) of 30 November 1978, p. 4: 'Priority attention for those who are suffering from radical poverty, for those who are suffering from injustice, certainly coincides with a fundamental concern of the Church . . .'
20. Address at Santa Cecilia district of Guadaljara, *AAS* 220, *John Paul II in Mexico* . . . 113; cf. address in Monterrey, para. 6, *AAS* 243, *John Paul II in Mexico* . . . 149.
21. Para. 4, *AAS* 242, *John Paul II in Mexico* . . . 148.
22. Address at Cuilapan near Oaxaca, para. 6, *AAS* 209, *John Paul II in Mexico* . . . 96. Translation emended slightly. Note that the pope refers twice to *Populorum Progressio* on this occasion.
23. Ibid. para. 9, *AAS* 210, *John Paul II in Mexico* . . . 97.
24. *Puebla*, 489, 1141, 538, 551-2.
25. Opening address, III, 7.
26. Marie-Dominique Chenu, *La 'doctrine sociale' de l'Église comme idéologie*, Paris (Cerf: 1979) 26. For a perceptive but highly acerbic and critical treatment of the issue see Peter Hebblethwaite, 'The Popes and Politics: Shifting Patterns in "Catholic Social Doctrine"', in *Daedalus: Journal of the American Academy of Arts and Sciences*, Winter 1982, 85-98.
27. Chenu, op. cit. 88-9.
28. Ibid. 87-8. Chenu notes angrily that the term 'social doctrine' was reintroduced into the text of para. 76 of *Gaudium et Spes*, 'by an illegal intervention after its promulgation' — ibid. 8, 88.
29. Ibid. 13. It may be noted in passing that Paul VI had not entirely abandoned the use of the term. In *Evangelii Nuntiandi* para. 38 he used it: 'Ecclesia . . . praebet . . . doctrinam socialem . . .' This weakens the case made by Chenu.
30. Cf. Roger Heckel, *The Social teaching of John Paul II, Booklet I, General aspects of the social catechesis of John Paul II; the use of the expression 'social doctrine' of the Church*, Vatican City (Pontifical Commission 'Justitia et Pax': 1980) 23: 'It is ordinarily a more *generic* (teaching of the Church on the life of societies) than a *specific* use (the historically and culturally dated doctrinal corpus and vocabulary — used more or less during the first half of the present century). But the Pope does not hesitate to use the specific sense . . . especially when referring to the major "social encyclicals" . . .'
31. Cf. Ibid.: The pope takes account of the fact that the term has created difficulties; while using the term he seeks to avoid getting involved 'in a dispute over words'.

311

32. Ibid. 21.
33. *Puebla*, 542-53.
34. *Puebla*, 553.
35. *Puebla*, 539.
36. Cf. *Puebla*, 472-6; it is clear that the drafters of the Puebla document preferred the term 'social teaching' to 'social doctrine'.
37. *Puebla*, 551, quoting John Paul's opening address III, 3.
38. *AAS* 71(1979) 257-324; English translation issued by Libreria Editrice Vaticana. References to the encyclical will be given by citing the number of the 'paragraph' preceded by the initials RH. Quotations in English will be from the Vatican text unless otherwise stated.
39. *AAS* 72(1980) 1177-1232; English translation issued by the Vatican Press. References to the encyclical will be given by citing the number of the 'paragraph', preceded by the initials DM. Quotations in English will be from the Vatican text.
40. RH 11 (my translation); cf. RH 10: 'Christ the Redeemer "fully reveals man to himself"'.
41. RH 14 title (my translation).
42. RH 14.
43. Opening address III, 4: 'Primacy must be given to that which is moral, to that which is spiritual, to that which flows from the full truth about the human being.'
44. *AAS* 71(1979) 1153-4 (para. 14).
45. RH 11.
46. Cf. Gregory Baum, 'The First Papal Encyclical', in *The Ecumenist: A Journal for Promoting Christian Unity*, 17 (1979) 57: 'The Pope stresses the spiritual in the world-historical sense. Spirit is always incarnate.'
47. RH 15 (my translation).
48. Address at Oaxaca and Cuilapan, *AAS* 71(1979) 206, 208; *John Paul II in Mexico* . . . 88, 92.
49. E.g. address to UNESCO, *AAS* 72(1980) 735-52.
50. RH 15; cf. DM 11.
51. DM 11.
52. RH 15. In translating papal statements I have tried as far as possible to use such words as 'person' or 'human' instead of 'man' (in its generic sense); but in cases like the present I can find no acceptable alternative to 'man as man'.
53. RH 16.
54. Ibid.
55. RH 15.
56. RH 16.
57. DM 11.
58. RH 16 (my translation).
59. Ibid.
60. Ibid. (my translation).
61. Ibid.
62. Cf. *Le Rédempteur de l'homme: lettre encyclique de Jean-Paul II: un guide de lecture par V. Cosmao*, Paris (Cerf: 1979) 24-5.

63. RH 17.
64. *AAS* 71(1979) 1147-8 (para. 7).
65. Ibid. 1156 (para. 17).
66. DM 12.
67. DM 14.
68. Ibid.
69. The text of the major addresses given by the pope in Brazil is available (in the original languages, Portuguese, Spanish, and French) in, *AAS* 72(1980) 825-961; but not all of his addresses are given there. The full text of all of his addresses is given in the various issues of *L'Osservatore Romano* from 2 July to 13 July 1980 (inclusive), which also contains an Italian translation in a series of supplements to these issues. An English translation of all the addresses is given in the English language weekly edition of *L'Osservatore Romano* of 7, 14, 21 and 28 July, and 4, 11, and 25 August 1980. The longer addresses are divided into numbered 'paragraphs'. References will be given by citing the paragraph number (where available) and the page reference to the original text as given in *AAS* (or, where the text is not given in *AAS*, to the original text as given in *L'Osservatore Romano*). Quotations in English will be from the translation referred to above unless otherwise stated.
70. Para. 4, *AAS* 831-2.
71. Paras. 5 and 6, *AAS* 832-3.
72. *AAS* 835.
73. Paras. 1 and 2, *AAS* 848-9.
74. *AAS* 858-73.
75. *AAS* 944-60.
76. III, 1, *AAS* 867. The Vatican translation is: 'I often had recourse to the Puebla Document, which I knew in detail and approved with joy after the clarification of some concepts.' (English ed. of *L'Osservatore Romano* of 14 July 1980, p. 7). The original Spanish text is '. . . tras precisar algunos conceptos'. For a list of the modifications that were made to the Puebla text (and an angry reaction to these changes) see, *Esperance des Pauvres: Revue de presse*, No. 183 (Septembre 1979).
77. III, 7, *AAS* 868.
78. Para. 6, *AAS* 868.
79. Para. 6.9. *AAS* 956 (translation from English ed. of *L'Osservatore Romano* of 11 August 1980, p. 10.) In the interests of clarity I have omitted a parenthetical remark made by the pope in the middle of the passage. The parenthesis is as follows: '— and in any case we must ask, what is the real meaning of this term "poor"? —' (my translation). The point of this 'aside' is to remind the audience that the word 'poor' is not to be restricted to those who are economically poor. Cf. also, address to Sao Paulo workers, paras. 2, 3 and 4, *AAS* 889-91.
80. To CELAM, II, 8, *AAS* 865; to Brazilian bishops, para. 6.9, *AAS* 957; at Vidigal, para. 5, *AAS* 856; to Sao Paulo workers, para. 4, *AAS* 890-1.

313

81. III, 8, *AAS* 870.
82. E.g. to São Paulo workers, para. 4, *AAS* 890; to diplomatic corps, *AAS* 835; at Vidigal, para. 5, *AAS* 857; to president, para. 5, *AAS* 832.
83. Para. 8, *AAS* 894-5.
84. Cf. Peadar Kirby, 'The Pope in Brazil', in *Doctrine and Life*, August/September 1980, 363.
85. Para. 7, *AAS* 893.
86. Para. 4, *AAS* 926 (my translation).
87. *AAS* 924.
88. Para. 1, *AAS* 853.
89. Para. 2, *AAS* 853.
90. Para. 3, *AAS* 854.
91. Para. 4, *AAS* 854.
92. Para. 4, *AAS* 855-6 (my translation).
93. Para. 5, *AAS* 857 (my translation).
94. Cf. Address to São Paulo workers, para. 4, *AAS* 890: 'This is especially the duty of those who hold power, whether economic or political, in society.'
95. Para. 4, *AAS* 855 (my translation).
96. This address is not given in *AAS*. Portuguese text in *L'Osservatore Romano*, 9 July 1981, pp. 1-2. Translation in English ed. of *L'Osservatore Romano*, 4 August, p. 7. This passage is para. 2, p. 1.
97. Ibid. para. 3 (translation emended).
98. Ibid.
99. Ibid. para. 3, pp. 1-2.
100. The text of the pope's addresses on his visit to the Philippines and the Far East is given in *AAS* 73(1981) 304-429. The address at Tondo is also available in English ed. of *L'Osservatore Romano*, 23 February 1981, pp. 13-14. The passage quoted is from para. 5.
101. Ibid. para. 6.
102. Ibid. para. 5.
103. Ibid.; cf. address at Alagados (note 96 above) para. 2, p. 1.


Chapter 11
(pp. 233-51)
1. Latin text in *L'Osservatore Romano*, 16 September 1981, pp. 1-6. English translation from Vatican Polyglot Press. The text is divided into numbered paragraphs. References will be given by citing the paragraph number, preceded by the initials LE. A useful help in studying the encyclical is: Campaign for Human Development and the Office of Domestic Social Development, *On Human Work: A Resource Book for the Study of Pope John Paul II's Third Encyclical*, Washington D.C. (United States Catholic Conference: 1982); this contains the text of LE as well as background articles and a valuable condensed paraphrase of the text by James R. Jennings (pp. 7-17).
2. LE 6.
3. LE 7, 8.

4. LE 12.
5. LE 13.
6. E.g. LE 12, 14, 15, 16.
7. LE 2.
8. E.g. LE 7, 8, 11, 14.
9. See Gregory Baum, 'John Paul II's Encyclical on Labor', in *The Ecumenist: A Journal for Promoting Christian Unity*, November-December 1981, 4; and idem, *The Priority of Labor: A Commentary on Laborem Exercens, Encyclical Letter of Pope John Paul II*, New York/Ramsey (Paulist: 1982) 55-6 and 80-6.
10. Carl Marzani, 'The Vatican as a Left Ally?', in *Monthly Review*, July/August 1982, 27.
11. E.g. LE 8, 13-9.
12. See LE 11, 13, 14; cf. Jan P. Schotte, *Reflections on 'Laborem Exercens'*, Vatican City (Pontifical Commission *'Justitia et Pax'*: 1982) 31: '. . . the Pope is cautiously not suggesting any concrete formula.' Ibid. 27: 'He does not propose a "third way" between liberal capitalism and Marxism. . . . In the debate between capitalism and communism, he offers elements for a critique of both systems. . .'
13. LE 17.
14. LE 16.
15. LE 17.
16. Ibid.
17. Ibid.
18. Ibid. Schotte makes the point that transnational enterprises should be seen both as direct and indirect employers — op. cit. (note 12 above) 30.
19. LE 22.
20. LE 19.
21. LE 1.
22. LE 1, 17, 18.
23. E.g. 'Final Document: International Ecumenical Congress of Theology, February 20-March 2, 1980, São Paulo, Brazil', in *Occasional Bulletin of Missionary Research*, July 1980, 127-33, notably 128 (paras. 12-7); cf. 'Delhi Conference of Theology (Fifth Conference of the Ecumenical Association of Third World Theologians): The Irruption of the Third World: A Challenge to Theology' (mimeographed), 2-3 (paras. 9-14). For a helpful treatment of poverty and oppression in the Bible see Elsa Tamez, *The Bible of the Oppressed*, Maryknoll (Orbis: 1982).
24. E.g. Leften Stavros Stavrianos, *Global Rift: The Third World Comes of Age*, New York (Morrow: 1981); Charles Elliot, *Patterns of Poverty in the Third World: A Study of Social and Economic Stratification* (New York: 1975).
25. Martin Tripole, 'A Church for the Poor and the World: At Issue with Moltmann's Ecclesiology', in *Theological Studies*, 42 (December 1981) 645-59.
26. Ibid. 652.
27. Ibid. 654.

28. Ibid.
29. LE 8.
30. E.g. LE 7, 8, 11, 14.
31. LE 20.
32. LE 8.
33. Ibid.
34. LE 8 (nine times) and LE 20.
35. The excerpts quoted here are from the second chapter (pp. 30-56) of *Karol Wojtyla (Pope John Paul II): An Anthology edited by Alfred Bloch and George T. Czuczka*, New York (Crossroad: 1981).
36. Ibid. 47.
37. Ibid. 48.
38. Ibid.
39. Ibid.
40. Ibid. 49.
41. Ibid.
42. Ibid. 49-50.
43. LE 8.
44. LE 20. It may be of interest here to look briefly at the way in which the issue of class warfare is treated by the Pastoral Commission of the Brazilian Bishops. The Commission states that the Church condemns the Marxist postulate of class war, in the sense that to promote such a struggle would be contrary to the Gospel and would not provide the solution to the real problems of today. But, it adds, the Church recognises realistically the existence of class conflicts — conflicts which ought to be overcome through the establishment of justice and of a spirit of brotherhood; see 'Fraternidade no Mundo do Trabalho', in *Trabalho e Justica para Todos, Campanha da Fraternidade 1978, CNBB* (Rio de Janeiro: 1977) 10.
45. LE 8.
46. Ibid.
47. Ibid.
48. Cf. LE 13.
49. LE 8.
50. Address at Quezaltenango, Guatamala, 7 March 1983, para. 5 (*Bollettino*, Sala Stampa della Santa Sede, Vatican City, No. 110, p. 5; my translation).


Chapter 12
(pp. 252-75)

1. Quentin L. Quade (ed.), *The Pope and Revolution: John Paul II confronts Liberation Theology*, Washington D.C. (Ethics and Public Policy Center: 1982) 6-10. (This section was written by the editor.) It may be noted that the writer apparently thinks that *Evangelii Nuntiandi* was issued by the 1974 Synod of Bishops — see ibid. 10.
2. Cf. Gregory Baum, *The Priority of Labor: A Commentary of*

'*Laborem Exercens*', *Encyclical Letter of Pope John Paul II*, New York (Paulist: 1982) 13.

3. Cf. Alfred T. Hennelly, 'A Spirituality of Work' in: Campaign for Human Development and the Office of Domestic Social Development, *On Human Work: A Resource Book for the Study of Pope John Paul II's Third Encyclical*, Washington D.C. (United States Catholic Conference: 1982), 34.

4. Cf. Jan P. Schotte, *Reflections on 'Laborem Exercens'*, Vatican City (Pontifical Commission '*Justitia et Pax*': 1982) 23.

5. *Laborem Exercens*, para. 11.

6. Ibid. para. 8.

7. Ibid. para. 11.

8. Cf. Baum, op. cit. (note 2 above) 29: 'Pope John Paul II offers . . . an imaginative rethinking of class conflict. The initiative for the struggle resides in the persons who recognise their common objective situation and freely commit themselves to solidarity in a joint struggle.'

9. Cf. ibid. 85: '. . . because ideologies are abstractions, they make people believe that they can analyse new historical situations without proper attention to what is taking place.'

10. Cf. José Porfirio Miranda, *Marx Against the Marxists: The Christian Humanism of Karl Marx*, Maryknoll (Orbis: 1980) 69-105.

11. Cf. Arthur F. McGovern, *Marxism: An American Christian Perspective*, Maryknoll (Orbis: 1980) 68-80; also, Miranda, op. cit. (note 10 above) passim.

12. Cf. Baum, op. cit. (note 2 above) 85-6.

13. E.g. Address of John Paul II to Council of Latin American Bishops (CELAM) at Port au Prince, Haiti, 9 March 1983, Section I, para. 3 (*Bollettino*, Sala Stampa della Santa Sede, Vatican City, No. 117, p. 6): 'You ought to have a preference in your hearts for those who are poorest of all. . . . But you know and proclaim that this option would be neither pastoral nor Christian if it were inspired by merely political or ideological criteria . . . or if it gave rise to feelings of hatred or struggle among brothers.' (My translation).

14. On the question of motivation of the poor in Marx see Miranda, op. cit. (note 10 above) 1-28. On the question of how, in John Paul's view, the struggle to overcome oppression goes beyond narrow 'class interest' see Baum, op. cit. (note 2 above) 30-1, 49, 69.

15. See, for instance, Michael Novak, ' "Creation Theology" — John Paul II and the American Experience' and Stanley Hauerwas, 'Work as "Co-Creation" — A Remarkably Bad Idea' in *This World*, No. 3, Fall 1982, 71-88 and 89-102 respectively.

16. See, for instance, the book mentioned in note 1 above; the author rests a good deal of his case on a remark of John Paul, made in the course of an address to *clergy* in Zaire, where he asks priests to leave politics to the politicians. One of the clearest instances of the pope himself, in the name of the Church, taking a very strong and specific stance on a burning issue of justice (which would inevitably be seen as a political matter) occurred in his address to American

317

Indians of Guatamala, at Quezaltenango, on 7 March 1983, para. 4 (*Bollettino*, Sala Stampa della Santa Sede, Vatican City, No. 119, p. 4): '. . . the Church at this moment knows the marginalization which you suffer, the injustices you endure, the serious difficulties you encounter in defending your lands and your rights. . . . So, in fulfilling her task of evangelization, she seeks to be near you and *to raise her voice in condemnation* when your dignity as human beings and children of God is violated. . . . For this reason, here and now, and in solemn form, in the name of the Church I call on the government to provide an ever more adequate legislation which will protect you effectively against abuses . . .' (my translation). In the same paragraph the pope very significantly demanded that the process of authentic evangelization should not be branded as subversion; in other words, he was vindicating the right of the Church to speak and act in the interests of justice even when this is interpreted by authorities such as those in Guatamala as a political activity, or even as subversive of the State authority. See also the outspoken demand made by the pope in Haiti that things must change — and his insistence on the crying need for justice, for equitable distribution of goods, as well as for participation by the people in decision-making and for freedom of expression of opinions — address at the airport of Port au Prince, 9 March 1983, para. 4 (ibid, No. 116, pp. 8-9).

17. E.g. Address to priests in San Salvador, 6 March 1983, para 4 (ibid, No. 198, p. 4): 'Remember, my dear brothers, that — as I said to the priests and religious of Mexico — you are not social directors, political leaders, or officials of a temporal power . . .' (my translation).

18. The visit of John Paul II to Central America and Haiti in March 1983 took place in a highly politicised atmosphere, where his words were bound to have an immediate impact both on the 'secular' politics of the region and on 'ecclesiastical politics'. Inevitably, then, the major interest of what he had to say turned more on papal *policy* than on papal *teaching* in a more 'doctrinal' sense. What he said in El Salvador and Nicaragua was of major importance from the point of view of Vatican policy, but it did not add significantly to his earlier teaching in terms of content — except to bring out more clearly than ever before his reservations about the Marxist answer to problems of social injustice; he objected to what he saw as an 'instrumentalization' of the Gospel and to its subjection to an 'ideology' (— see especially his address in Managua, Nicaragua, 4 March 1983, paras. 4-6 — ibid, No. 194, pp. 3-7). It is appropriate to quote here from two passages in his address to the Council of Latin American Bishops (CELAM) at Port au Prince on 9 March 1983, since they are typical. The first is from Section I, para. 3 (ibid, No. 117, p. 5) and it expresses his concern about poverty and injustice: 'A sincere analysis of the situation shows that at its root one finds painful injustices, exploitation of some by others, and a serious lack of equity in the distribution of wealth

318

and the benefits of culture.' The second passage comes towards the end of Section III of the address and it indicates his concern about distortions of the Gospel and one-sided or partial interpretations of Puebla: '. . . it is necessary to spread and . . . to recover *the wholeness* of the message of Puebla, without deformed interpretations or deformed reductions, and without unwarranted applications of some parts and the eclipse of others.' (my translation).

# Select Bibliography

(The following list does not include the titles of articles in periodicals, or the titles of individual documents issued by popes or councils; these can be found in the notes to the various chapters.)

Abbott, Walter M. (ed.), *The Documents of Vatican II*, New York (America Press: 1966) and London (Chapman: 1967)

Antonchic, Ricardo, *Los Cristianos ante la Injusticia: Hacia un lectura latinamericano de la doctrina social de la Iglesia*, Bogota (Ediciones Grupo Social: 1980). (To be published in English by Orbis Press.)

Aubert, Roger *et al*, *The Christian Centuries, Vol 5: The Church in a Secularized Society*, London (Darton, Longman and Todd: 1978) and New York (Paulist: 1978)

Baum, Gregory, *The Priority of Labor: A Commentary on Laborem Exercens, Encyclical Letter of Pope John Paul II*, New York/Ramsey (Paulist: 1982)

Bloch, Alfred and Czuczka, George T. (eds), *Karol Wojtyla (Pope John Paul II): An Anthology*, New York (Crossroad: 1981)

Bolté, Paul-Emile, *Mater et Magistra: texte latin, nouvelle traduction, index analytique* Montréal (Univ. de Montréal: 1968)

Bolté, Paul-Emile, *Mater et Magistra, commentaire*, Vol I 1964, Vol II 1966, Vol III 1967, Vol IV 1968, Montréal (Univ. de Montréal)

Brookfield, Harold, *Interdependent Development*, London (Methuen: 1975)

Calvez, Jean-Yves, *The Social Thought of John XXIII: Mater et Magistra*, London (Burns and Oates: 1964)

Calvez, Jean-Yves and Perrin, Jacques, *The Church and Social Justice: The Social Teaching of the Popes from Leo XIII to Pius XII (1878–1958*, Chicago (Regnery: 1961)

Camp, Richard L., *The Papal Ideology of Social Reform: A Study in Historical Development 1878–1967*, Leiden (E.J. Brill: 1969)

Campaign for Human Development and the Office of Domestic Social Development, *On Human Work: A Resource Book for the Study of Pope John Paul II's Third Encyclical*, Washington D.C. (United States Catholic Conference: 1982)

Chenu, Marie-Dominique, *La 'doctrine sociale' de l'Église comme idéologie*, Paris (Cerf: 1979)

Chiavacci, Enrico, *La costituzione pastorale sulla Chiesa nel mondo contemporaneo: Gaudium et Spes*, Roma (Studium: 1967)

Congar, Yves M.J. and Peuchmaurd, M., (ed.), *L'Église dans le monde de ce temps: Constitution pastoral 'Gaudium et Spes': Tome III, Reflections et perspectives* (Unam Sanctam 65c), Paris (Cerf: 1967)

Cosmao, Vincent, *Changer le monde: une tâche pour l'Église*, Paris (Cerf: 1979)

Cosmao, Vincent, *Dossier: nouvel ordre mondial; les chrétiens provoqués par le développement* (Chalet: 1978)

Cosmao, Vincent, *Le Rédempteur de l'homme: lettre encyclique de Jean-Paul II: un guide de lecture par V. Cosmao*, Paris (Cerf: 1979)

de Soras, Alfred, *International Morality (Faith and Fact Books, no 58)*, London (Burns and Oates: 1963)

de Riedmatten, H. *et al*, *La Chiesa nel mondo contemporaneo: commento alla costituzione pastorale: 'Gaudium et Spes'*, Brescia (Queriniana: 1966)

Eagleson, John and Sharper, Philip (eds.), *Puebla and Beyond: Documentation and Commentary*, Maryknoll (Orbis: 1979)

Elliot, Charles, *Patterns of Poverty in the Third World: A Study of Social and Economic Stratification*, New York (Praeger: 1975)

Flannery, Austin (ed.), *Vatican Council II The Conciliar and Post Conciliar Documents*, Northport, New York (Costello: 1975, 1977)

Gilson, Etienne (ed.), *The Church Speaks to the Modern World: The Social Teachings of Leo XIII*, Garden City (Doubleday Image: 1954)

Gremillion, Joseph (ed.), *The Gospel of Peace and Justice: Catholic Social Teaching since Pope John*, Maryknoll (Orbis: 1976)

Guano, E. *et al*, *La costituzione pastorale sulla Chiesa nel mondo contemporaneo: introduzione storico-dottrinale; testo latino e traduzione italiano; esposizione e commento*, Torino-Leamann (Elle di Ci: 1966)

Gudorf, Christine E., *Catholic Social Teaching on Liberation Themes*, Lanham (University Press of America: 1980

Gutierrez, Gustavo, *A Theology of Liberation: History, Politics and Salvation*, Maryknoll (Orbis: 1973) and London (SCM: 1974)

Heckel, Roger, *The Social Teaching of John Paul II, Booklet I, General aspects of the social catechesis of John Paul II; the use of the expression 'social doctrine' of the Church*, Vatican City (Pontifical Commission 'Justitia et Pax': 1980)

Holland, Joe and Henriot, Peter, *Social Analysis: Linking Faith and Justice*, Washington D.C. (Center of Concern: 1980)

Hollenback, David, *Claims in Conflict: Retrieving and Renewing the Catholic Human Rights Tradition*, New York (Paulist: 1979)

John XXIII, *The Encyclicals and Other Messages of John XXIII*, Washington D.C. (T.P.S. Press: 1964)

John Paul II, *John Paul II in Mexico: His Collected Speeches*, London and New York (Collins: 1979)

Latin American Bishops, *The Church in the Present-Day Transformation of Latin America in the Light of the Council* (Medellín docu-

321

ments), Washington D.C. (Secretariat for Latin America, National Conference of Bishops: 3rd ed., 1979)

Leclercq, J., *Leçons de droit naturel, II: L'État ou la politique* (2ieme ed), Namur (Wesmael-Charlier: 1934)

Leo XIII, *Actes de Léon XIII, Encycliques, Moto Proprio, Brefs, Allocutions, Actes de Dicastrères etc.*, Paris (Bonne Presse: n.d.)

Leo XIII, *The Great Encyclical Letters of Pope Leo XIII*, New York (Benziger Brothers: 1903)

Leo XIII, *The Pope and the People: Select Letters and Addresses on Social Questions by Pope Leo XIII* (revised edition), London (CTS: 1913)

Leo XIII *et al*, *The Pope and the People: Select Letters and Addresses on Social Questions by Pope Leo XIII, Pope Pius X, Pope Benedict XV and Pope Pius XI* (1929 ed.), London (CTS: 1937 reprint)

Kirwan, J.R., *The Social Thought of John XXIII*, Oxford (Catholic Social Guild: 1964)

Masse, Benjamin L. (ed.), *The Church and Social Progress: Background Readings for Pope John's Mater et Magistra*, Milwaukee (Bruce: 1966)

McGovern, Arthur F., *Marxism: An American Christian Perspective*, Maryknoll (Orbis: 1980)

Miller, Raymond J., *Forty Years After: Pius XI and the Social Order: A Commentary*, St Paul, Minn. (Radio Replies Press: 1947)

Miranda, José Porfirio, *Marx Against the Marxists: The Christian Humanism of Karl Marx*, Maryknoll (Orbis: 1980)

Moody, Josph N., *Church and Society: Catholic Social and Political Thought and Movements 1789–1950*, New York (Arts Inc.: 1953)

O'Brien, David J. and Shannon, Thomas A. (ed.), *Renewing the Earth: Catholic Documents on Peace, Justice and Liberation*, Garden City (Doubleday Image: 1977)

Paul VI, *Encyclical Letter of his Holiness Pope Paul VI: On the Development of Peoples* (with commentary by Barbara Ward), New York (Paulist: 1967)

Pius XI, *Twelve Encyclicals of Pius XI* (with a foreword by Mgr P.E. Hallett), London (CTS: 1943)

Pius XII, *Selected Letters and Addresses of Pius XII*, London (CTS: 1949)

Quade, Quentin L. (ed.), *The Pope and Revolution: John Paul II Confronts Liberation Theology*, Washington D.C. (Ethics and Public Policy Center: 1982)

Ryan, John A., *A Better Economic Order*, New York (Harper: 1935)

Savignat, Alain (ed.), *Relations humaines et société contemporaine: synthèse chrétienne directives de S.S. Pie XII*, Fribourg (St Paul: 1956)

Schotte, Jan P., *Reflections on 'Laborem Exercens'*, Vatican City (Pontifical Commission 'Justitia et Pax': 1982)

Stavrianos, Leften Stavros, *Global Rift: The Third World Comes of Age*, New York (Morrow: 1981)

Tamez, Elsa, *The Bible of the Oppressed*, Maryknoll (Orbis: 1982)

Theas, Pierre Marie *et al. Guerre révolutionnaire et conscience chrétienne*, Paris (Pax Christi: 1963)

Todaro, Michael P., *Economic Development in the Third World: An introduction to problems and policies in a global perspective*, London (Longman: 1977)

Utz, Arthur Fridolin, *Die Friedensenzyklika Papst Johannes: XXIII: Pacem in Terris*, Freiburg (Herder: 1963)

Vidler, Alec R., *A Century of Social Catholicism*, London (SPCK: 1964)

Villain, Jean, *L'enseignement social de l'Église, t.I: Introduction, capitalisme et socialisme*, Paris (Spes: 1953)

Von Nell-Breuning, Oswald, *Reorganization of Social Economy: The Social Encyclical Developed and Explained* (English edition prepared by Bernard W. Dempsey), Milwaukee (Bruce: 1936)

Vorgrimmler, Herbert (ed.), *Commentary on the Documents of Vatican II*, Vol 5, London (Burns and Oates: 1969) and New York (Herder and Herder: 1969)

Ward-Jackson, Barbara, *The Angry Seventies: The Second Development Decade: A Call to the Church*, Vatican City (Pontifical Commission 'Justitia et Pax': 1970)

Williams, Raymond, *Keywords: A Vocabulary of Culture and Society*, Glasgow (Collins Fontana: 1976)

# Index

324

325

326

239, 256, 261, 263

power, economic, 16, 17, 58, 61, 91; political, 16, 17, 58, 61; social, 16; abuse of, 40, 70-1; depends on wealth, 60, 140; other references, 68, 130, 145

property, ownership of, 18, 83, 96, 129, 142; damage to, 21; private, 64, 83-4, 87, 108, 111, 113, 127, 213, 255, 261, 263; distribution of, 93

Puebla, 2, 7, 207-17, 224, 258, 265

*Quadragesimo Anno*, 57-70, 74, 79, 80, 81, 84, 100, 107, 109, 128, 142, 143, 235, 254

*Quod Apostolici Muneris*, 30-1, 33

*Quod Multum*, 32

Recife, 226

*Redemptor Hominis*, 217-22

religion, 18, 31, 32-4, 35-6, 59-60, 76, 135

*Rerum Novarum*, 7, 11-28, 29, 45, 48, 50, 51, 52, 53, 56, 57, 59, 62, 80, 83, 84, 128, 139, 142, 162, 205, 233, 234, 253, 260

revolution, danger of, 30; justified, 40, 41; Leo XIII's fear of, 44, 45-9, 253; other references, 43, 146-9, 155, 162, 164, 170-1, 194, 200

rich, the, 12, 16-23 passim, 26, 33, 34, 47, 48, 49, 53, 58, 68, 93, 94, 105, 126, 128, 131, 138, 139, 145, 152, 182, 204, 227, 240, 241

rights, of workers, 18, 19, 21; individual, human 82, 112, 137, 185-6, 221-2, 224, 231, 257, 259; to private ownership, 84; to personal freedom, 90

Rio de Janeiro, 224

Roman Republic, 1848, 46

Romero, Oscar, 264

Russia, 72, 73, 77

St Francis Xavier, association of, 29

Sao Paulo, 225

Scripture *see* Bible

Second Vatican Council *see* Vatican II

Sobrino, Jon, 208

social injustice *see* injustice, social

social issues, 12-13, 22, 51, 57-8, 66, 87, 102, 162, 211, 213, 214, 215, 254

social justice *see* justice, social

social need, 38, 39

*Social Order, The* see *Quadragesimo Anno*

social problems, 15-16, 17, 18, 45, 52, 60, 62, 65-7, 77, 79, 80-1, 84, 87, 91, 107, 164, 165, 175, 216, 258

social services *see* Welfare State

socialisation, 103-5, 107

socialism, rejected by Leo XIII, 14-15, 28, 32, 33, 45, 47, 48; rejected by Pius XI, 57, 67; and capitalism, 94, 234, 235, 255; other references, 64, 65, 68, 98, 108, 109, 110, 111, 143, 167, 168, 170, 181, 235, 254, 262

society, structures of, 3, 19, 25, 28, 57, 58-9, 60, 62-3, 69, 88, 105, 130, 141, 144, 152, 192; stability in, 19, 42, 43, 46, 59, 68, 74, 83, 173, 253; justice in, 19, 23, 24, 27, 187, 210; socio-economic order of, 58, 166; other references, 138, 183, 216

solidarity, with the poor, 4, 78, 115, 135, 159, 183, 210, 225; of rich and poor, 143, other references, 170, 221, 232, 233, 244, 245-50, 251, 259-60, 264, 266, 268

South Africa, 48, 263

South America *see* America, Latin

Spain, 79, 262

spirituality *see* religion

State, its role, 16-17, 18, 64; its apparatus, 16, 17, 49, 107; institutions of, 17, 22, 23; cooperation with the Church, 30-1, 138; other references, 14-15, 35, 60, 70, 80, 109-10, 167, 270

strikes, 21, 22, 29, 50, 133, 171, 172, 173, 174

subsidiarity, 106, 107

Synod of Bishops in Rome 1971, 7, 177, 193, 209, 212, 273, 274

Synod of Bishops in Rome 1974, 177, 187, 189, 190-1

Third World, 1, 25, 94, 95, 99, 119-20, 124, 126, 131, 132, 133, 134, 140, 179, 181, 190, 198, 214, 236, 237, 238, 239, 249, 264

Tondo, 226